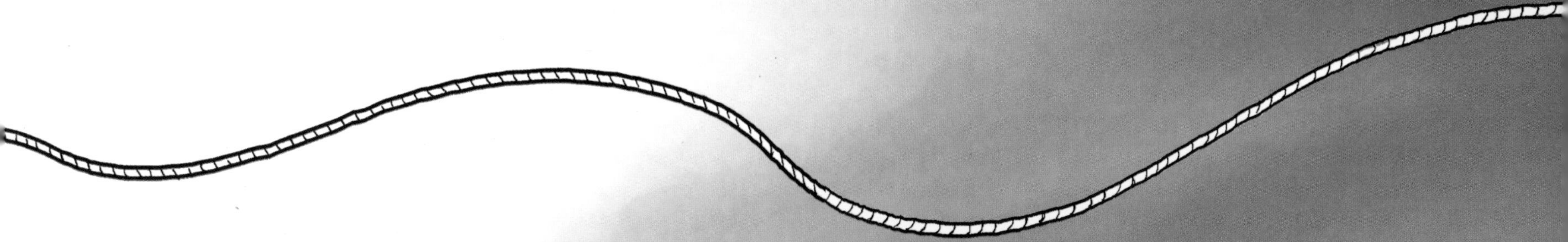

"...babies of course are not human - they are animals, and have a very ancient and ramified culture, as cats have, and fishes, and even snakes: the same in kind as these, but much more complicated and vivid, since babies are, after all, one of the most developed species of the lower vertebrates.

In short, babies have minds which work in terms and categories of their own which cannot be translated into the terms and categories of the human mind.

It is true they look human - but not so human, to be quite fair, as many monkeys."

—Richard Hughes, A High Wind In Jamaica

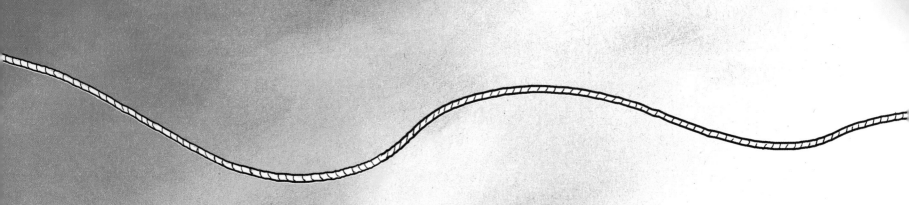

SORT OF BOOKS
*presents*

# THE BOOK OF
# LEVIATHAN

## by Peter Blegvad

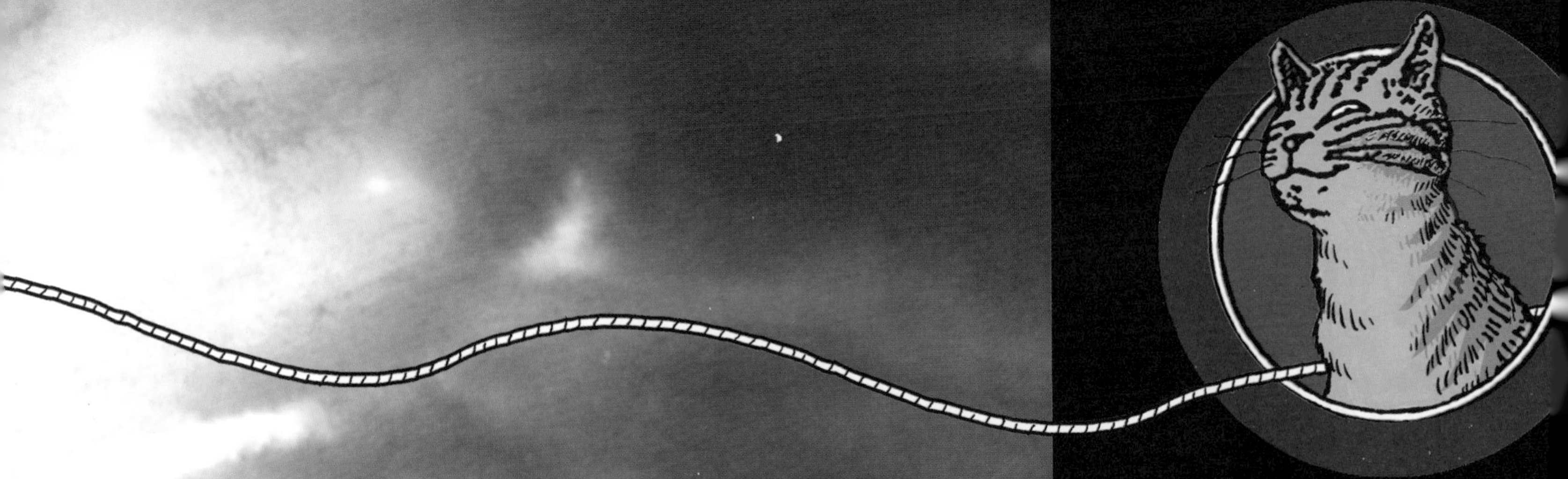

*By the seat of our pants ad astr*

The Book of Leviathan

*for Chloë, Kaye and Viggo*

Thanks to Mark Ellingham, Natania Jansz, Rafi Zabor, Julian Rothenstein, Edwin Belchamber, Tim Chester, John Paige, amd Simon Lucas. Also to Richard Williams, Liz Jobey, Ian Jack, Nikki Moore, Ruth Metzstein, Henry Porter, et al (especially in scanning) at the *Independent on Sunday Review,* 1991-1999



Published in 2000 by Sort Of Books
PO Box 18678, London NW3 2FL

Distributed by the Penguin Group in all territories excluding the United States and Canada: Penguin Books, 27 Wrights Lane, London W8 5TZ

Printed in Hong Kong by South Sea International Press

160pp
A catalogue record for this book is available from the British Library
ISBN 0-9535227-2-5

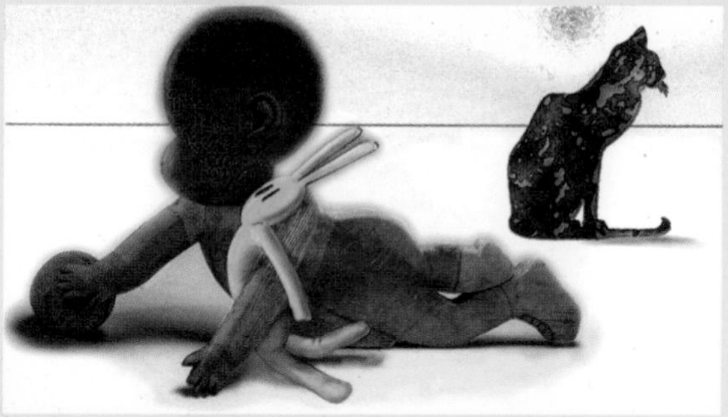

"OUR DOLLS DON'T LIVE THROUGH US, WE LIVE THROUGH OUR DOLLS." — WALTER BENJAMIN

# TABLE of CONTENTS

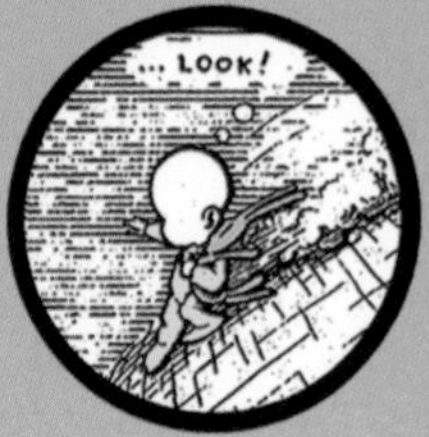
... LOOK!



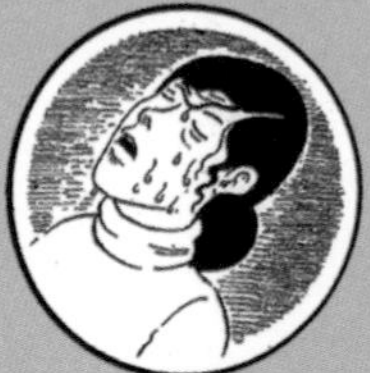



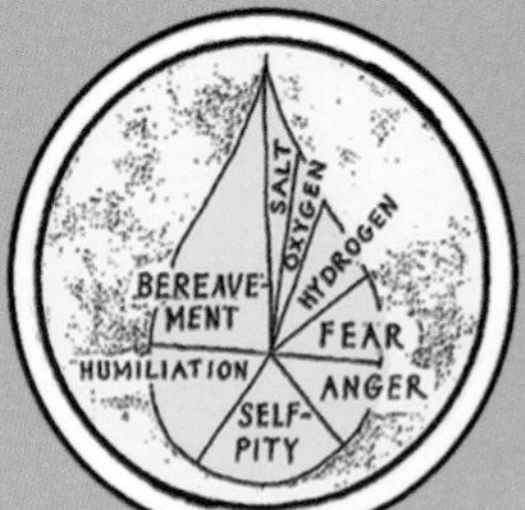
SALT
OXYGEN
HYDROGEN
BEREAVE-MENT
FEAR
HUMILIATION
ANGER
SELF-PITY



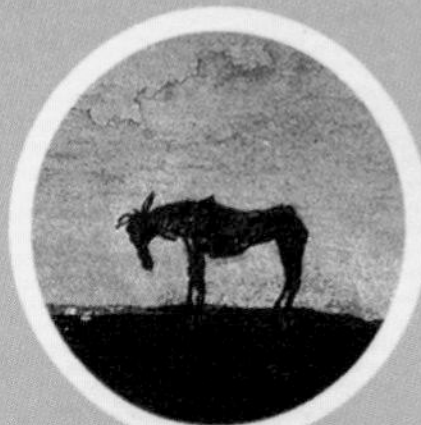



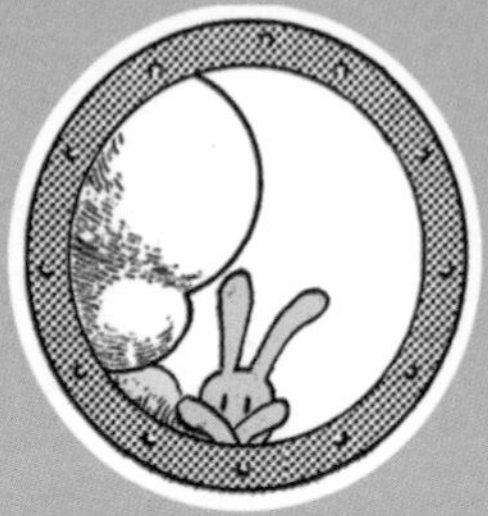

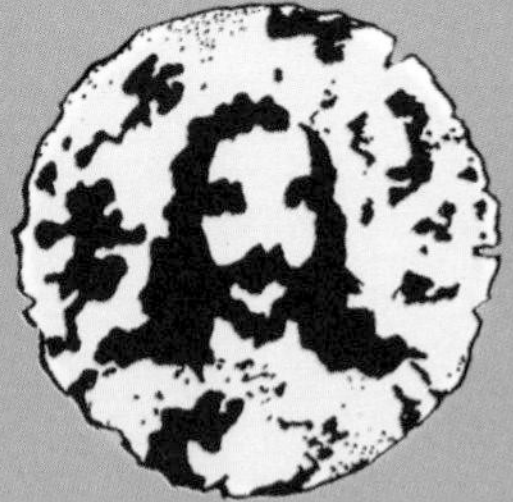



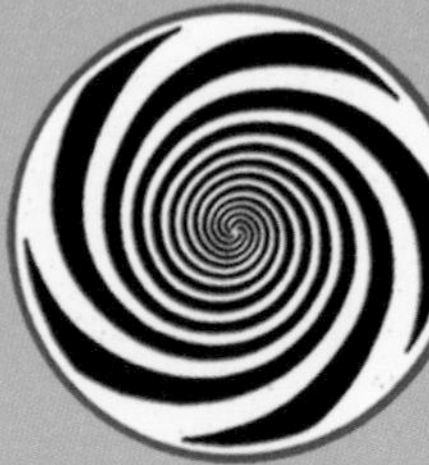

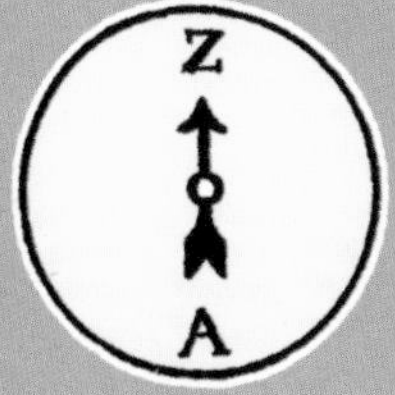
Z
A

## VIII — Words Enough & Time
*Tempus fuggit.*

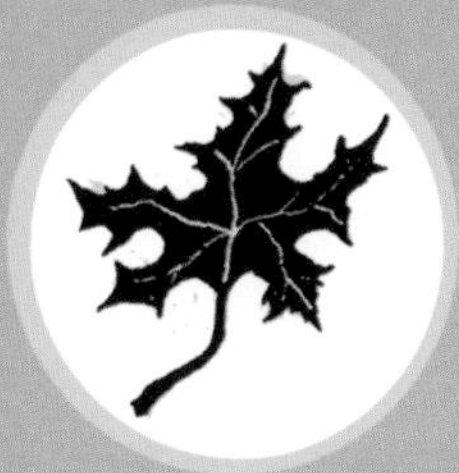

## IX — Wilds, Woods & Gas
*101 Damnations*

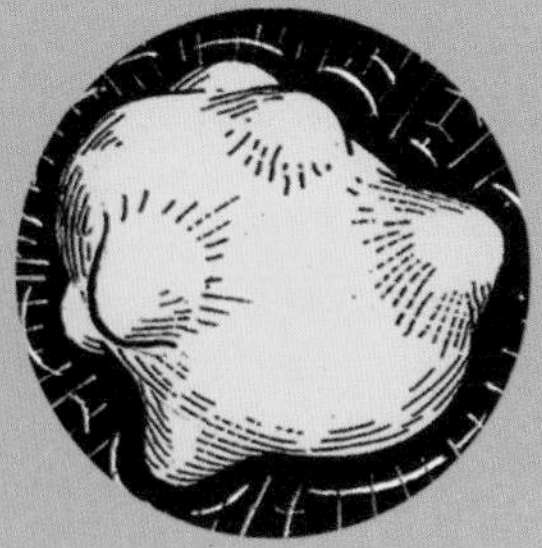

## X — I Got a Million of 'em
*An oasis of sanity in a world GONE MAD.*

## XI — Hell
*Come on down!*

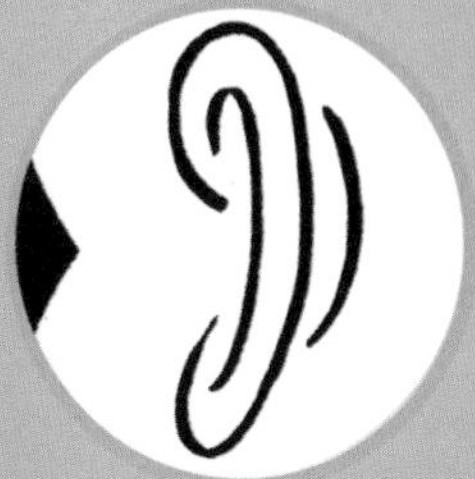

## XII — Escape
*There's one bored every minute.*

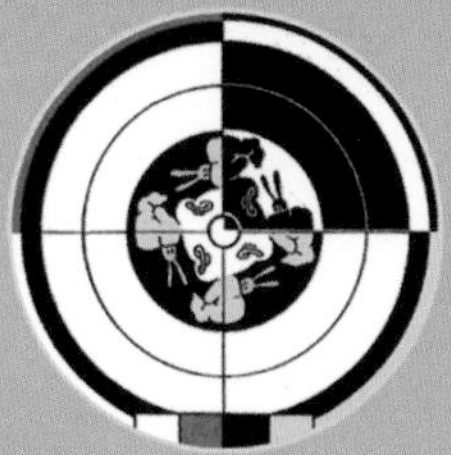

## XIII — Tell Me a Story
*Beginning, muddle & end.*

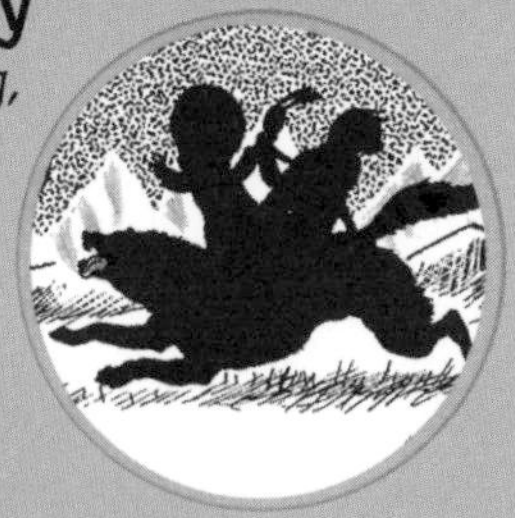

## XIV — Songs
*In which things too foolish to be said are sung.*

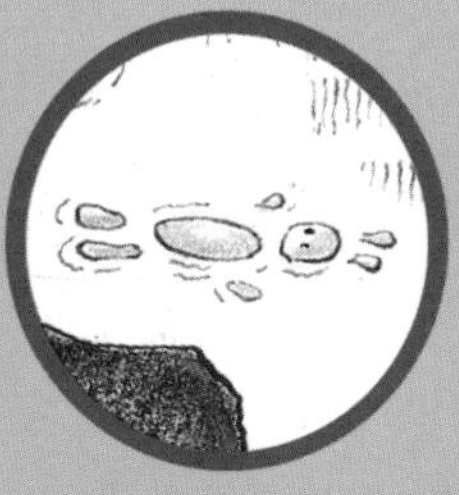

## XV — This Way Up
*To be taken lying down.*

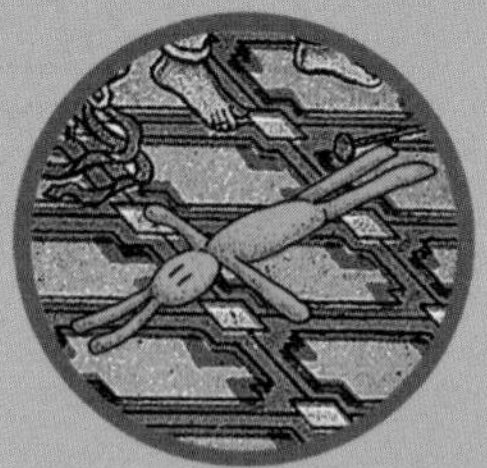

## XVI — A Problem Aired
*To air is human.*

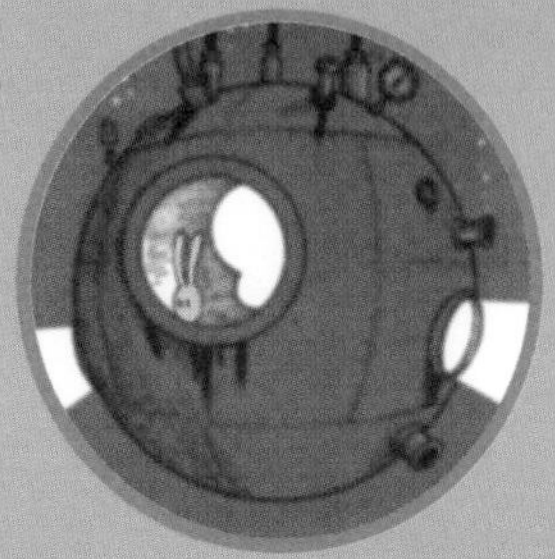

## XVII — The Truck is Stuck
*Tale fin.*

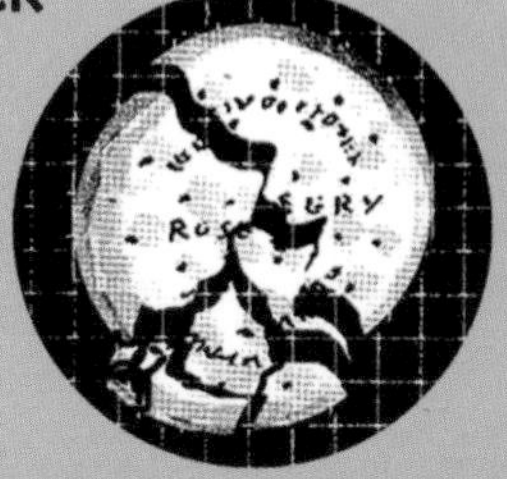

# Introduction
## by Rafi Zabor

Q: How did you get the idea of naming a tiny baby Leviathan?

A: From my own kids: they're born, you bring them home and they're bigger than anything else in your life.

Q: Why did you switch from Levi's parents to the Cat?

A: The Cat was easier to draw.

The first time I saw Peter Blegvad's *Leviathan* in *The Independent on Sunday*—and as an American wandering back and forth across the Atlantic in the early nineties, I tended to see it in fragmentary fashion, on visits to France and England—I responded with a spontaneous yelp of pleasure, and within a few encounters with the strip it was clear to me that it was one of the very best things being written, drawn, sung, sculpted, played, danced or acted at the time, an impression the intervening years have done nothing to dim, harumph et cetera. I knew Blegvad's name—it's one you don't easily forget—because about ten years earlier I had reviewed a record, *Kew. Rhone*, he'd been involved with, and he'd sent me a postcard to say thanks for the nice review and to point out that a lyric I had praised as an instance of intelligent surrealism—"Peel's foe, not a set animal, laminates a tone of sleep"—was also a palindrome; but that was it, we'd had no further contact and I had no personal or ulterior motive for going bughouse about his brainchild. I just did. Whenever I was in Europe, spontaneous yelp of pleasure followed spontaneous yelp of pleasure in a tight weekly sequence, nipping at each others' heels, frolicking in the roadside pastures, and assuming looser formations when I could find a copy Stateside or convince a friend to clip an installment and send it over.

It is also true that I have met a few intelligent, literate, artistically sophisticated people who just don't *get* it, and their non-response to what is obviously and just for starters a classic of its kind, assuming it has a kind, has always puzzled me. Maybe they lack an appetite for metaphysical funnies, or are plagued by an allergy to the air of other planets—who knows?—but they're missing out on one of the treats of the present age, and a whole series of bracing violations of the stale prosy treaties of quotidian perception.

This collection tilts away from the metaphysical intricacies of some of Leviathan's darker passages—although in fact it opens with one of the eeriest of these—and treats the reader to a purer oxygen of comedy. The first couple of sections anchor the strip in relatively terrestrial and psychological reality—childhood cognition and miscognition, makeshift household cosmologies, parental incomprehension, sibling rivalry—the better to support the unearthly oddities to come when—Cat replacing Parents and a cosmic puzzlement overwhelming the family dynamic—*Leviathan* decants us into a world not so much fallen as tipped over: realms of dimensional slippage, cognitive puns, and mirrored halls of infinite paradox and *double-comprendre*. It is strange but finally not unfamiliar country.

Installments that continue to leave me fairly helpless with laughter even after many viewings include the conjunction of a heavily armored robot and a Hamlin Garland poem, the appearance of a frothing ectoplasmic Hegel to explain "the opposite of bunny", the ludicrously funny Bark Ode panel (in which, *sotto voce*, that hymning, lyring dog and his rapt audience index an elemental feel for the vanity, poignancy and limits of life in any species: the strip in general sounds a persistent note whose music might humble human supposition), the flawless tautological humor of Leviathan and the locomotive (though note that most people, had they come up with the gag, wouldn't have written the Cat's line, which perfects it), and many, many more. Blegvad's expansive gift for concision may be most evident in the one-panel episode concerning the cut of the other guy's jib (notice also: those boats are round: the sense of detail just doesn't quit). He also seems to own precise access to preconscious memory, of which the alchemical formula for milk may be the most acute example. None of this resembles anything I've seen or read anywhere else, ever.

The drawing ranges from the defiantly home-made to the surprisingly beautiful. It is always apt, and sometimes it can be the key to a subtle door. "Cat's New Look," introduced in the first panel of the sequence in which Leviathan visits Hell, seems a good example. Deciding to draw the Cat differently one week first struck me as an instance of the freedom and simplicity of motion only first-rate talents can manage, that and an unwillingness to be hobgobbled by smallminded consistencies. After a while it emerged as not just a clever-clever demonstration of authorial smarts but as a subtle injunction to remain unruffled, in life as in more quickly passing comix, by the unexpected lurch of secondary elements—all appearances in the strip are subject to unexplained mutation—the better perhaps to pursue a sustaining central essence beyond the noise of change. Blegvad keeps burying the bone deeper and inviting us behind the stage-set and the changing-rooms with their stash of costumes, masks and mirrors to what might actually endure but eludes being nailed in place with a name. (As for the altered Cat, note that in order to make so apparently arbitrary a move and allow it due meaning you need to have invented a master narrative, characters and world that can take such flux without snapping.)

 *Leviathan* does sometimes set an epistemological terror whickering beneath the skin of things, since for all its comedy and obliquity the strip engages straight the strangeness, peril and beauty of finding oneself alive—is this what puts off the odd unreceptive sophisticado? I really couldn't say. I seldom read it without being rewarded by a dose of liberating light, a freshening of perception, and a reanimation of the normal sluggard crawl and stumble of the working brain: Blegvad's baby leaves fresh script incised upon the mind.

 But—aside from the obvious fact that we're all faceless babies wandering through a shifting, barely scrutable world with only a cat for tutelary spirit—like what's it all mean, man? As the Lord rhetorically inquired in another publication, "Canst thou draw out Leviathan with an hook?" The answer, I think, is a resounding *nyet*. The Fudd of intellect will never capture the Wabbit of true vision. Words fail. Times change. Cats meow. Leviathan swims in its native deep, glistening through serial sea-green layers, sending off spectra of intelligible light as it steers with ribbed and radiant fins. Whut? It is the finest gnostic comic strip to come out of Britain since the heyday of William Blake, and it's a treat to have this book available. Invite it home. Share it with family and friends. Spend the money. It will make us all a little happier, and welcome a classic into our midst.

Rafi Zabor is the author of *The Bear Comes Home*

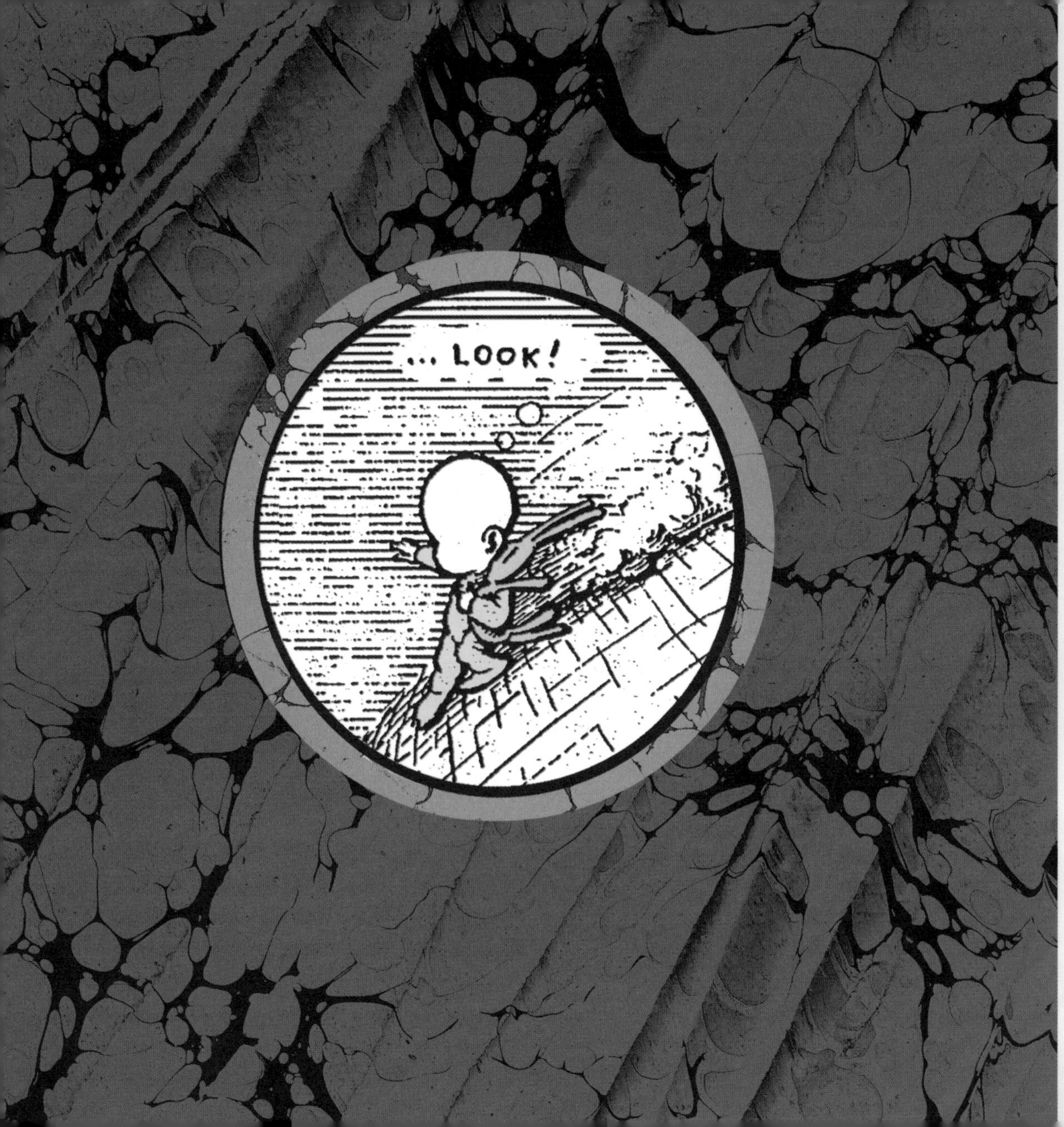
...LOOK!

# I. LOST & FOUNDLING

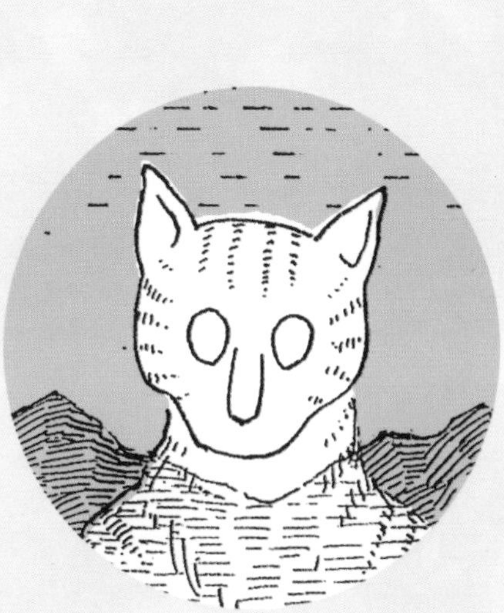

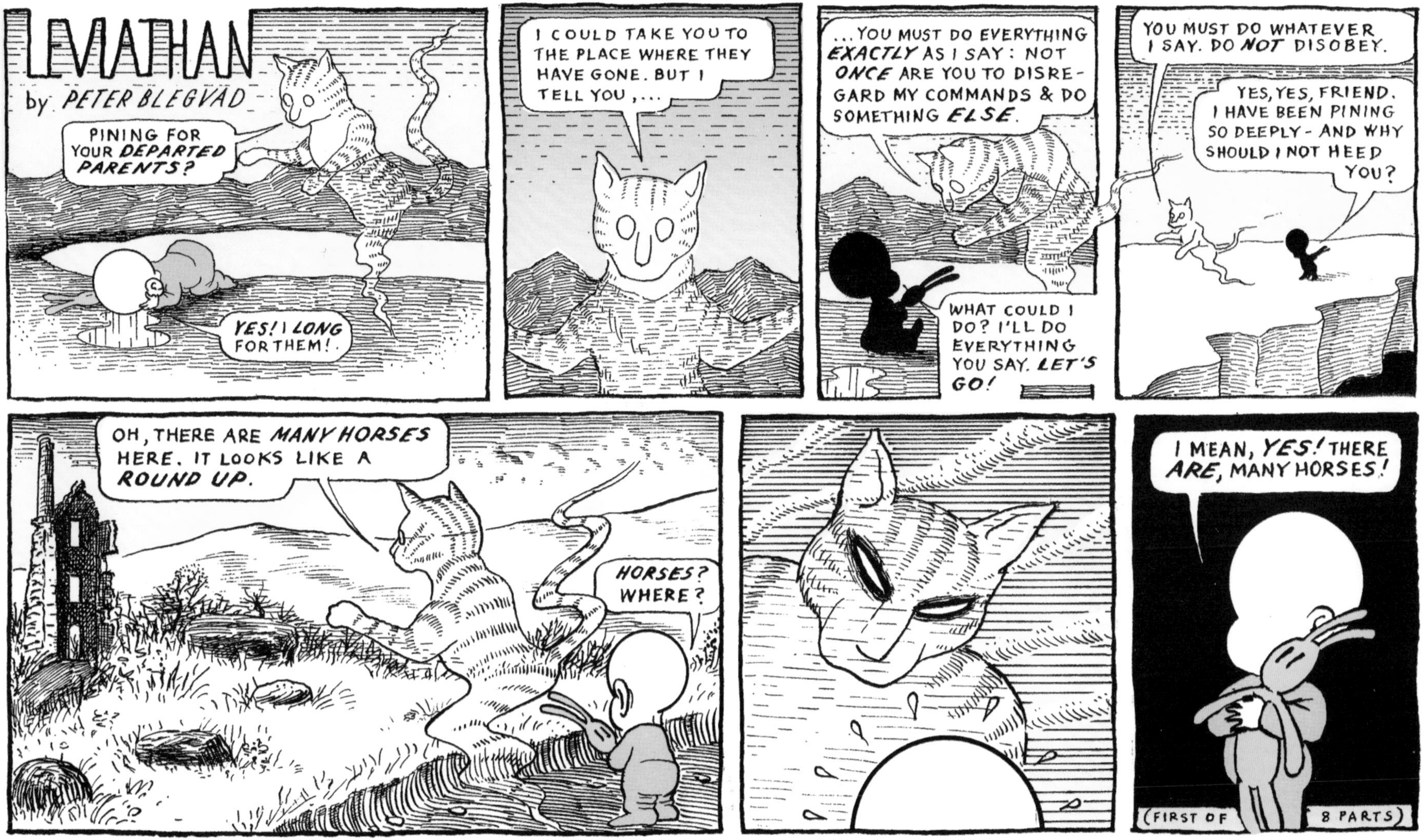
LEVIATHAN
by PETER BLEGVAD
PINING FOR YOUR DEPARTED PARENTS?
YES! I LONG FOR THEM!
I COULD TAKE YOU TO THE PLACE WHERE THEY HAVE GONE. BUT I TELL YOU, ...
... YOU MUST DO EVERYTHING EXACTLY AS I SAY: NOT ONCE ARE YOU TO DISREGARD MY COMMANDS & DO SOMETHING ELSE.
WHAT COULD I DO? I'LL DO EVERYTHING YOU SAY. LET'S GO!
YOU MUST DO WHATEVER I SAY. DO NOT DISOBEY.
YES, YES, FRIEND. I HAVE BEEN PINING SO DEEPLY - AND WHY SHOULD I NOT HEED YOU?
OH, THERE ARE MANY HORSES HERE. IT LOOKS LIKE A ROUND UP.
HORSES? WHERE?
I MEAN, YES! THERE ARE, MANY HORSES!
(FIRST OF 8 PARTS)

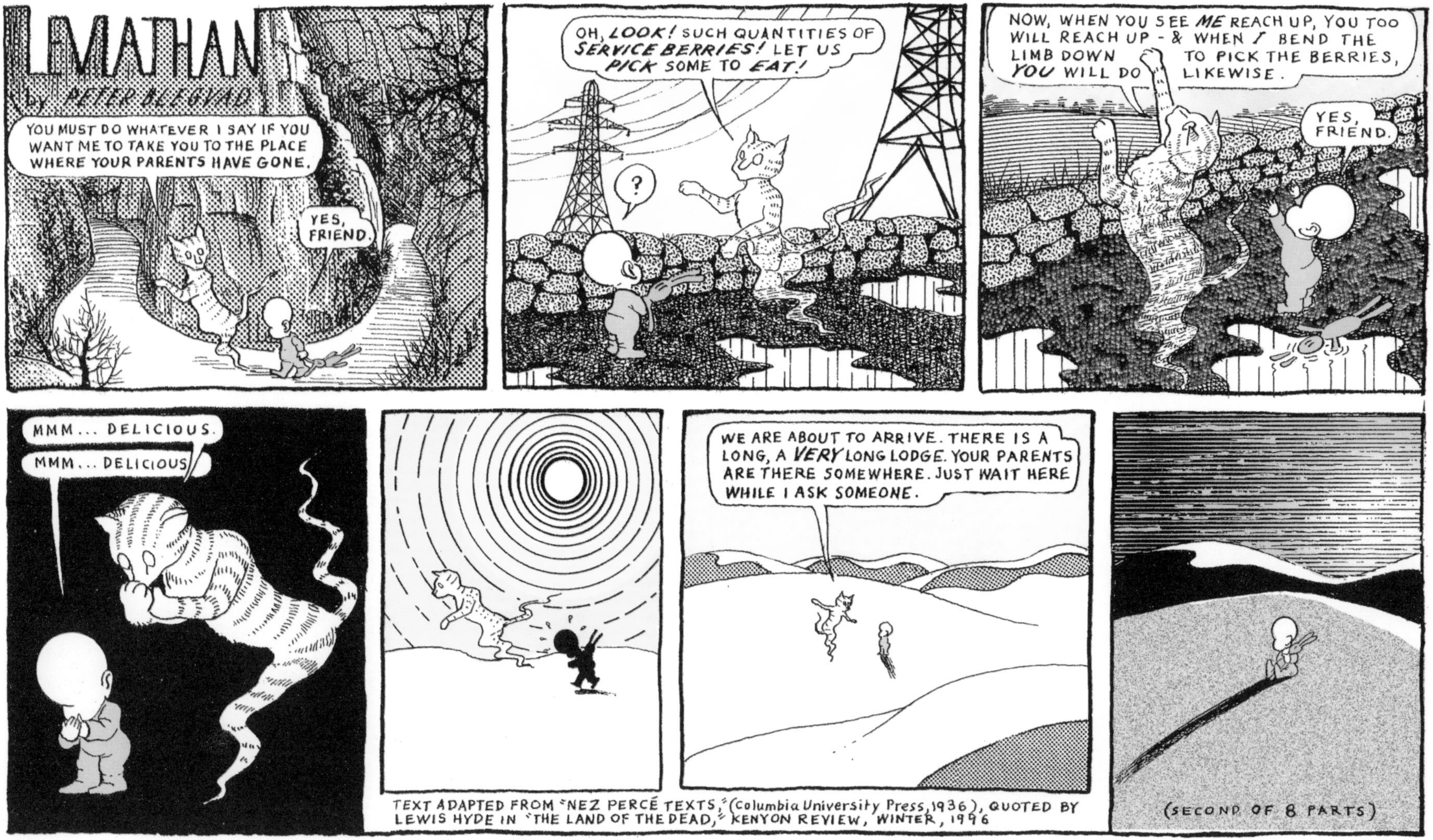
LEVIATHAN
by PETER BLEGVAD
YOU MUST DO WHATEVER I SAY IF YOU WANT ME TO TAKE YOU TO THE PLACE WHERE YOUR PARENTS HAVE GONE.
YES, FRIEND.
OH, LOOK! SUCH QUANTITIES OF SERVICE BERRIES! LET US PICK SOME TO EAT!
?
NOW, WHEN YOU SEE ME REACH UP, YOU TOO WILL REACH UP - & WHEN I BEND THE LIMB DOWN TO PICK THE BERRIES, YOU WILL DO LIKEWISE.
YES, FRIEND.
MMM... DELICIOUS.
MMM... DELICIOUS.
WE ARE ABOUT TO ARRIVE. THERE IS A LONG, A VERY LONG LODGE. YOUR PARENTS ARE THERE SOMEWHERE. JUST WAIT HERE WHILE I ASK SOMEONE.
(SECOND OF 8 PARTS)

TEXT ADAPTED FROM "NEZ PERCÉ TEXTS," (Columbia University Press, 1936), QUOTED BY LEWIS HYDE IN "THE LAND OF THE DEAD," KENYON REVIEW, WINTER, 1996

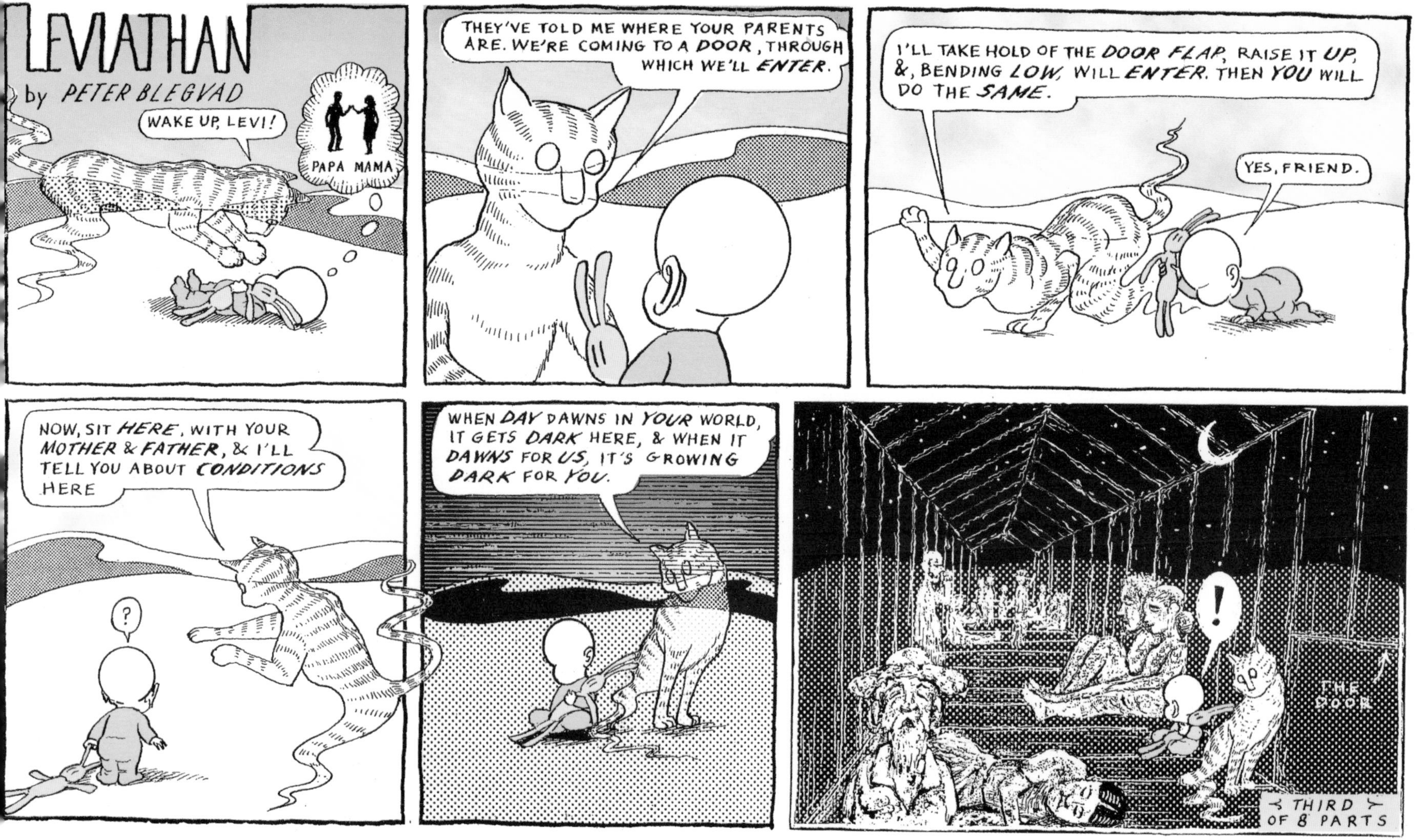
LEVIATHAN
by PETER BLEGVAD
WAKE UP, LEVI!
PAPA MAMA
THEY'VE TOLD ME WHERE YOUR PARENTS ARE. WE'RE COMING TO A DOOR, THROUGH WHICH WE'LL ENTER.
I'LL TAKE HOLD OF THE DOOR FLAP, RAISE IT UP, &, BENDING LOW, WILL ENTER. THEN YOU WILL DO THE SAME.
YES, FRIEND.
NOW, SIT HERE, WITH YOUR MOTHER & FATHER, & I'LL TELL YOU ABOUT CONDITIONS HERE
?
WHEN DAY DAWNS IN YOUR WORLD, IT GETS DARK HERE, & WHEN IT DAWNS FOR US, IT'S GROWING DARK FOR YOU.
!
THE DOOR
THIRD OF 8 PARTS

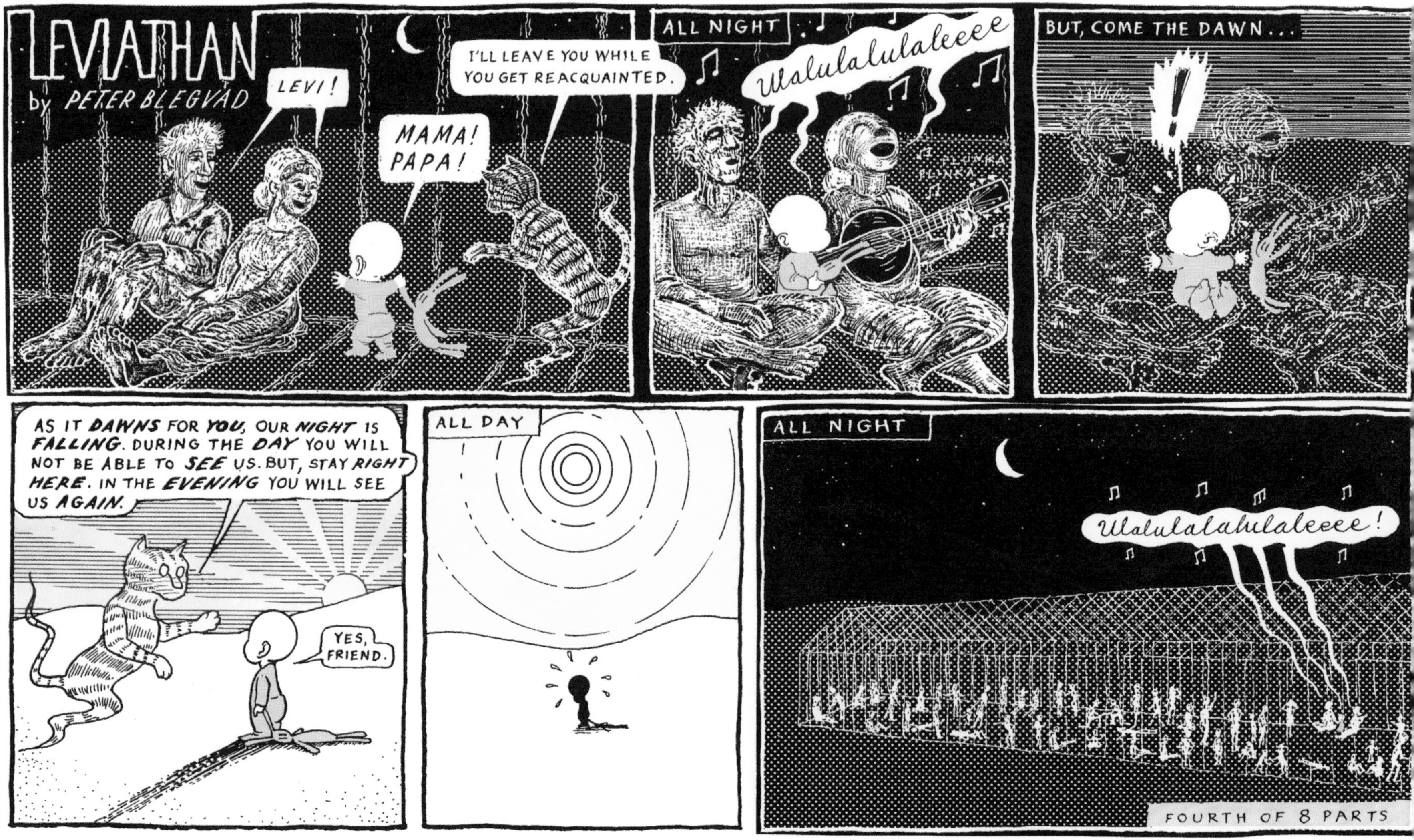
LEVIATHAN
by PETER BLEGVAD
LEVI!
MAMA! PAPA!
I'LL LEAVE YOU WHILE YOU GET REACQUAINTED.
ALL NIGHT
Ulalulalulaleeee
BUT, COME THE DAWN...
!
AS IT DAWNS FOR YOU, OUR NIGHT IS FALLING. DURING THE DAY YOU WILL NOT BE ABLE TO SEE US. BUT, STAY RIGHT HERE. IN THE EVENING YOU WILL SEE US AGAIN.
YES, FRIEND.
ALL DAY
ALL NIGHT
Ulalulalalulaleeee!
FOURTH OF 8 PARTS

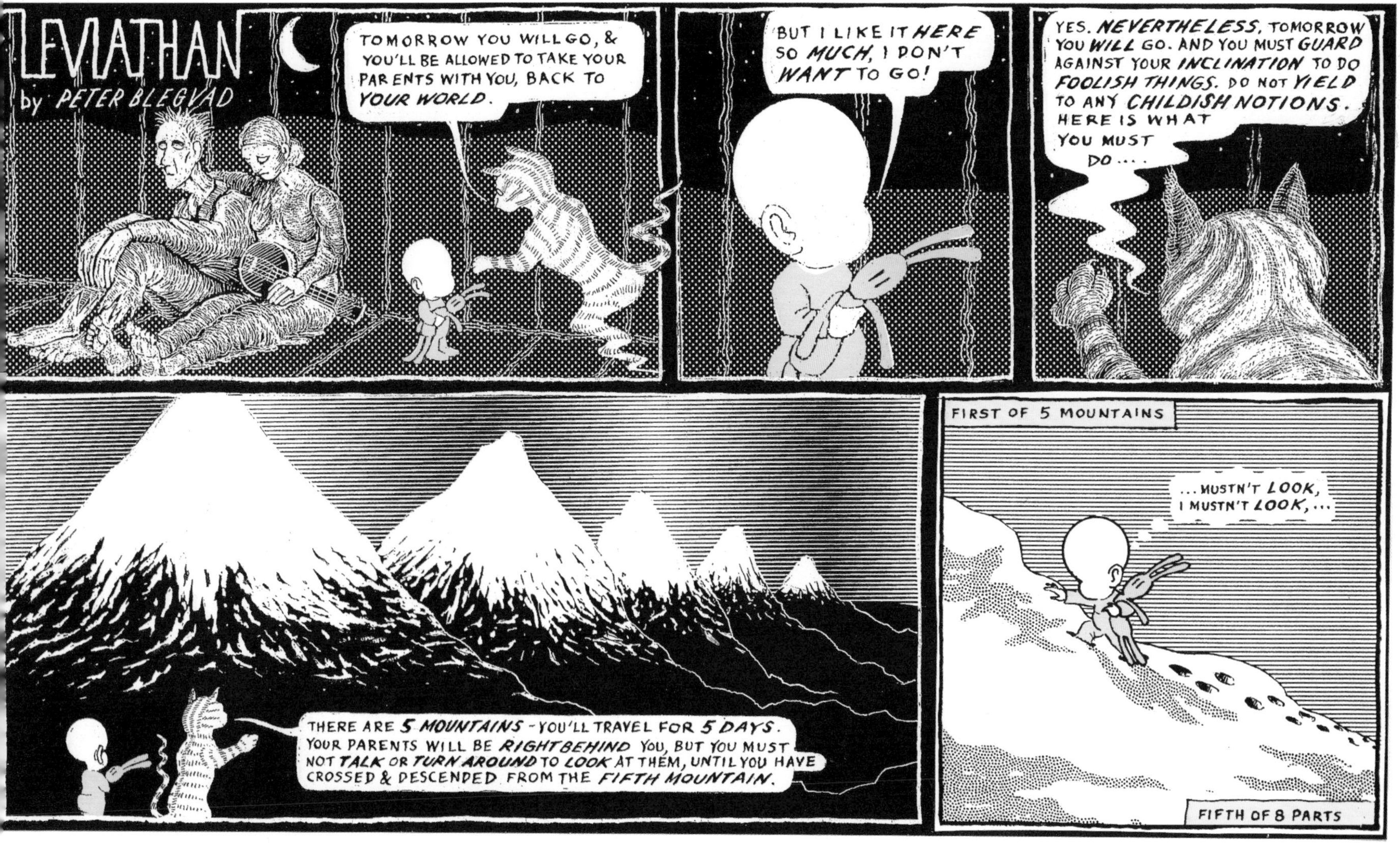
LEVIATHAN
by PETER BLEGVAD
TOMORROW YOU WILL GO, & YOU'LL BE ALLOWED TO TAKE YOUR PARENTS WITH YOU, BACK TO YOUR WORLD.
BUT I LIKE IT HERE SO MUCH, I DON'T WANT TO GO!
YES. NEVERTHELESS, TOMORROW YOU WILL GO. AND YOU MUST GUARD AGAINST YOUR INCLINATION TO DO FOOLISH THINGS. DO NOT YIELD TO ANY CHILDISH NOTIONS. HERE IS WHAT YOU MUST DO....
THERE ARE 5 MOUNTAINS - YOU'LL TRAVEL FOR 5 DAYS. YOUR PARENTS WILL BE RIGHT BEHIND YOU, BUT YOU MUST NOT TALK OR TURN AROUND TO LOOK AT THEM, UNTIL YOU HAVE CROSSED & DESCENDED FROM THE FIFTH MOUNTAIN.
FIRST OF 5 MOUNTAINS
...MUSTN'T LOOK, I MUSTN'T LOOK,...
FIFTH OF 8 PARTS

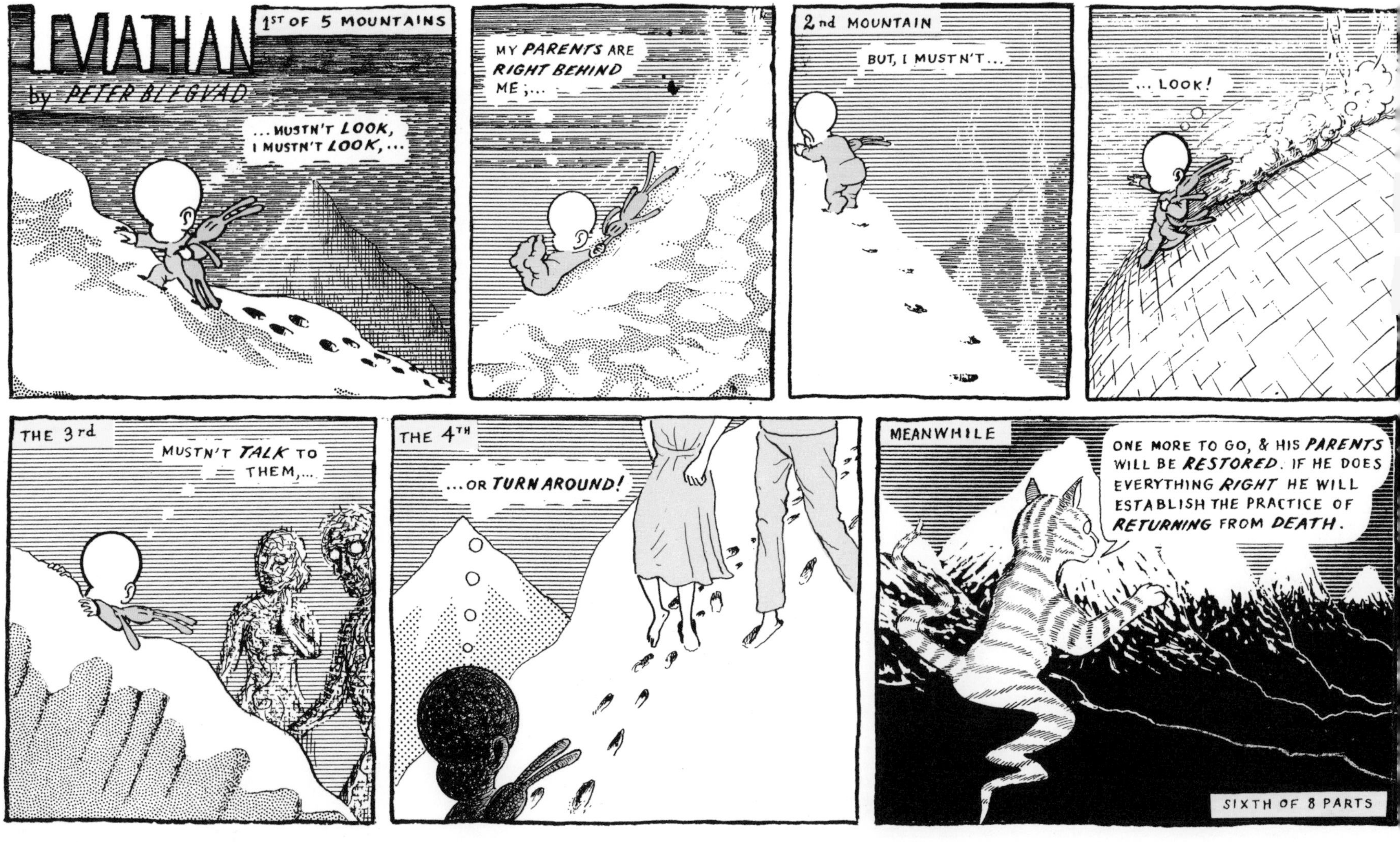
LEVIATHAN
by PETER BLEGVAD
1ST OF 5 MOUNTAINS
...MUSTN'T LOOK, I MUSTN'T LOOK,...
MY PARENTS ARE RIGHT BEHIND ME;...
2nd MOUNTAIN
BUT, I MUSTN'T...
...LOOK!
THE 3rd
MUSTN'T TALK TO THEM,...
THE 4TH
...OR TURN AROUND!
MEANWHILE
ONE MORE TO GO, & HIS PARENTS WILL BE RESTORED. IF HE DOES EVERYTHING RIGHT HE WILL ESTABLISH THE PRACTICE OF RETURNING FROM DEATH.
SIXTH OF 8 PARTS

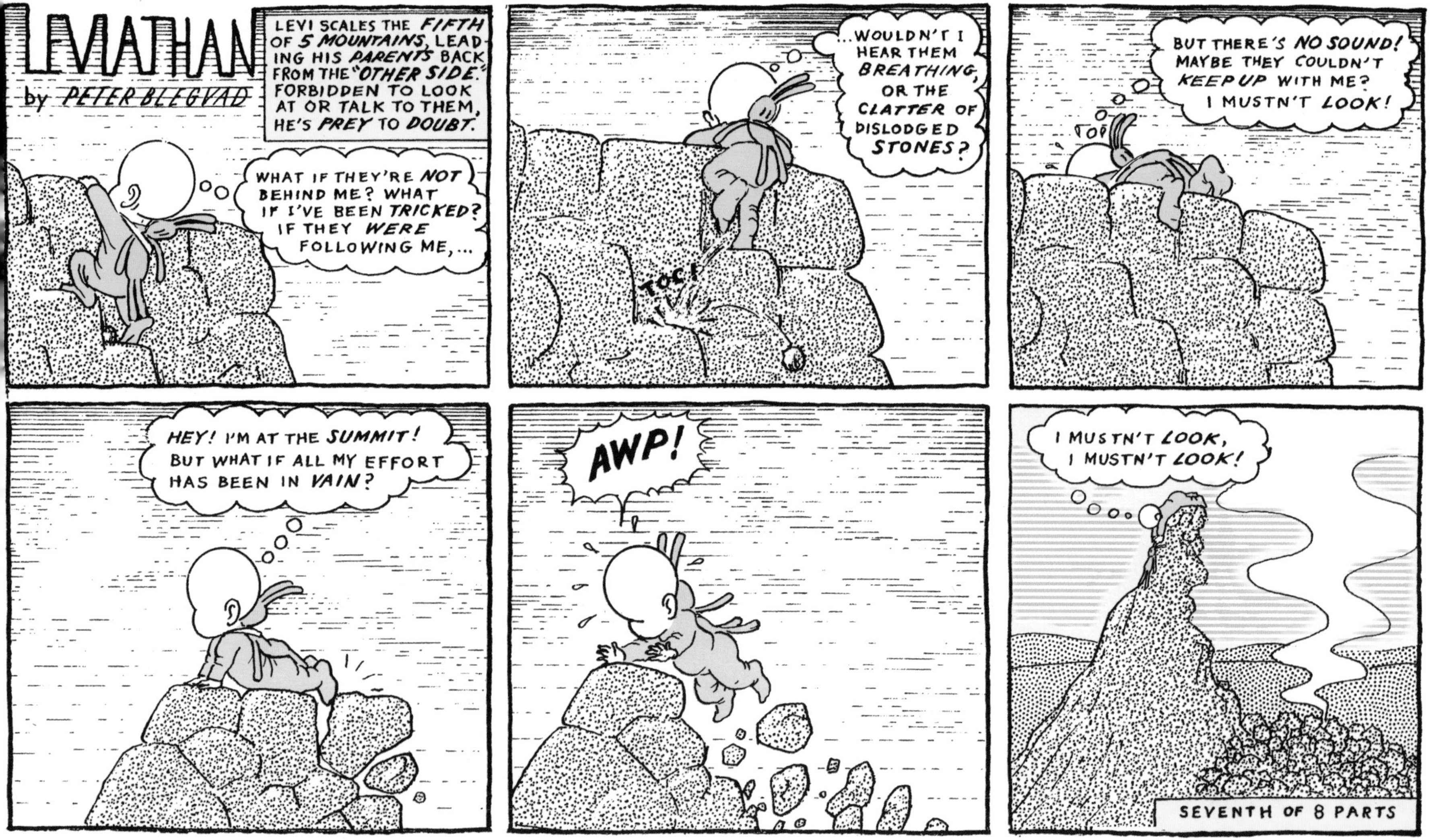
LEVIATHAN
by PETER BLEGVAD
LEVI SCALES THE FIFTH OF 5 MOUNTAINS, LEADING HIS PARENTS BACK FROM THE "OTHER SIDE." FORBIDDEN TO LOOK AT OR TALK TO THEM, HE'S PREY TO DOUBT.
WHAT IF THEY'RE NOT BEHIND ME? WHAT IF I'VE BEEN TRICKED? IF THEY WERE FOLLOWING ME,...
...WOULDN'T I HEAR THEM BREATHING, OR THE CLATTER OF DISLODGED STONES?
TOC!
BUT THERE'S NO SOUND! MAYBE THEY COULDN'T KEEP UP WITH ME? I MUSTN'T LOOK!
HEY! I'M AT THE SUMMIT! BUT WHAT IF ALL MY EFFORT HAS BEEN IN VAIN?
AWP!
I MUSTN'T LOOK, I MUSTN'T LOOK!
SEVENTH OF 8 PARTS

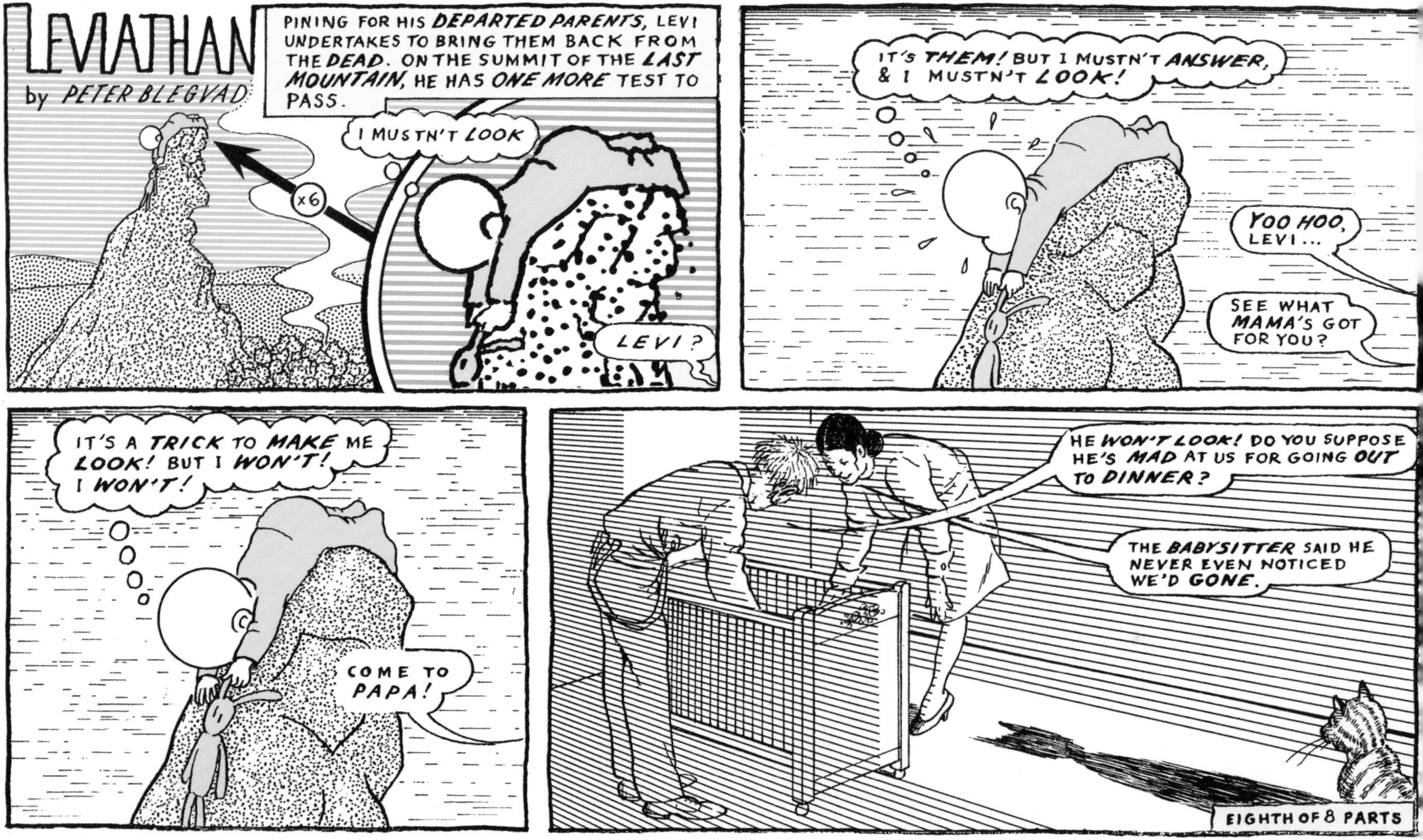
LEVIATHAN
by PETER BLEGVAD
PINING FOR HIS DEPARTED PARENTS, LEVI UNDERTAKES TO BRING THEM BACK FROM THE DEAD. ON THE SUMMIT OF THE LAST MOUNTAIN, HE HAS ONE MORE TEST TO PASS.
x6
I MUSTN'T LOOK
LEVI?
IT'S THEM! BUT I MUSTN'T ANSWER, & I MUSTN'T LOOK!
YOO HOO, LEVI...
SEE WHAT MAMA'S GOT FOR YOU?
IT'S A TRICK TO MAKE ME LOOK! BUT I WON'T! I WON'T!
COME TO PAPA!
HE WON'T LOOK! DO YOU SUPPOSE HE'S MAD AT US FOR GOING OUT TO DINNER?
THE BABYSITTER SAID HE NEVER EVEN NOTICED WE'D GONE.
EIGHTH OF 8 PARTS

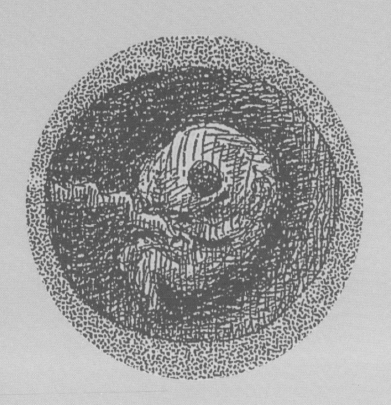

# II. MILK

LEVIATHAN
by PETER BLEGVAD

"a suit of clothes, like a body, spotted with food & shameful behaviour, ..." Volodia Teitelboim, Neruda

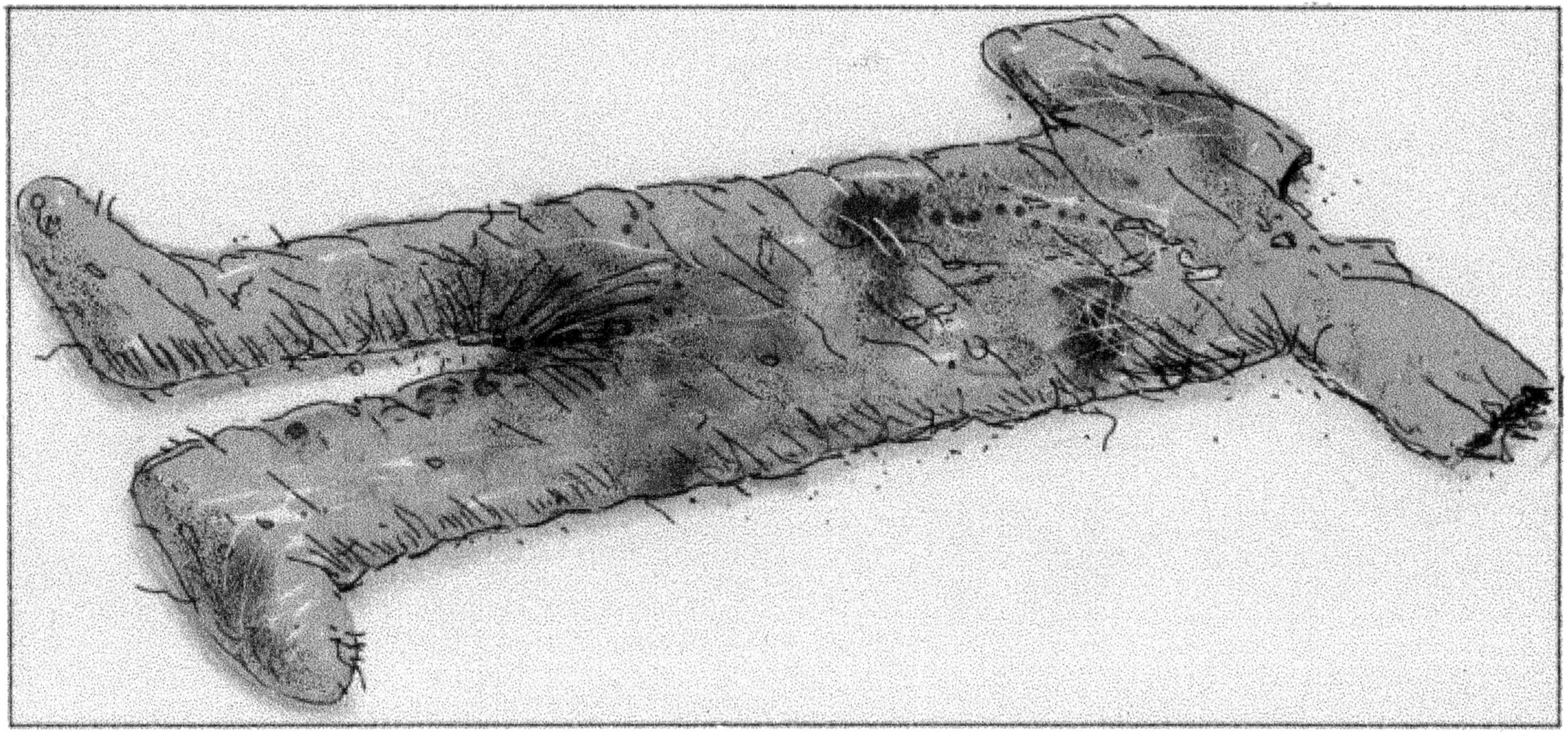

UNITED COLOURS OF LEVIATHAN

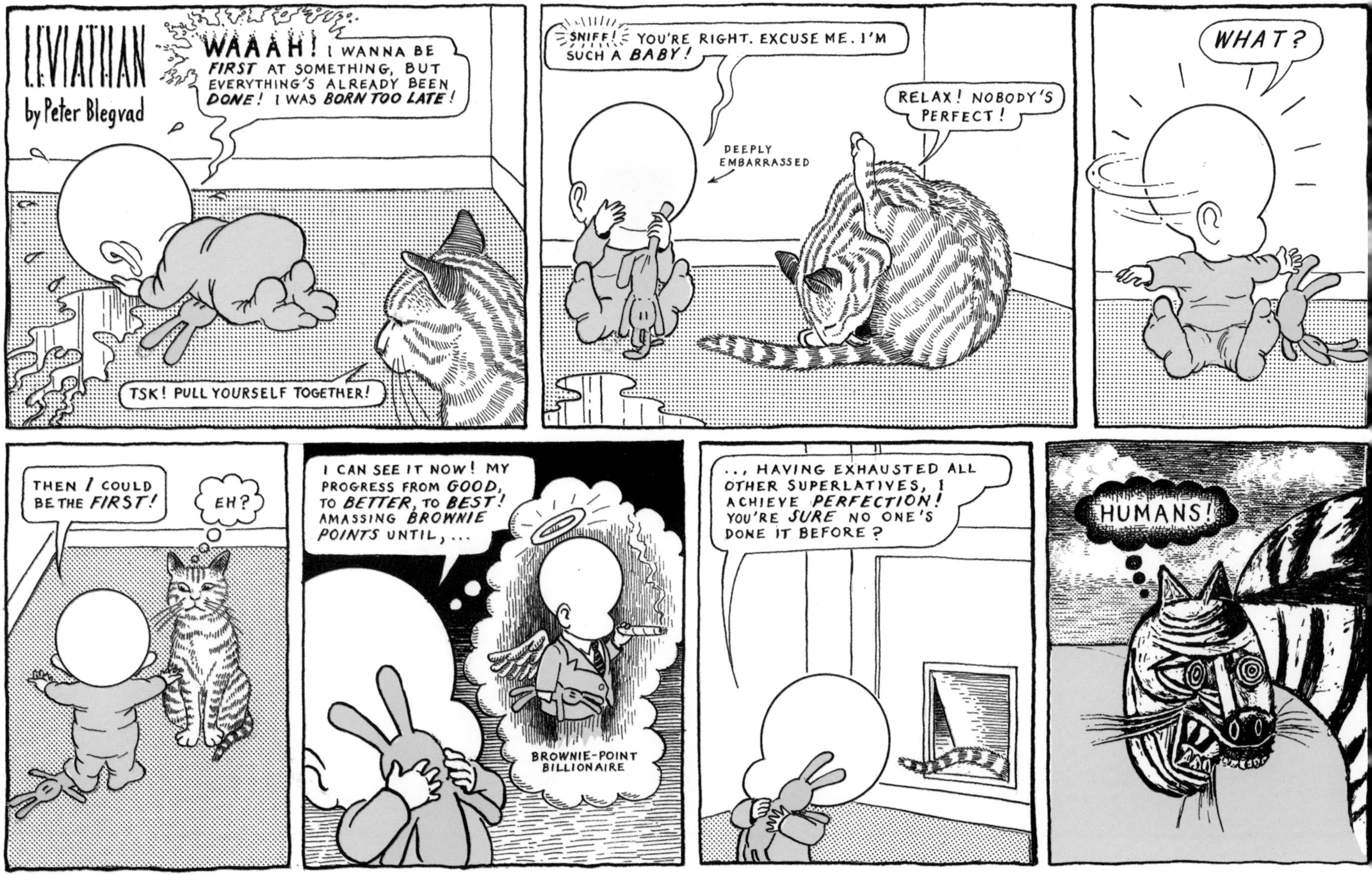
LEVIATHAN
by Peter Blegvad
WAAAH! I WANNA BE FIRST AT SOMETHING, BUT EVERYTHING'S ALREADY BEEN DONE! I WAS BORN TOO LATE!
TSK! PULL YOURSELF TOGETHER!
SNIFF! YOU'RE RIGHT. EXCUSE ME. I'M SUCH A BABY!
DEEPLY EMBARRASSED
RELAX! NOBODY'S PERFECT!
WHAT?
THEN I COULD BE THE FIRST!
EH?
I CAN SEE IT NOW! MY PROGRESS FROM GOOD, TO BETTER, TO BEST! AMASSING BROWNIE POINTS UNTIL, ...
BROWNIE-POINT BILLIONAIRE
.., HAVING EXHAUSTED ALL OTHER SUPERLATIVES, I ACHIEVE PERFECTION! YOU'RE SURE NO ONE'S DONE IT BEFORE?
HUMANS!

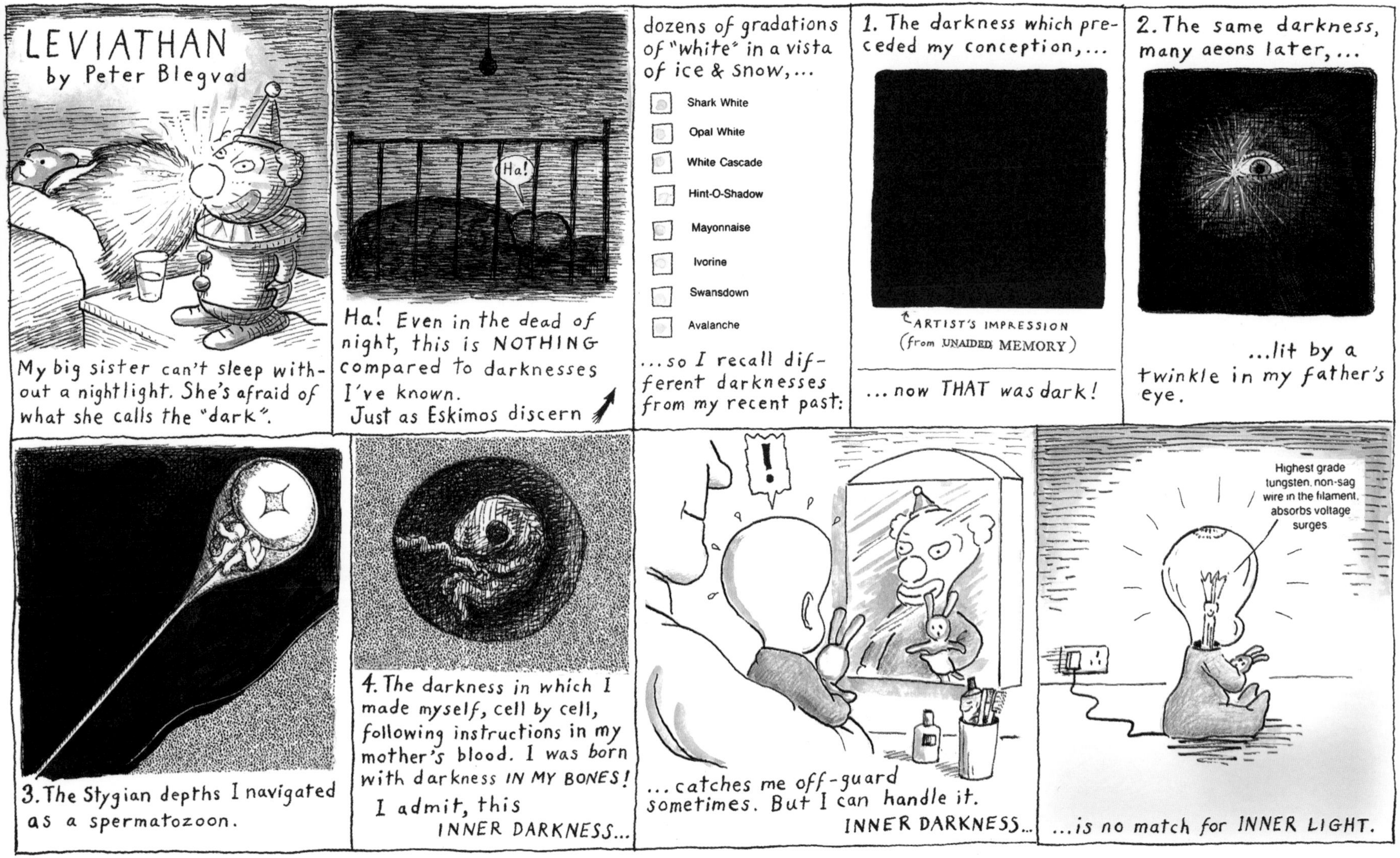
LEVIATHAN
by Peter Blegvad
My big sister can't sleep without a nightlight. She's afraid of what she calls the "dark".
Ha!
Ha! Even in the dead of night, this is NOTHING compared to darknesses I've known.
Just as Eskimos discern
dozens of gradations of "white" in a vista of ice & snow,...
Shark White
Opal White
White Cascade
Hint-O-Shadow
Mayonnaise
Ivorine
Swansdown
Avalanche
...so I recall different darknesses from my recent past:
1. The darkness which preceded my conception,...
ARTIST'S IMPRESSION
(from UNAIDED MEMORY)
... now THAT was dark!
2. The same darkness, many aeons later,...
...lit by a twinkle in my father's eye.
3. The Stygian depths I navigated as a spermatozoon.
4. The darkness in which I made myself, cell by cell, following instructions in my mother's blood. I was born with darkness IN MY BONES!
I admit, this INNER DARKNESS...
!
... catches me off-guard sometimes. But I can handle it.
INNER DARKNESS...
Highest grade tungsten, non-sag wire in the filament, absorbs voltage surges
...is no match for INNER LIGHT.

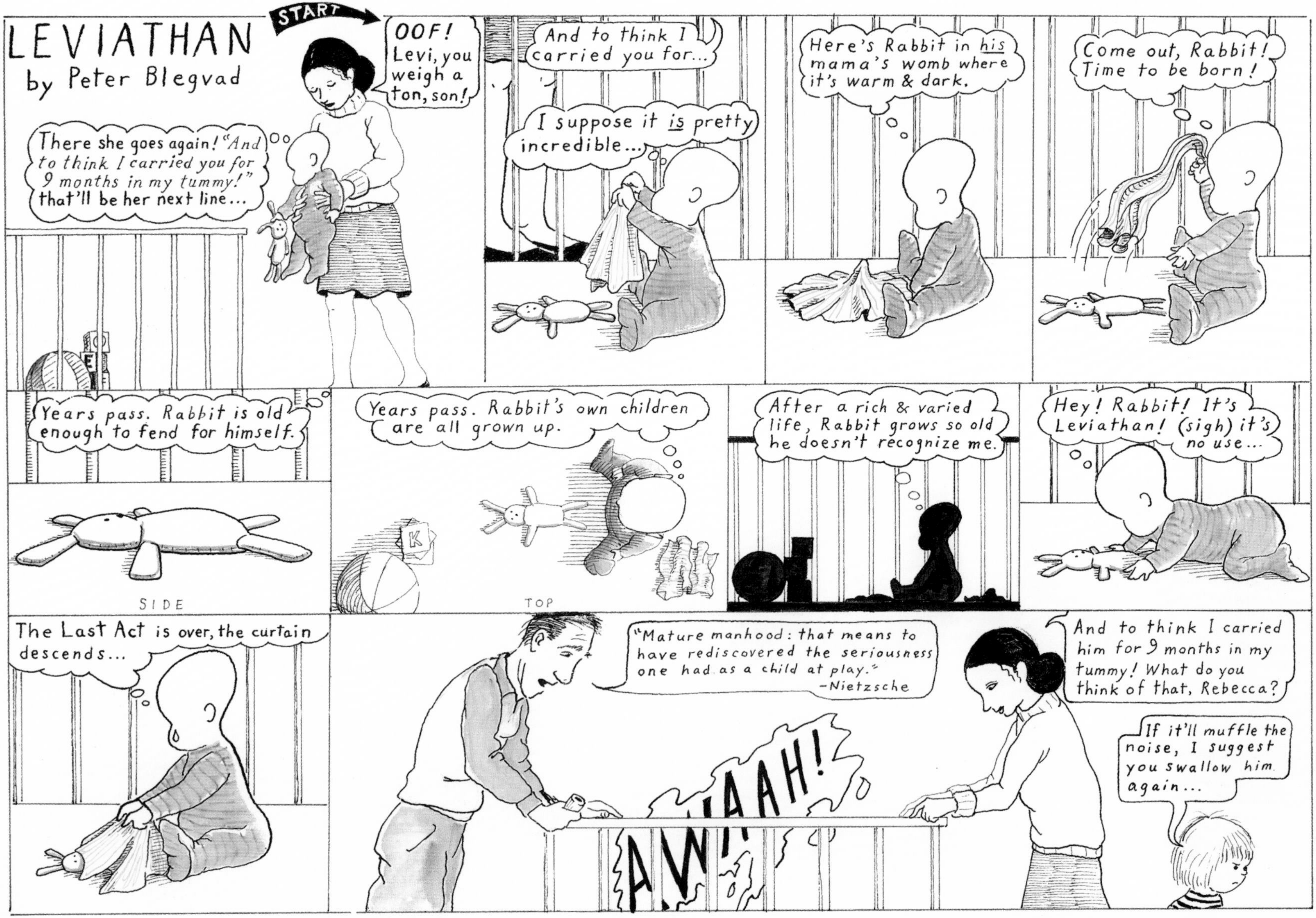
LEVIATHAN
by Peter Blegvad
START
OOF! Levi, you weigh a ton, son!
There she goes again! "And to think I carried you for 9 months in my tummy!" that'll be her next line...
And to think I carried you for...
I suppose it is pretty incredible...
Here's Rabbit in his mama's womb where it's warm & dark.
Come out, Rabbit! Time to be born!
Years pass. Rabbit is old enough to fend for himself.
SIDE
Years pass. Rabbit's own children are all grown up.
TOP
After a rich & varied life, Rabbit grows so old he doesn't recognize me.
Hey! Rabbit! It's Leviathan! (sigh) it's no use...
The Last Act is over, the curtain descends...
"Mature manhood: that means to have rediscovered the seriousness one had as a child at play." –Nietzsche
AWAAAH!
And to think I carried him for 9 months in my tummy! What do you think of that, Rebecca?
If it'll muffle the noise, I suggest you swallow him again...

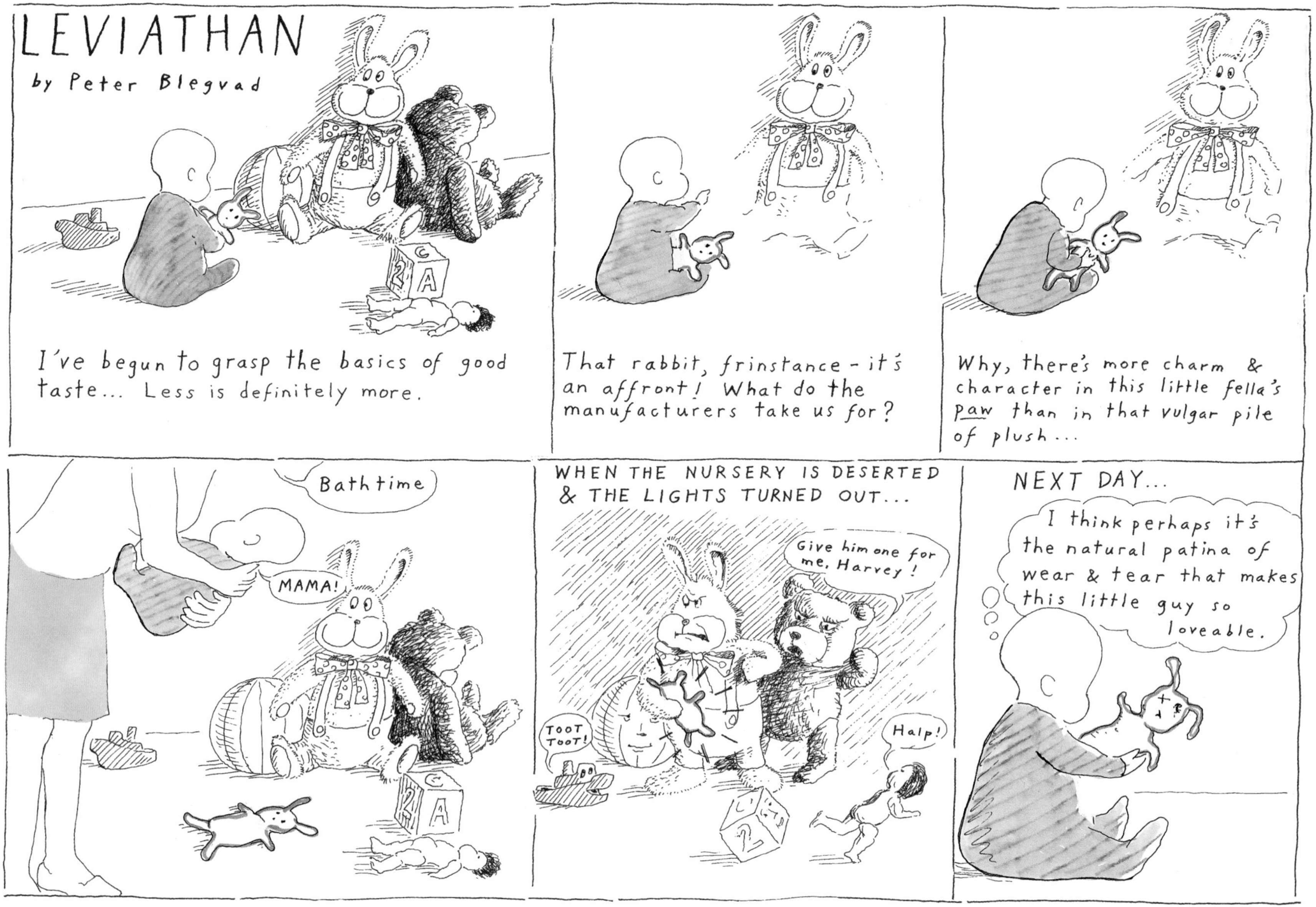
LEVIATHAN
by Peter Blegvad
I've begun to grasp the basics of good taste... Less is definitely more.
That rabbit, frinstance - it's an affront! What do the manufacturers take us for?
Why, there's more charm & character in this little fella's paw than in that vulgar pile of plush...
Bathtime
MAMA!
WHEN THE NURSERY IS DESERTED & THE LIGHTS TURNED OUT...
Give him one for me, Harvey!
TOOT TOOT!
Halp!
NEXT DAY...
I think perhaps it's the natural patina of wear & tear that makes this little guy so loveable.

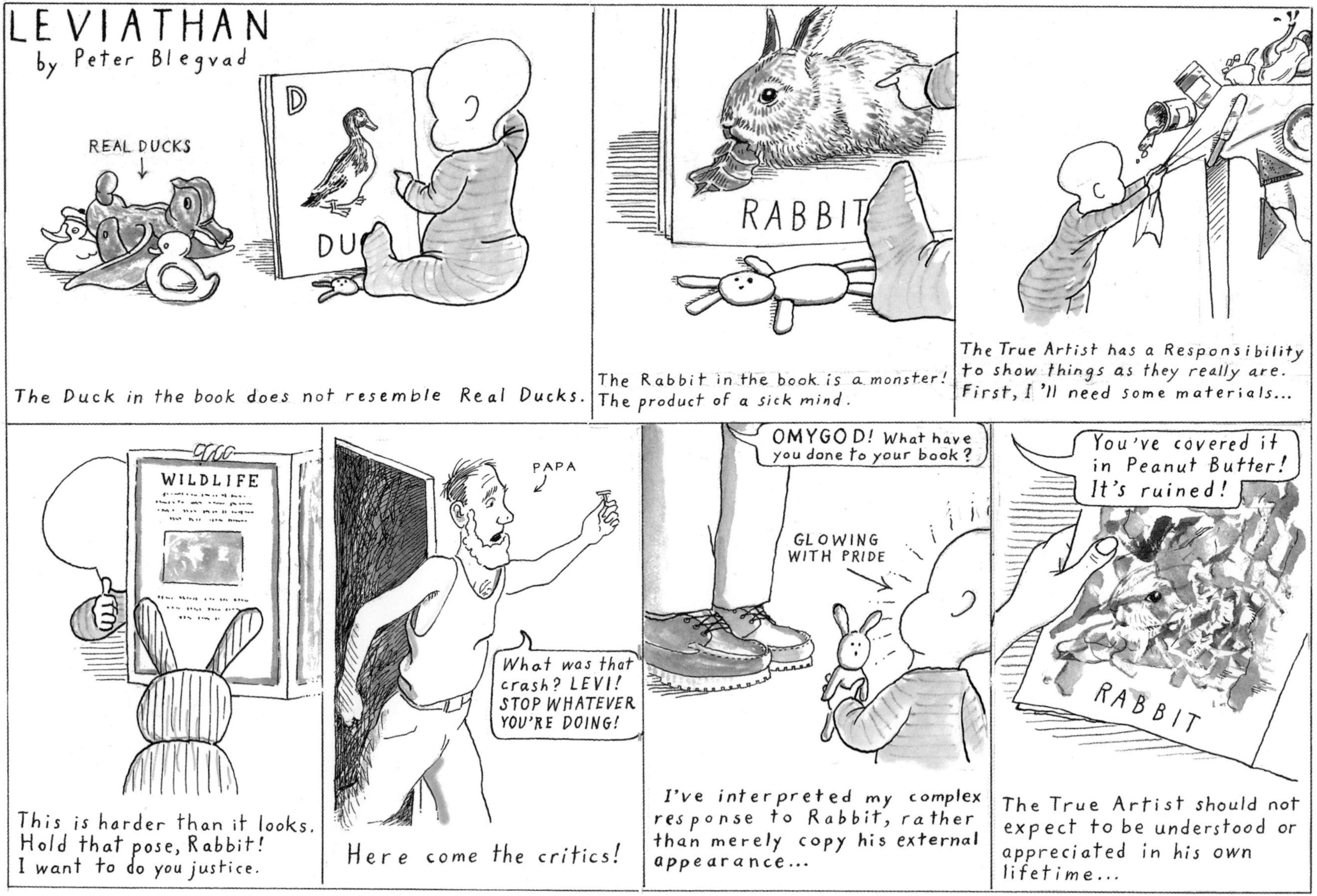

LEVIATHAN
by Peter Blegvad
D
DU
REAL DUCKS
The Duck in the book does not resemble Real Ducks.
RABBIT
The Rabbit in the book is a monster! The product of a sick mind.
The True Artist has a Responsibility to show things as they really are. First, I'll need some materials...
WILDLIFE
This is harder than it looks. Hold that pose, Rabbit! I want to do you justice.
PAPA
What was that crash? LEVI! STOP WHATEVER YOU'RE DOING!
Here come the critics!
OMYGOD! What have you done to your book?
GLOWING WITH PRIDE
I've interpreted my complex response to Rabbit, rather than merely copy his external appearance...
You've covered it in Peanut Butter! It's ruined!
RABBIT
The True Artist should not expect to be understood or appreciated in his own lifetime...

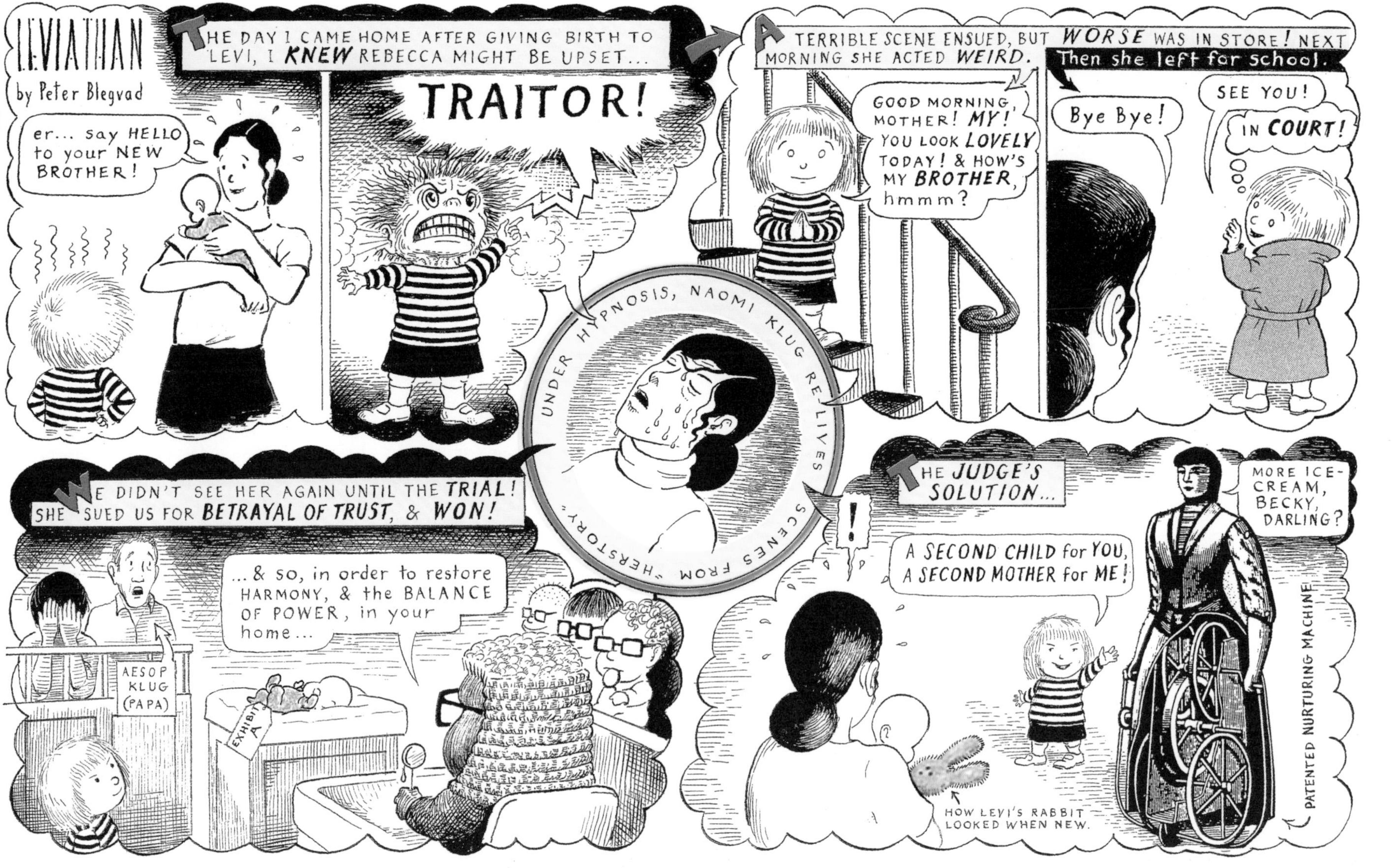

LEVIATHAN
by Peter Blegvad
THE DAY I CAME HOME AFTER GIVING BIRTH TO LEVI, I KNEW REBECCA MIGHT BE UPSET...
er... say HELLO to your NEW BROTHER!
TRAITOR!
A TERRIBLE SCENE ENSUED, BUT WORSE WAS IN STORE! NEXT MORNING SHE ACTED WEIRD.
GOOD MORNING, MOTHER! MY! YOU LOOK LOVELY TODAY! & HOW'S MY BROTHER, hmmm?
Then she left for school.
Bye Bye!
SEE YOU!
IN COURT!
UNDER HYPNOSIS, NAOMI KLUG RE-LIVES SCENES FROM "HERSTORY"
WE DIDN'T SEE HER AGAIN UNTIL THE TRIAL! SHE SUED US FOR BETRAYAL OF TRUST, & WON!
AESOP KLUG (PAPA)
EXHIBIT A
...& so, in order to restore HARMONY, & the BALANCE OF POWER, in your home...
THE JUDGE'S SOLUTION...
!
A SECOND CHILD for YOU, A SECOND MOTHER for ME!
MORE ICE-CREAM, BECKY, DARLING?
HOW LEVI'S RABBIT LOOKED WHEN NEW.
PATENTED NURTURING MACHINE

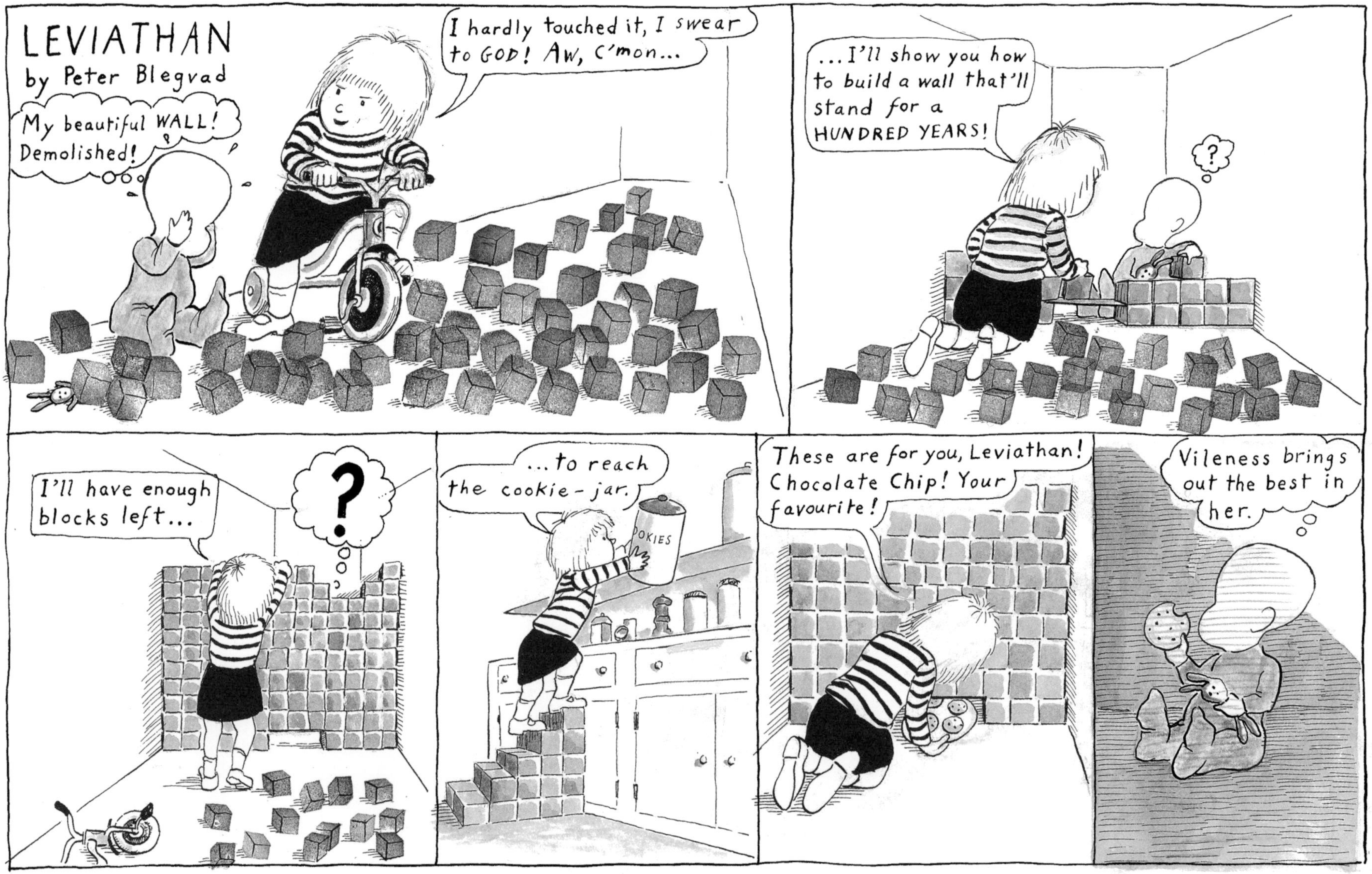
LEVIATHAN
by Peter Blegvad
My beautiful WALL! Demolished!
I hardly touched it, I swear to GOD! Aw, C'mon...
...I'll show you how to build a wall that'll stand for a HUNDRED YEARS!
?
I'll have enough blocks left...
?
...to reach the cookie-jar.
COOKIES
These are for you, Leviathan! Chocolate Chip! Your favourite!
Vileness brings out the best in her.

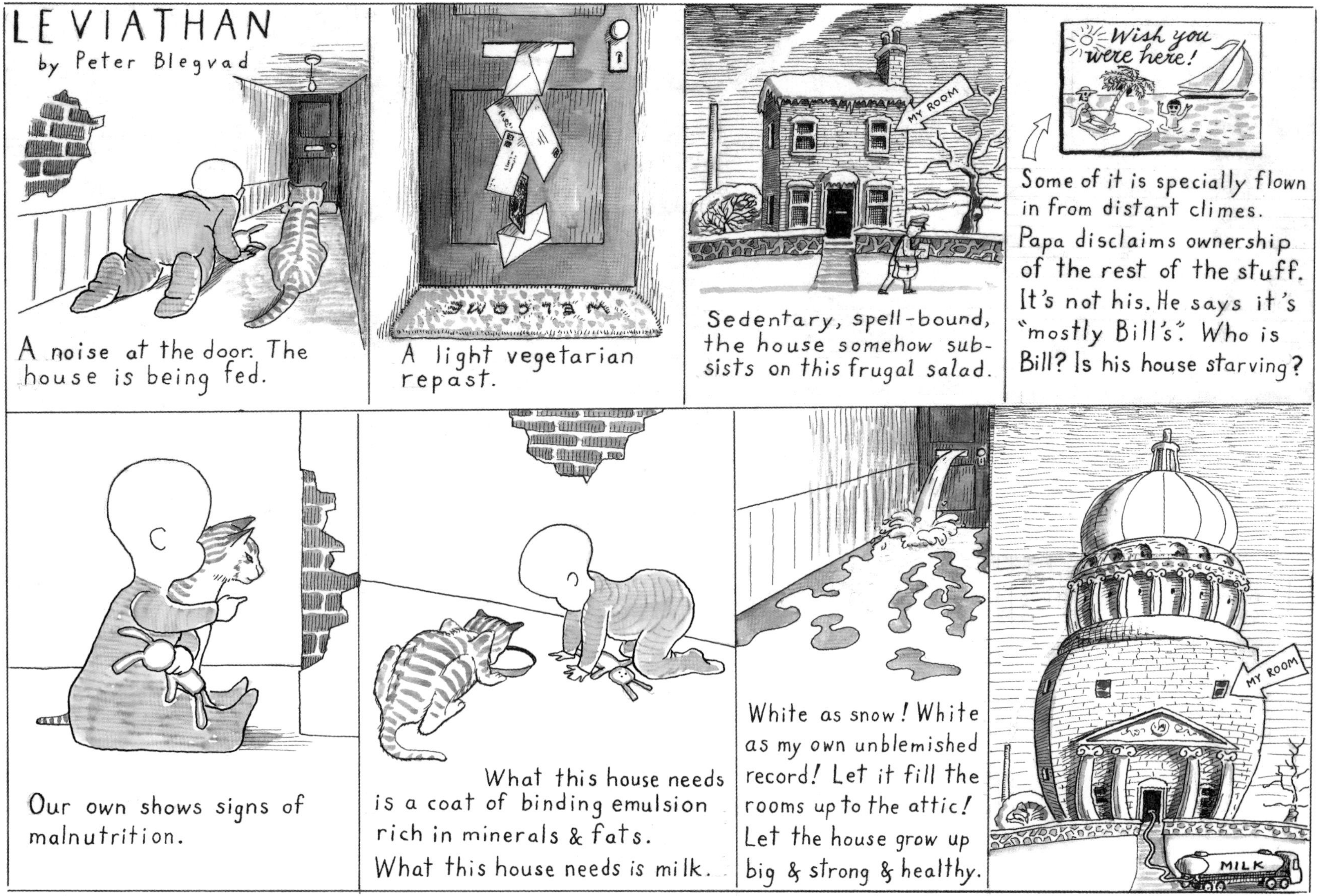
LEVIATHAN
by Peter Blegvad
A noise at the door. The house is being fed.
WELCOME
A light vegetarian repast.
MY ROOM
Sedentary, spell-bound, the house somehow subsists on this frugal salad.
Wish you were here!
Some of it is specially flown in from distant climes. Papa disclaims ownership of the rest of the stuff. It's not his. He says it's "mostly Bill's". Who is Bill? Is his house starving?
Our own shows signs of malnutrition.
What this house needs is a coat of binding emulsion rich in minerals & fats. What this house needs is milk.
White as snow! White as my own unblemished record! Let it fill the rooms up to the attic! Let the house grow up big & strong & healthy.
MY ROOM
MILK

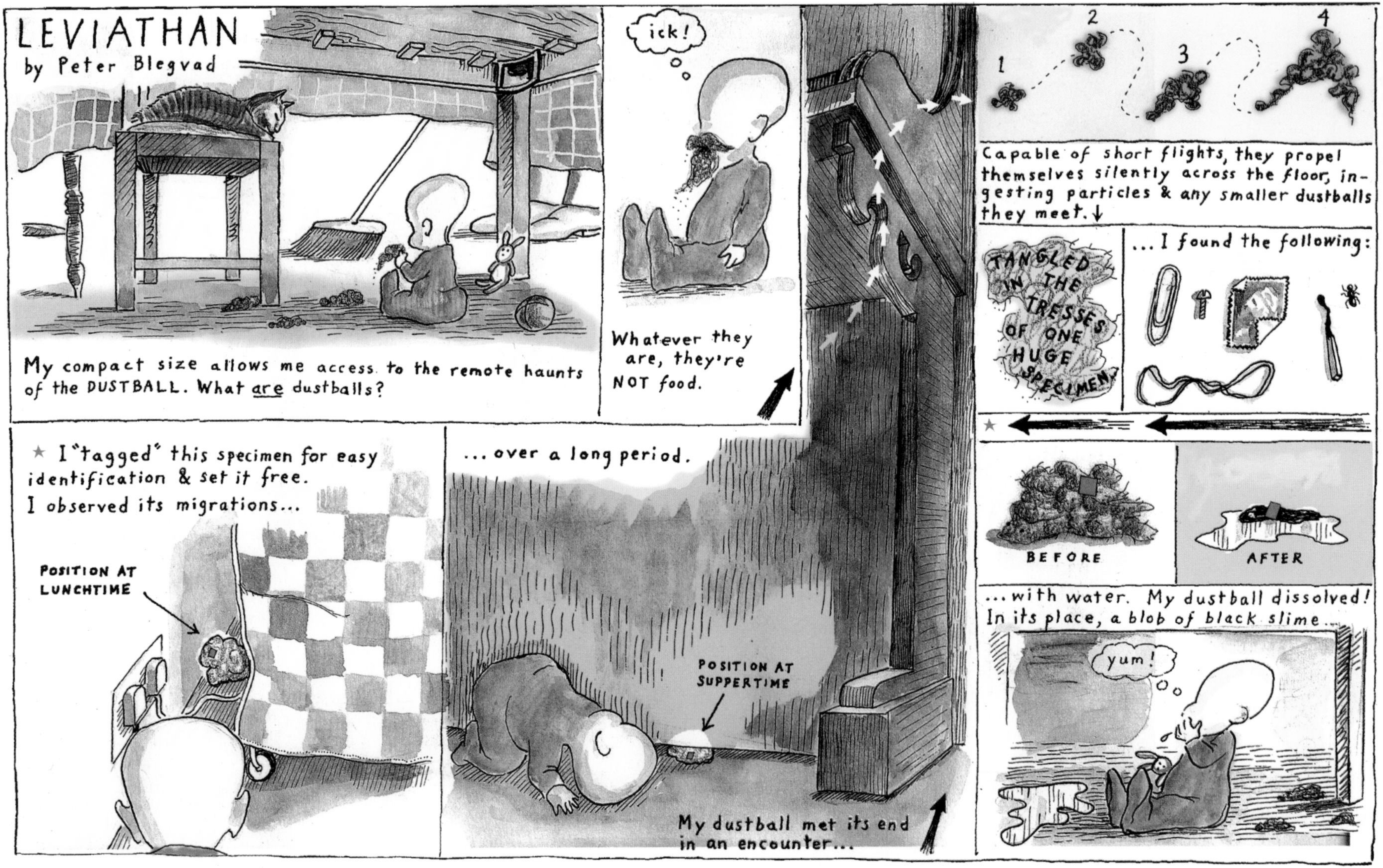
LEVIATHAN
by Peter Blegvad
My compact size allows me access to the remote haunts of the DUSTBALL. What are dustballs?
ick!
Whatever they are, they're NOT food.
1
2
3
4
Capable of short flights, they propel themselves silently across the floor, ingesting particles & any smaller dustballs they meet.
TANGLED IN THE TRESSES OF ONE HUGE SPECIMEN
...I found the following:
★ I "tagged" this specimen for easy identification & set it free. I observed its migrations...
POSITION AT LUNCHTIME
...over a long period.
POSITION AT SUPPERTIME
My dustball met its end in an encounter...
BEFORE
AFTER
...with water. My dustball dissolved! In its place, a blob of black slime...
yum!

The Tear of a Clown

SALT · OXYGEN · HYDROGEN · BEREAVEMENT · FEAR · HUMILIATION · ANGER · SELF-PITY

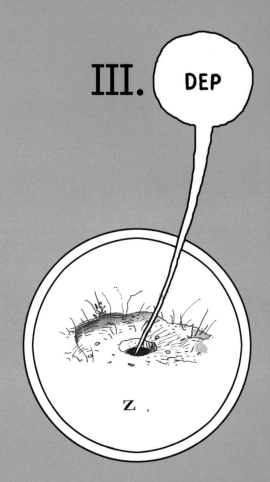

III. DEP

Z.

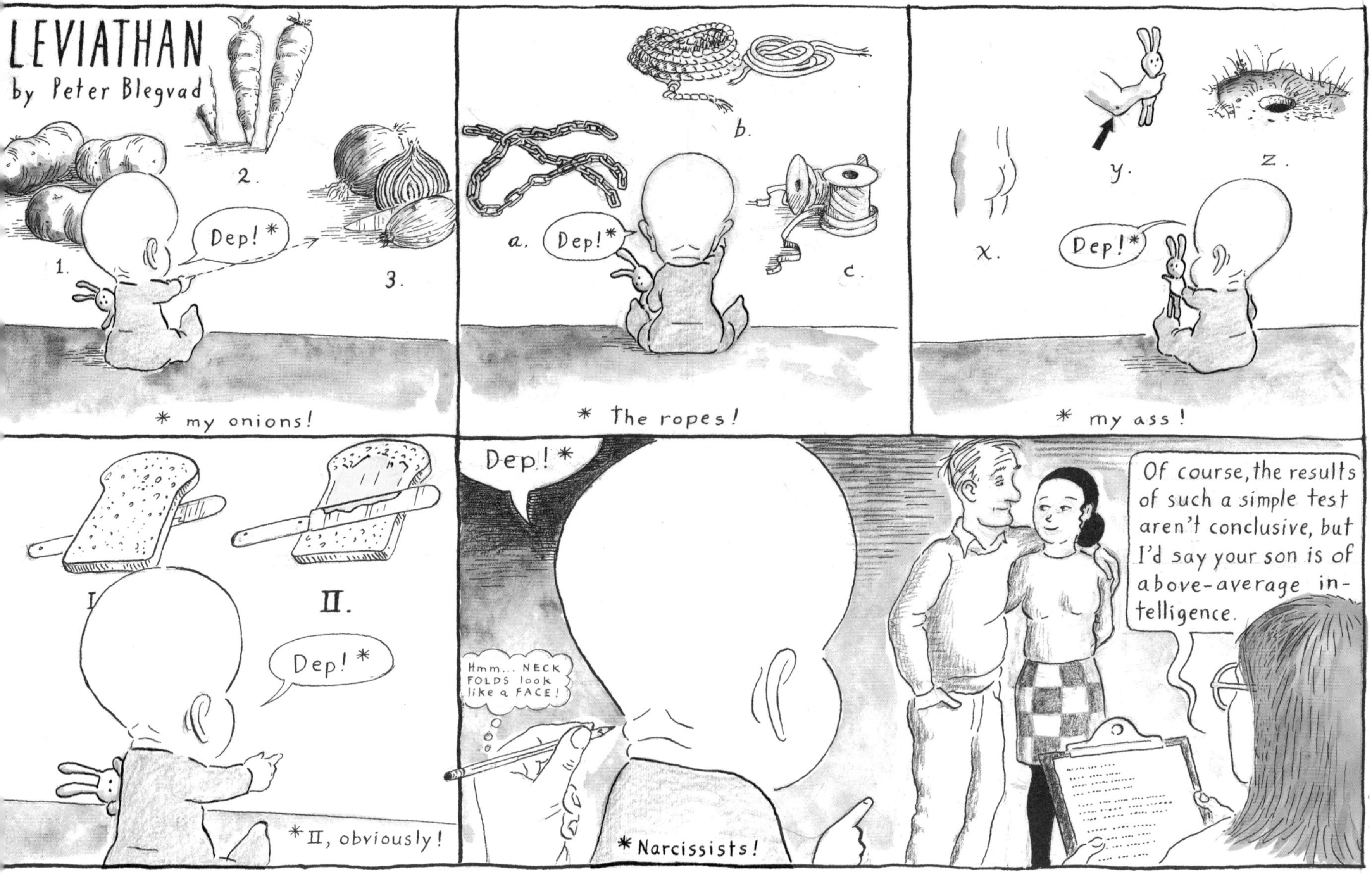

LEVIATHAN
by Peter Blegvad
1.
2.
3.
Dep! *
* my onions!
a.
b.
c.
Dep! *
* The ropes!
x.
y.
z.
Dep! *
* my ass!
I.
II.
Dep! *
* II, obviously!
Dep! *
Hmm... NECK FOLDS look like a FACE!
* Narcissists!
Of course, the results of such a simple test aren't conclusive, but I'd say your son is of above-average intelligence.

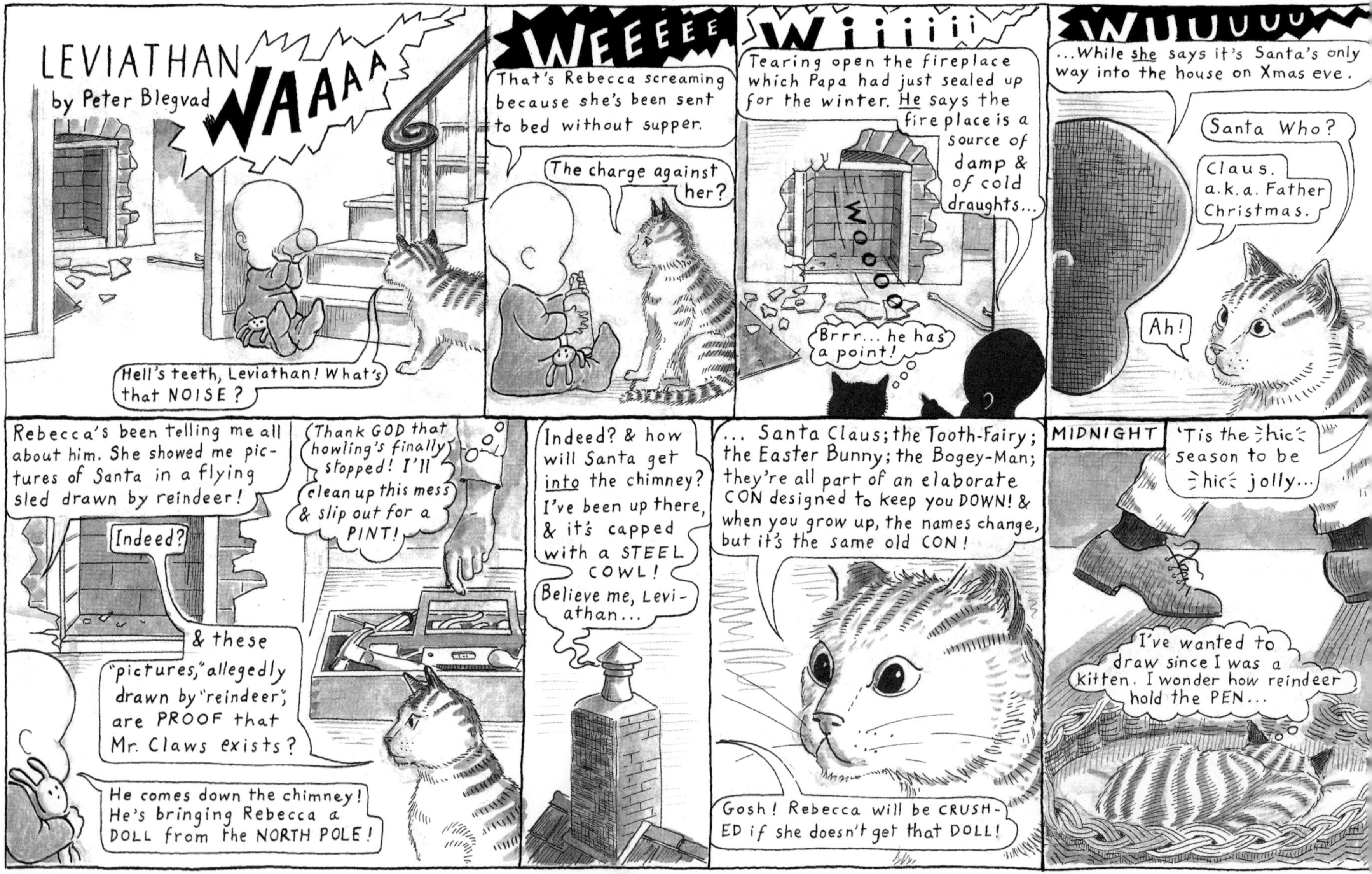

LEVIATHAN
by Peter Blegvad
WAAAA
Hell's teeth, Leviathan! What's that NOISE?
WEEEEE
That's Rebecca screaming because she's been sent to bed without supper.
The charge against her?
Wiiiiii
Tearing open the fireplace which Papa had just sealed up for the winter. He says the fire place is a source of damp & of cold draughts...
WOOOOO
Brrr... he has a point!
WUUUUU
...While she says it's Santa's only way into the house on Xmas eve.
Santa Who?
Claus. a.k.a. Father Christmas.
Ah!
Rebecca's been telling me all about him. She showed me pictures of Santa in a flying sled drawn by reindeer!
Indeed?
& these "pictures," allegedly drawn by "reindeer", are PROOF that Mr. Claws exists?
He comes down the chimney! He's bringing Rebecca a DOLL from the NORTH POLE!
Thank GOD that howling's finally stopped! I'll clean up this mess & slip out for a PINT!
Indeed? & how will Santa get into the chimney? I've been up there, & it's capped with a STEEL COWL!
Believe me, Leviathan...
... Santa Claus; the Tooth-Fairy; the Easter Bunny; the Bogey-Man; they're all part of an elaborate CON designed to keep you DOWN! & when you grow up, the names change, but it's the same old CON!
Gosh! Rebecca will be CRUSHED if she doesn't get that DOLL!
MIDNIGHT
'Tis the hic season to be hic jolly...
I've wanted to draw since I was a kitten. I wonder how reindeer hold the PEN...

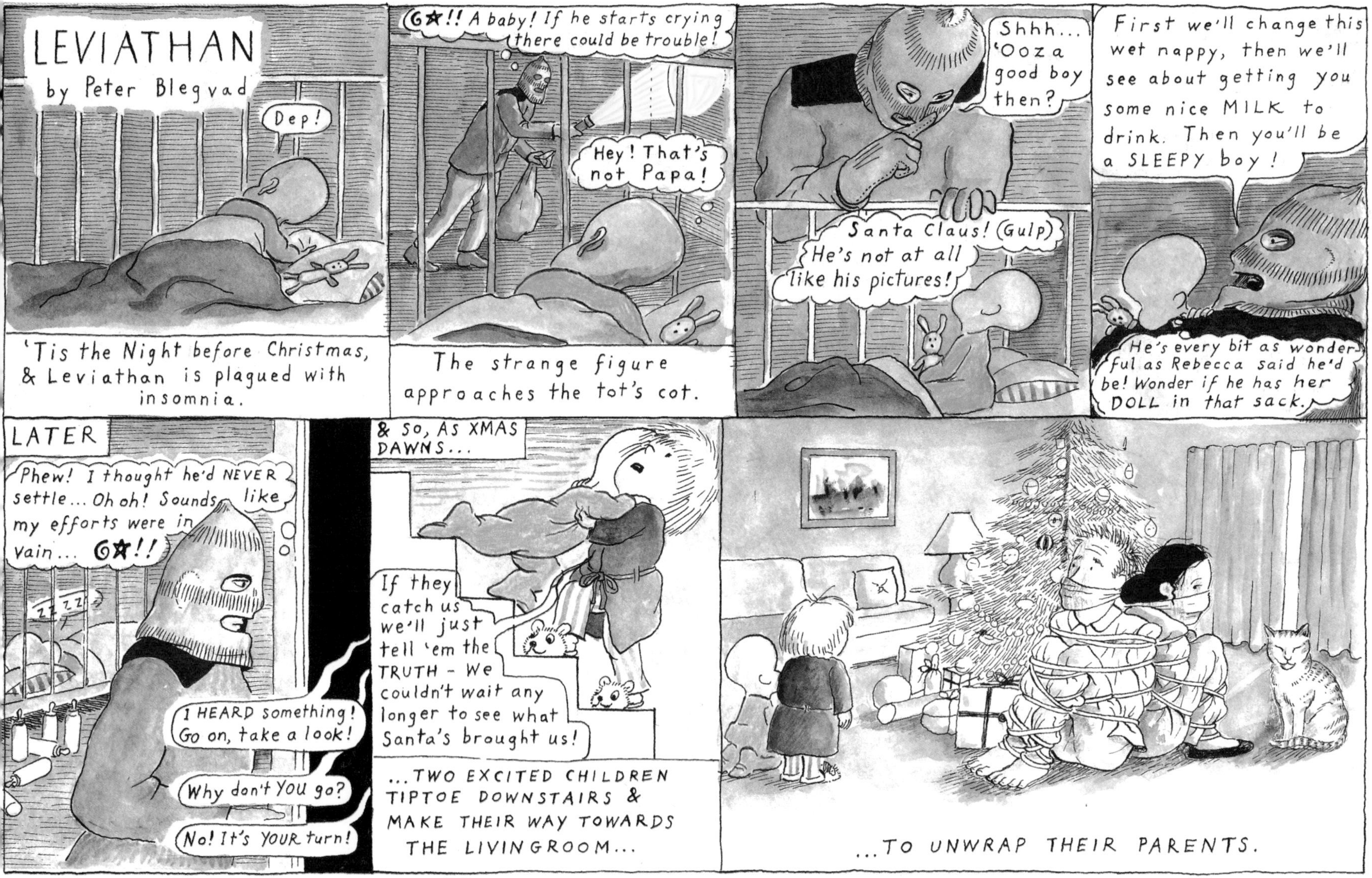

LEVIATHAN
by Peter Blegvad
Dep!
'Tis the Night before Christmas, & Leviathan is plagued with insomnia.
G✫!! A baby! If he starts crying there could be trouble!
Hey! That's not Papa!
The strange figure approaches the tot's cot.
Shhh... 'Ooza good boy then?
Santa Claus! (Gulp)
He's not at all like his pictures!
First we'll change this wet nappy, then we'll see about getting you some nice MILK to drink. Then you'll be a SLEEPY boy!
He's every bit as wonderful as Rebecca said he'd be! Wonder if he has her DOLL in that sack.
LATER
Phew! I thought he'd NEVER settle... Oh oh! Sounds like my efforts were in vain... G✫!!
ZZZZ
I HEARD something! Go on, take a look!
Why don't YOU go?
No! It's YOUR turn!
& SO, AS XMAS DAWNS...
If they catch us we'll just tell 'em the TRUTH - We couldn't wait any longer to see what Santa's brought us!
...TWO EXCITED CHILDREN TIPTOE DOWNSTAIRS & MAKE THEIR WAY TOWARDS THE LIVINGROOM...
...TO UNWRAP THEIR PARENTS.

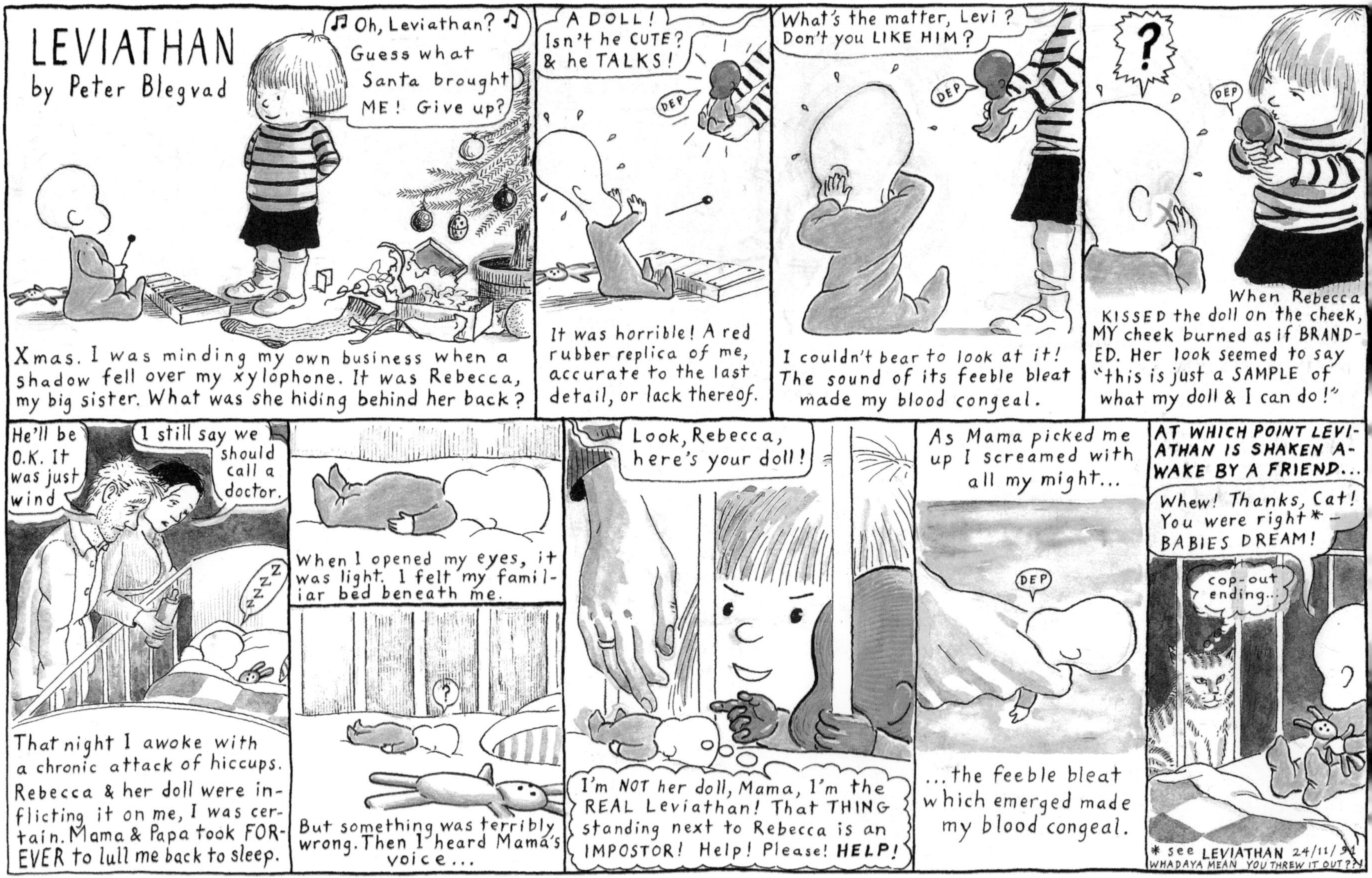
LEVIATHAN
by Peter Blegvad
♫ Oh, Leviathan? ♫ Guess what Santa brought ME! Give up?
Xmas. I was minding my own business when a shadow fell over my xylophone. It was Rebecca, my big sister. What was she hiding behind her back?
A DOLL! Isn't he CUTE? & he TALKS!
DEP
It was horrible! A red rubber replica of me, accurate to the last detail, or lack thereof.
What's the matter, Levi? Don't you LIKE HIM?
DEP
I couldn't bear to look at it! The sound of its feeble bleat made my blood congeal.
?
DEP
When Rebecca KISSED the doll on the cheek, MY cheek burned as if BRANDED. Her look seemed to say "this is just a SAMPLE of what my doll & I can do!"
He'll be O.K. It was just wind
I still say we should call a doctor.
ZZZZ
That night I awoke with a chronic attack of hiccups. Rebecca & her doll were inflicting it on me, I was certain. Mama & Papa took FOREVER to lull me back to sleep.
When I opened my eyes, it was light. I felt my familiar bed beneath me.
?
But something was terribly wrong. Then I heard Mama's voice...
Look, Rebecca, here's your doll!
I'm NOT her doll, Mama, I'm the REAL Leviathan! That THING standing next to Rebecca is an IMPOSTOR! Help! Please! HELP!
As Mama picked me up I screamed with all my might...
DEP
...the feeble bleat which emerged made my blood congeal.
AT WHICH POINT LEVIATHAN IS SHAKEN AWAKE BY A FRIEND...
Whew! Thanks, Cat! You were right* — BABIES DREAM!
cop-out ending...
* see LEVIATHAN 24/11/91
WHADAYA MEAN YOU THREW IT OUT??!

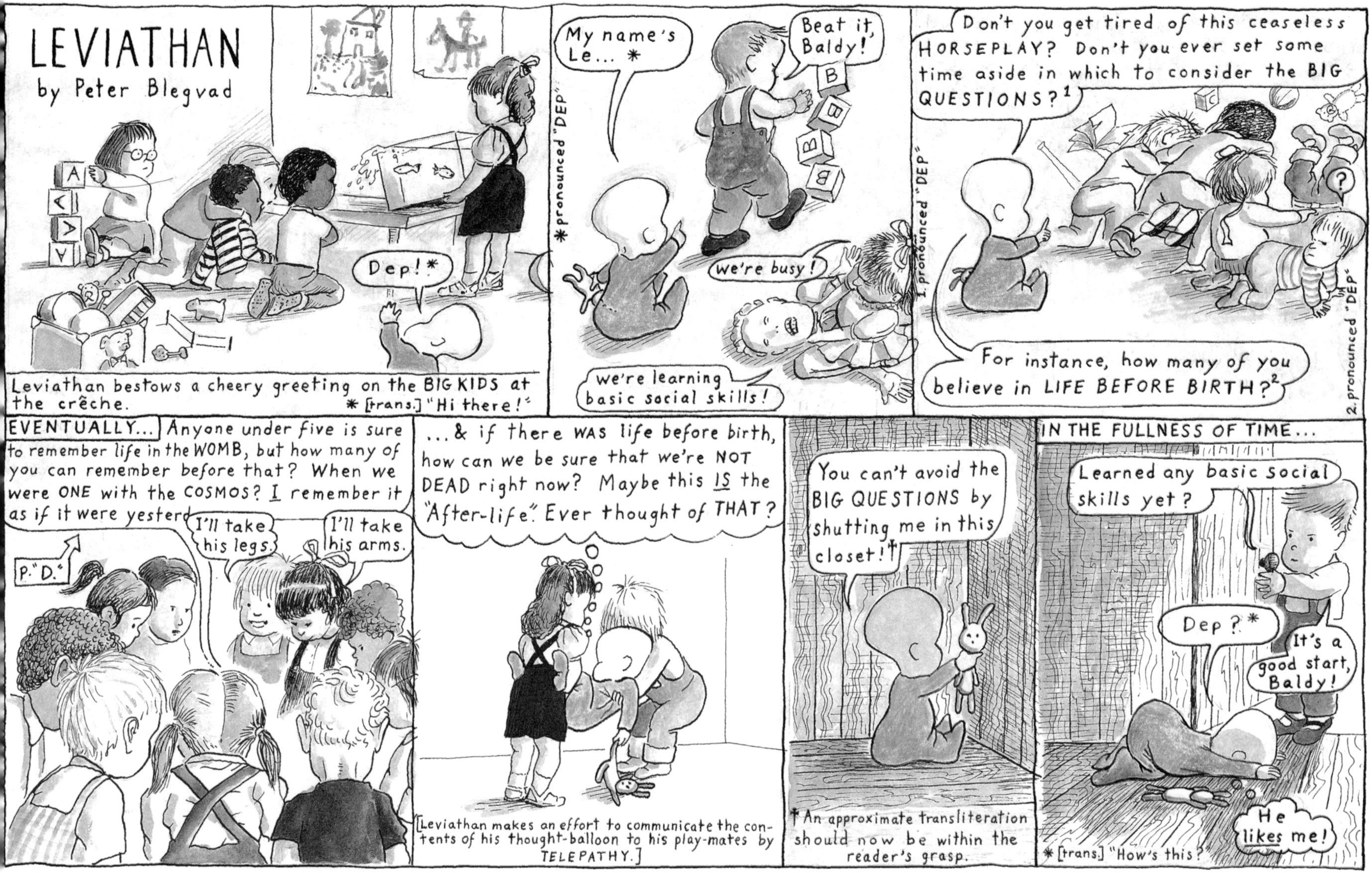
LEVIATHAN
by Peter Blegvad
Dep!*
Leviathan bestows a cheery greeting on the BIG KIDS at the crêche.
* [trans.] "Hi there!"
My name's Le... *
Beat it, Baldy!
we're busy!
we're learning basic social skills!
* pronounced "DEP"
Don't you get tired of this ceaseless HORSEPLAY? Don't you ever set some time aside in which to consider the BIG QUESTIONS?1
For instance, how many of you believe in LIFE BEFORE BIRTH?2
1. pronounced "DEP"
2. pronounced "DEP"
EVENTUALLY...
Anyone under five is sure to remember life in the WOMB, but how many of you can remember before that? When we were ONE with the COSMOS? I remember it as if it were yesterd
P. "D."
I'll take his legs.
I'll take his arms.
...& if there WAS life before birth, how can we be sure that we're NOT DEAD right now? Maybe this IS the "After-life". Ever thought of THAT?
[Leviathan makes an effort to communicate the contents of his thought-balloon to his play-mates by TELEPATHY.]
You can't avoid the BIG QUESTIONS by shutting me in this closet!†
† An approximate transliteration should now be within the reader's grasp.
IN THE FULLNESS OF TIME...
Learned any basic social skills yet?
Dep?*
It's a good start, Baldy!
He likes me!
* [trans] "How's this?"

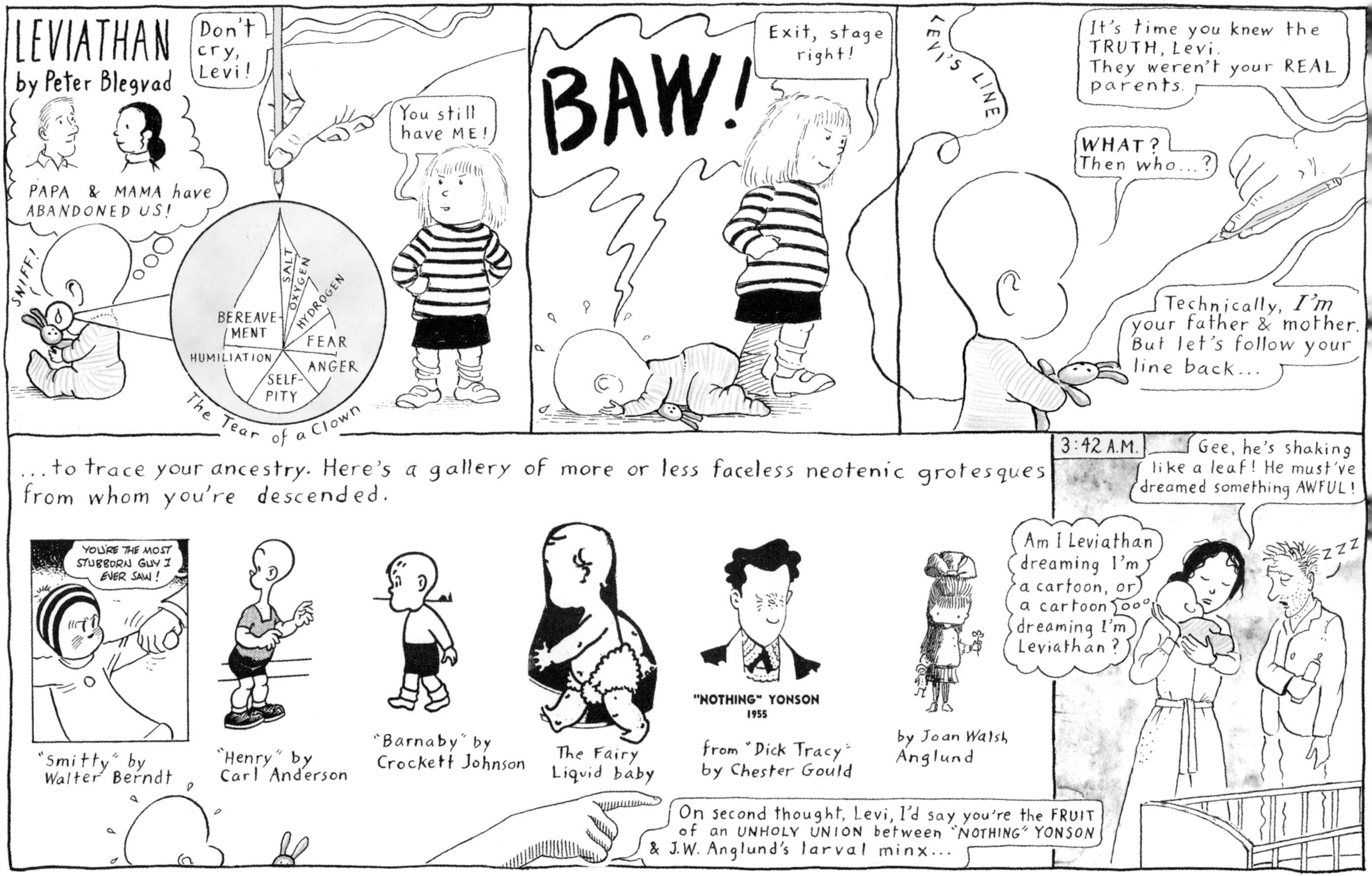
LEVIATHAN
by Peter Blegvad
PAPA & MAMA have ABANDONED US!
SNIFF!
Don't cry, Levi!
You still have ME!
SALT
OXYGEN
HYDROGEN
BEREAVEMENT
FEAR
HUMILIATION
ANGER
SELF-PITY
The Tear of a Clown
BAW!
Exit, stage right!
LEVI'S LINE
It's time you knew the TRUTH, Levi. They weren't your REAL parents.
WHAT? Then who...?
Technically, I'm your father & mother. But let's follow your line back...
...to trace your ancestry. Here's a gallery of more or less faceless neotenic grotesques from whom you're descended.
YOU'RE THE MOST STUBBORN GUY I EVER SAW!
"Smitty" by Walter Berndt
"Henry" by Carl Anderson
"Barnaby" by Crockett Johnson
The Fairy Liquid baby
"NOTHING" YONSON
1955
from "Dick Tracy" by Chester Gould
by Joan Walsh Anglund
On second thought, Levi, I'd say you're the FRUIT of an UNHOLY UNION between "NOTHING" YONSON & J.W. Anglund's larval minx...
3:42 A.M.
Gee, he's shaking like a leaf! He must've dreamed something AWFUL!
ZZZ
Am I Leviathan dreaming I'm a cartoon, or a cartoon dreaming I'm Leviathan?

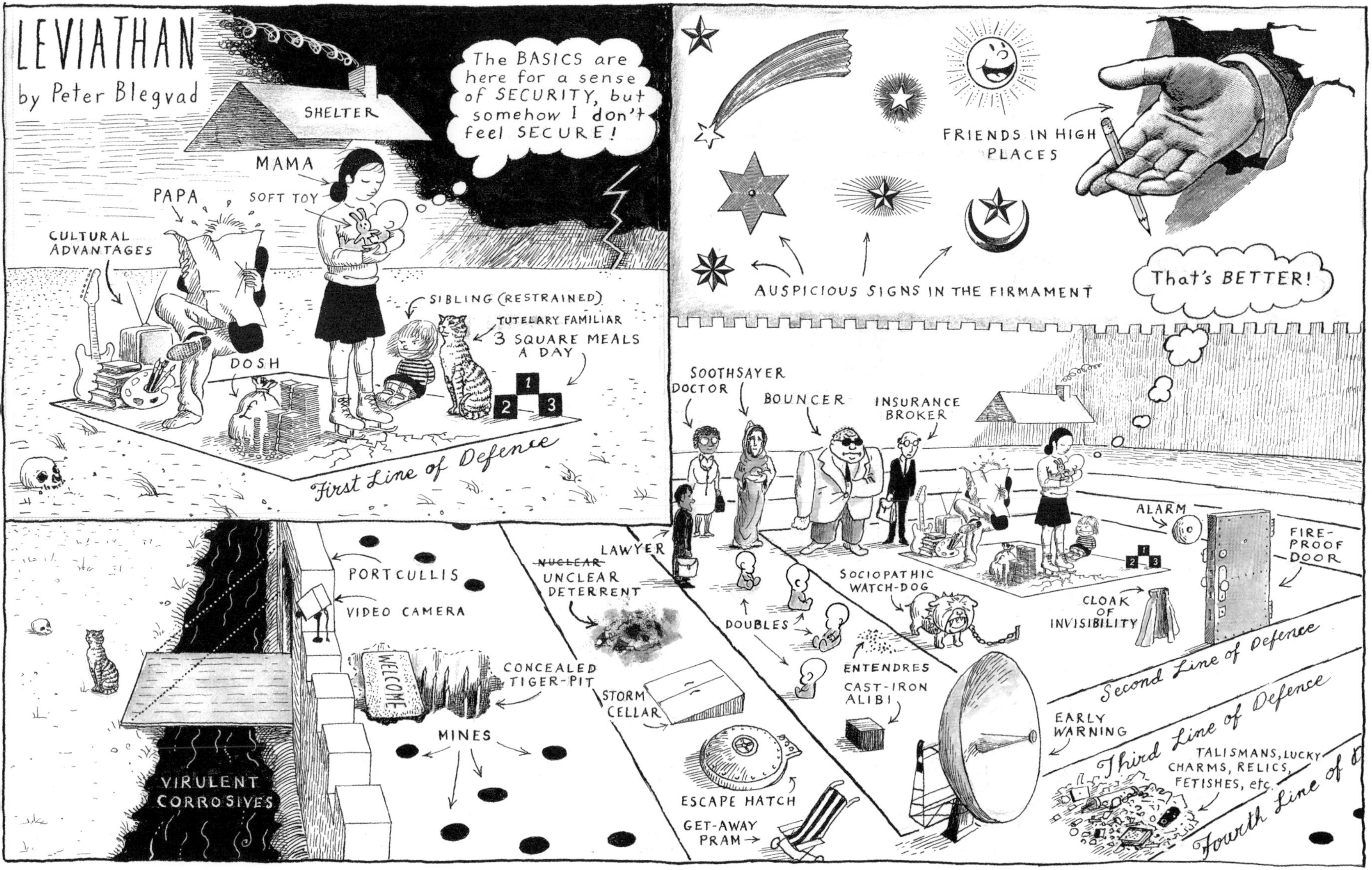

LEVIATHAN
by Peter Blegvad
The BASICS are here for a sense of SECURITY, but somehow I don't feel SECURE!
SHELTER
MAMA
PAPA
SOFT TOY
CULTURAL ADVANTAGES
SIBLING (RESTRAINED)
TUTELARY FAMILIAR
3 SQUARE MEALS A DAY
DOSH
First Line of Defence
FRIENDS IN HIGH PLACES
AUSPICIOUS SIGNS IN THE FIRMAMENT
That's BETTER!
SOOTHSAYER
DOCTOR
BOUNCER
INSURANCE BROKER
ALARM
FIRE-PROOF DOOR
LAWYER
~~NUCLEAR~~ UNCLEAR DETERRENT
PORTCULLIS
VIDEO CAMERA
SOCIOPATHIC WATCH-DOG
CLOAK OF INVISIBILITY
DOUBLES
ENTENDRES
CAST-IRON ALIBI
Second Line of Defence
WELCOME
CONCEALED TIGER-PIT
STORM CELLAR
MINES
EARLY WARNING
Third Line of Defence
TALISMANS, LUCKY CHARMS, RELICS, FETISHES, etc.
ESCAPE HATCH
GET-AWAY PRAM
VIRULENT CORROSIVES
Fourth Line of

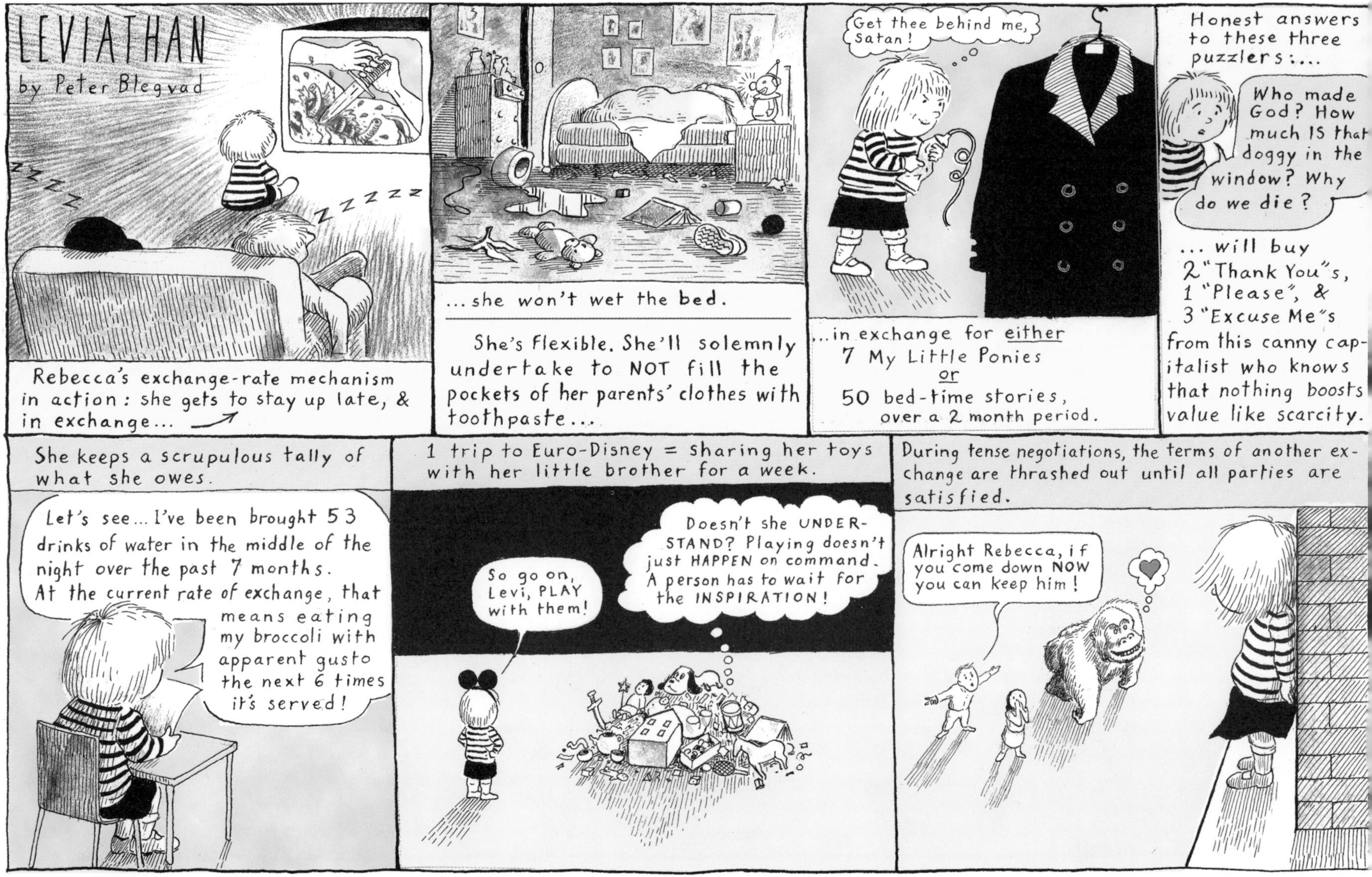
LEVIATHAN
by Peter Blegvad
Z Z Z Z Z
Z Z Z Z Z Z
Rebecca's exchange-rate mechanism in action: she gets to stay up late, & in exchange...
...she won't wet the bed.
She's flexible. She'll solemnly undertake to NOT fill the pockets of her parents' clothes with toothpaste...
Get thee behind me, Satan!
...in exchange for either
7 My Little Ponies
or
50 bed-time stories, over a 2 month period.
Honest answers to these three puzzlers:...
Who made God? How much IS that doggy in the window? Why do we die?
... will buy
2 "Thank You"s,
1 "Please", &
3 "Excuse Me"s
from this canny capitalist who knows that nothing boosts value like scarcity.
She keeps a scrupulous tally of what she owes.
Let's see... I've been brought 53 drinks of water in the middle of the night over the past 7 months. At the current rate of exchange, that means eating my broccoli with apparent gusto the next 6 times it's served!
1 trip to Euro-Disney = sharing her toys with her little brother for a week.
So go on, Levi, PLAY with them!
Doesn't she UNDERSTAND? Playing doesn't just HAPPEN on command. A person has to wait for the INSPIRATION!
During tense negotiations, the terms of another exchange are thrashed out until all parties are satisfied.
Alright Rebecca, if you come down NOW you can keep him!

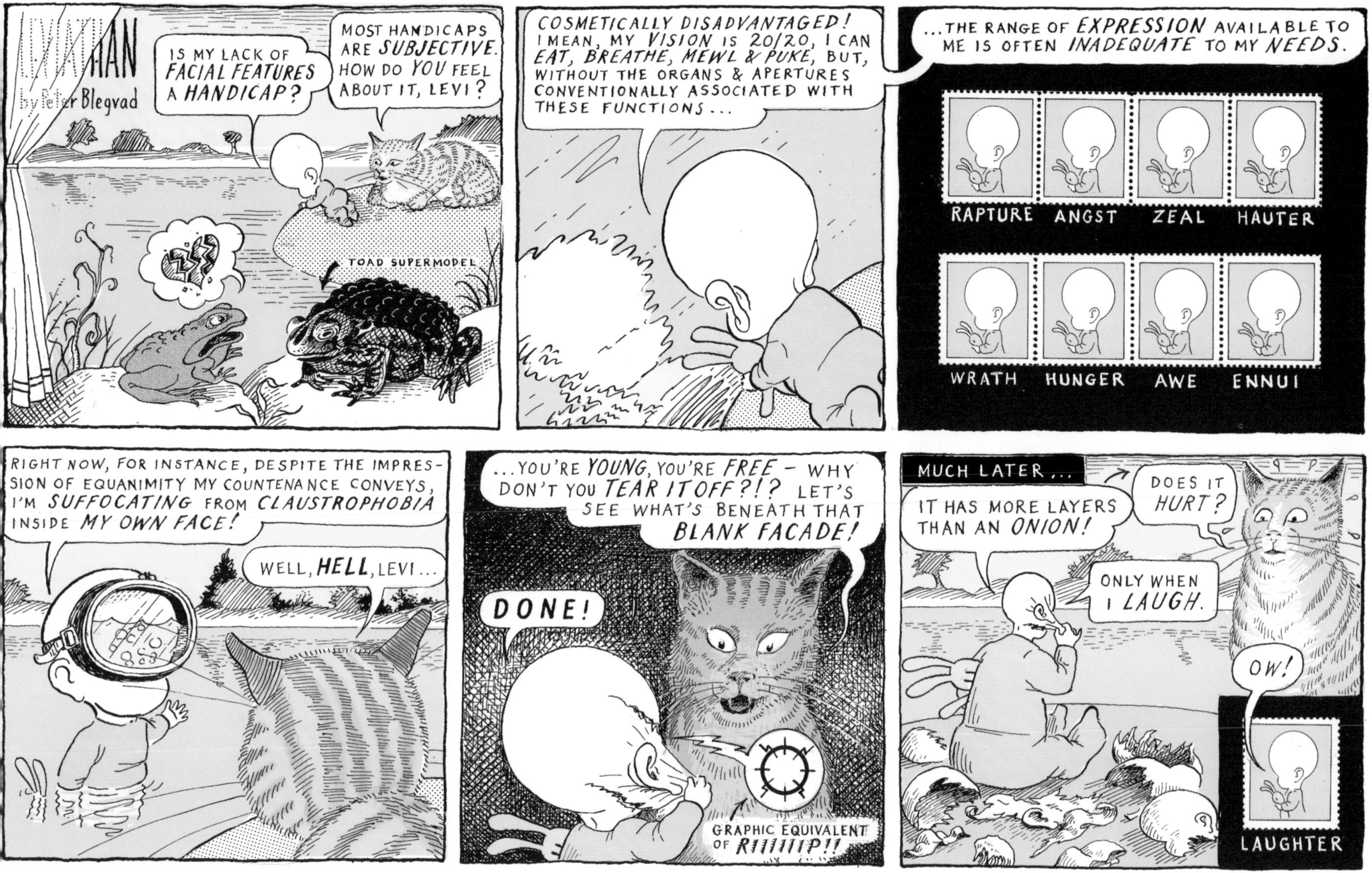

LEVIATHAN
by Peter Blegvad
IS MY LACK OF FACIAL FEATURES A HANDICAP?
MOST HANDICAPS ARE SUBJECTIVE. HOW DO YOU FEEL ABOUT IT, LEVI?
TOAD SUPERMODEL
COSMETICALLY DISADVANTAGED! I MEAN, MY VISION IS 20/20, I CAN EAT, BREATHE, MEWL & PUKE, BUT, WITHOUT THE ORGANS & APERTURES CONVENTIONALLY ASSOCIATED WITH THESE FUNCTIONS...
...THE RANGE OF EXPRESSION AVAILABLE TO ME IS OFTEN INADEQUATE TO MY NEEDS.
RAPTURE
ANGST
ZEAL
HAUTER
WRATH
HUNGER
AWE
ENNUI
RIGHT NOW, FOR INSTANCE, DESPITE THE IMPRESSION OF EQUANIMITY MY COUNTENANCE CONVEYS, I'M SUFFOCATING FROM CLAUSTROPHOBIA INSIDE MY OWN FACE!
WELL, HELL, LEVI...
...YOU'RE YOUNG, YOU'RE FREE – WHY DON'T YOU TEAR IT OFF?!? LET'S SEE WHAT'S BENEATH THAT BLANK FACADE!
DONE!
GRAPHIC EQUIVALENT OF RIIIIIIIP!!
MUCH LATER...
IT HAS MORE LAYERS THAN AN ONION!
DOES IT HURT?
ONLY WHEN I LAUGH.
OW!
LAUGHTER

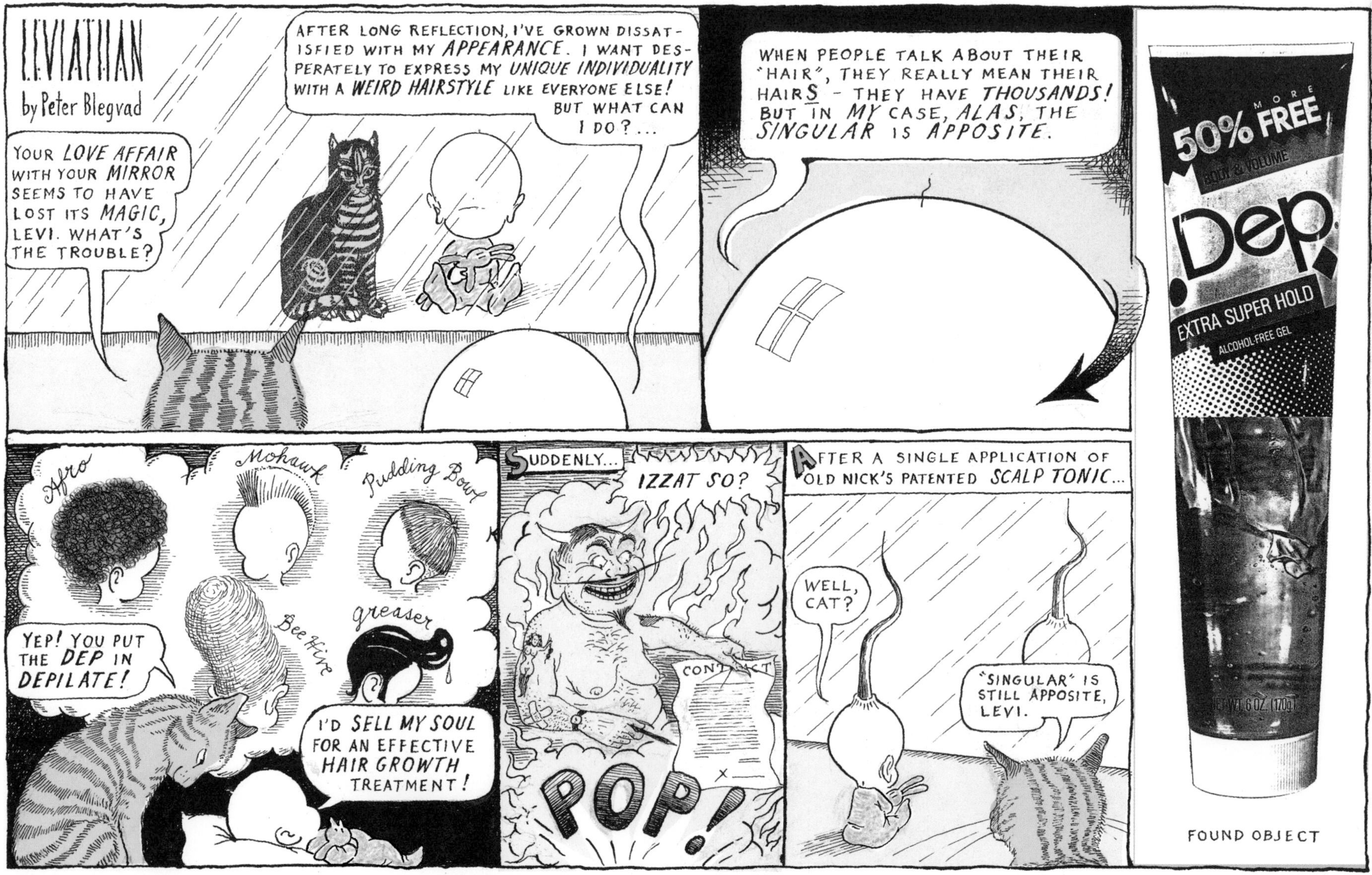

LEVIATHAN
by Peter Blegvad
YOUR LOVE AFFAIR WITH YOUR MIRROR SEEMS TO HAVE LOST ITS MAGIC, LEVI. WHAT'S THE TROUBLE?
AFTER LONG REFLECTION, I'VE GROWN DISSATISFIED WITH MY APPEARANCE. I WANT DESPERATELY TO EXPRESS MY UNIQUE INDIVIDUALITY WITH A WEIRD HAIRSTYLE LIKE EVERYONE ELSE!
BUT WHAT CAN I DO?...
WHEN PEOPLE TALK ABOUT THEIR "HAIR", THEY REALLY MEAN THEIR HAIRS - THEY HAVE THOUSANDS! BUT IN MY CASE, ALAS, THE SINGULAR IS APPOSITE.
50% MORE FREE
BODY & VOLUME
.Dep.
EXTRA SUPER HOLD
ALCOHOL-FREE GEL
NET WT. 6 OZ. (170g)
FOUND OBJECT
Afro
Mohawk
Pudding Bowl
Bee Hive
greaser
YEP! YOU PUT THE DEP IN DEPILATE!
I'D SELL MY SOUL FOR AN EFFECTIVE HAIR GROWTH TREATMENT!
SUDDENLY...
IZZAT SO?
CONTRACT
X
POP!!
AFTER A SINGLE APPLICATION OF OLD NICK'S PATENTED SCALP TONIC...
WELL, CAT?
"SINGULAR" IS STILL APPOSITE, LEVI.

# IV. SURELY YOU JEST

*Chable/Tair thanks to Chris McCourt (see page 46)*

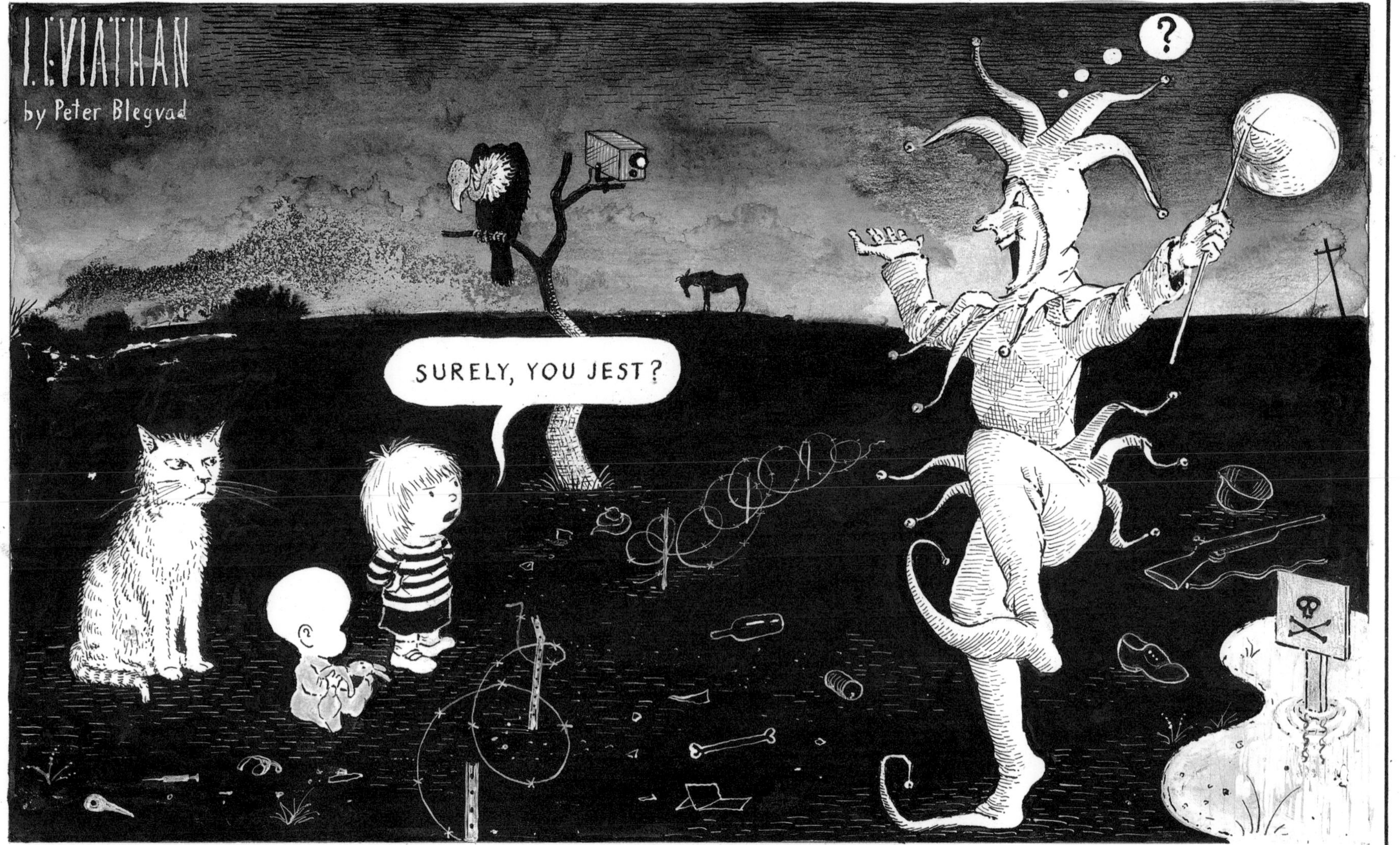
LEVIATHAN
by Peter Blegvad
SURELY, YOU JEST?
?

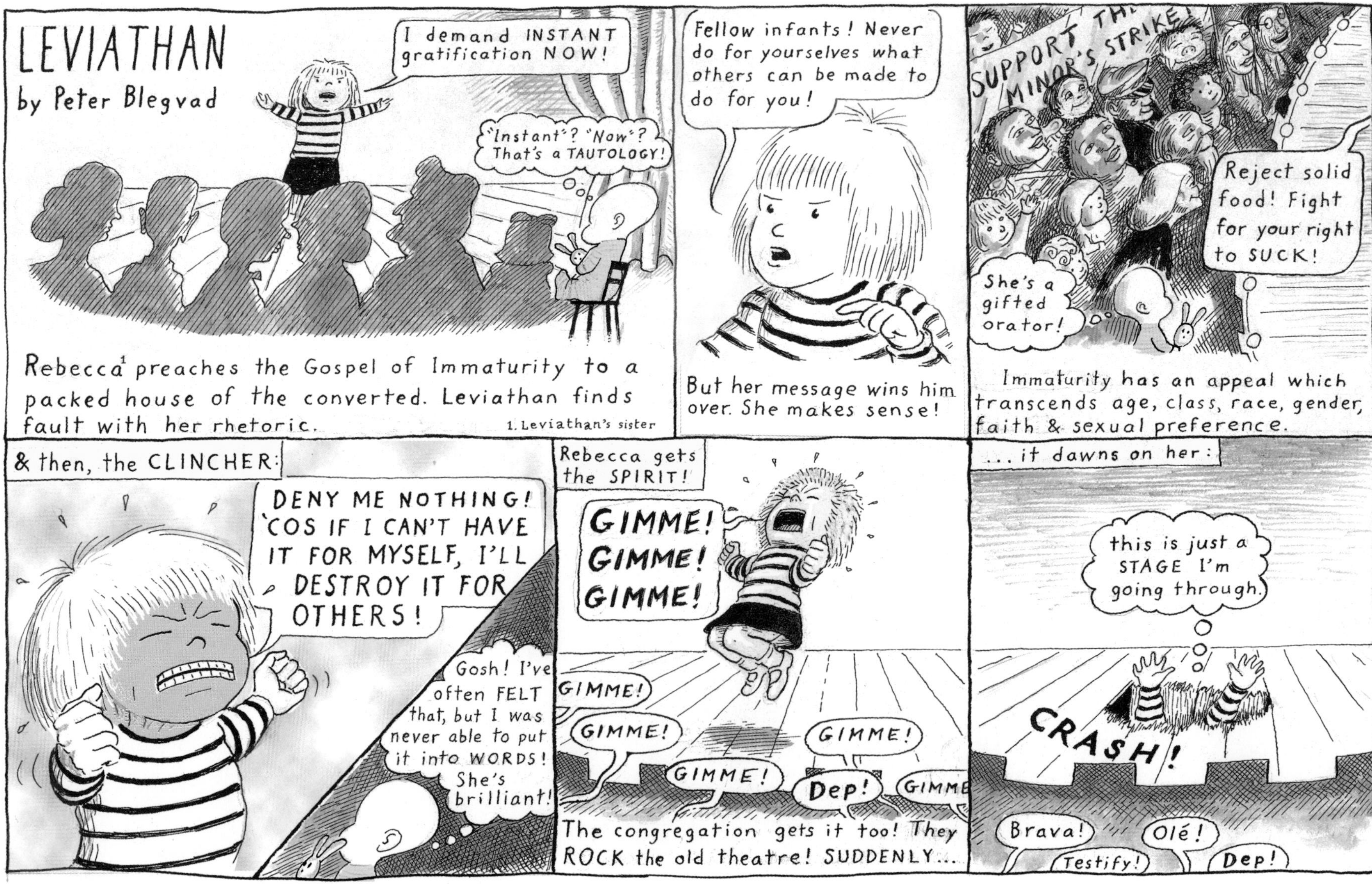
LEVIATHAN
by Peter Blegvad
I demand INSTANT gratification NOW!
"Instant"? "Now"? That's a TAUTOLOGY!
Rebecca[1] preaches the Gospel of Immaturity to a packed house of the converted. Leviathan finds fault with her rhetoric.
1. Leviathan's sister
Fellow infants! Never do for yourselves what others can be made to do for you!
But her message wins him over. She makes sense!
SUPPORT THE MINOR'S STRIKE!
Reject solid food! Fight for your right to SUCK!
She's a gifted orator!
Immaturity has an appeal which transcends age, class, race, gender, faith & sexual preference.
& then, the CLINCHER:
DENY ME NOTHING! 'COS IF I CAN'T HAVE IT FOR MYSELF, I'LL DESTROY IT FOR OTHERS!
Gosh! I've often FELT that, but I was never able to put it into WORDS! She's brilliant!
Rebecca gets the SPIRIT!
GIMME! GIMME! GIMME!
GIMME!
GIMME!
GIMME!
GIMME!
Dep!
GIMME
The congregation gets it too! They ROCK the old theatre! SUDDENLY...
... it dawns on her:
this is just a STAGE I'm going through.
CRASH!
Brava!
Testify!
Olé!
Dep!

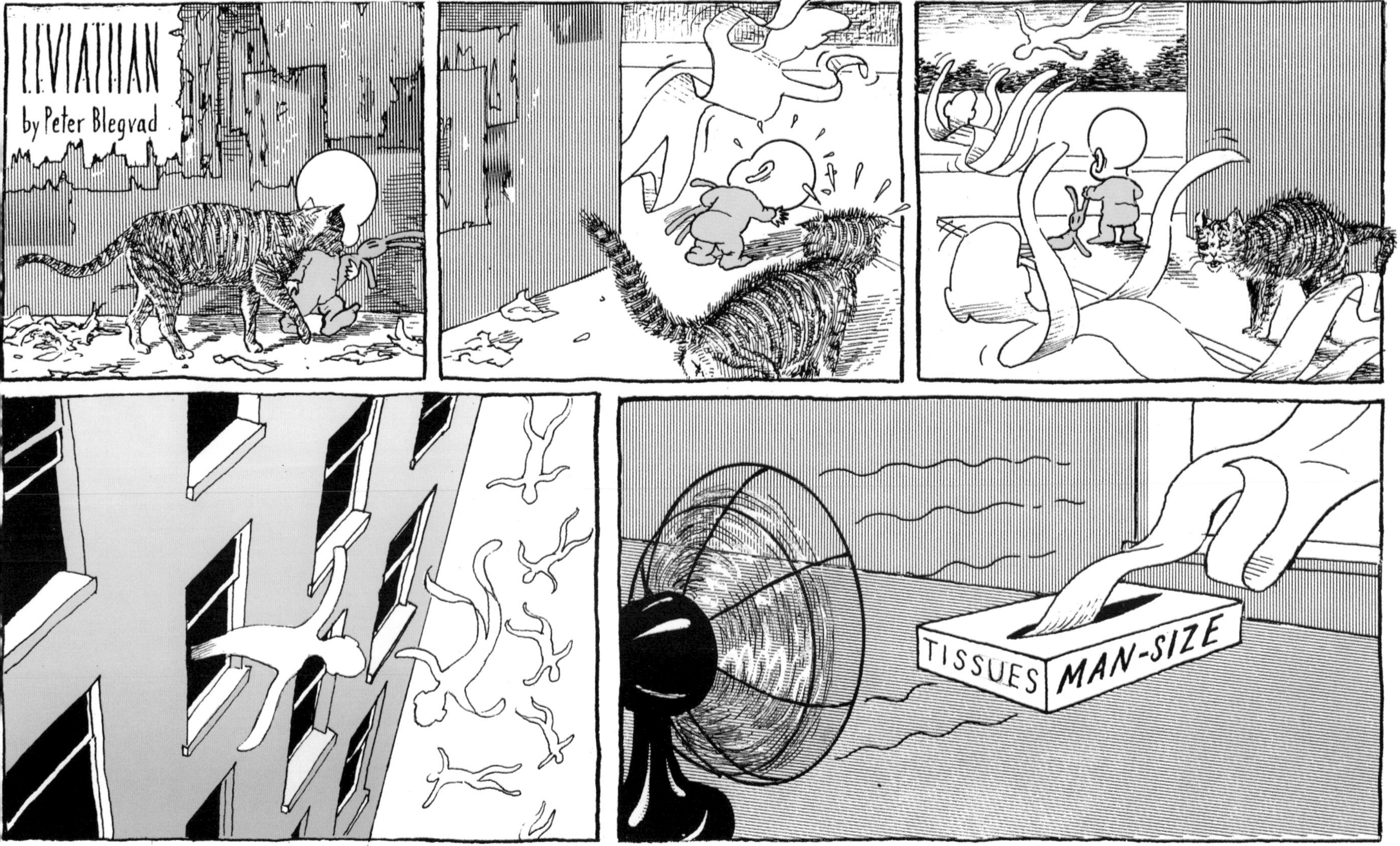
LEVIATHAN
by Peter Blegvad
TISSUES
MAN-SIZE

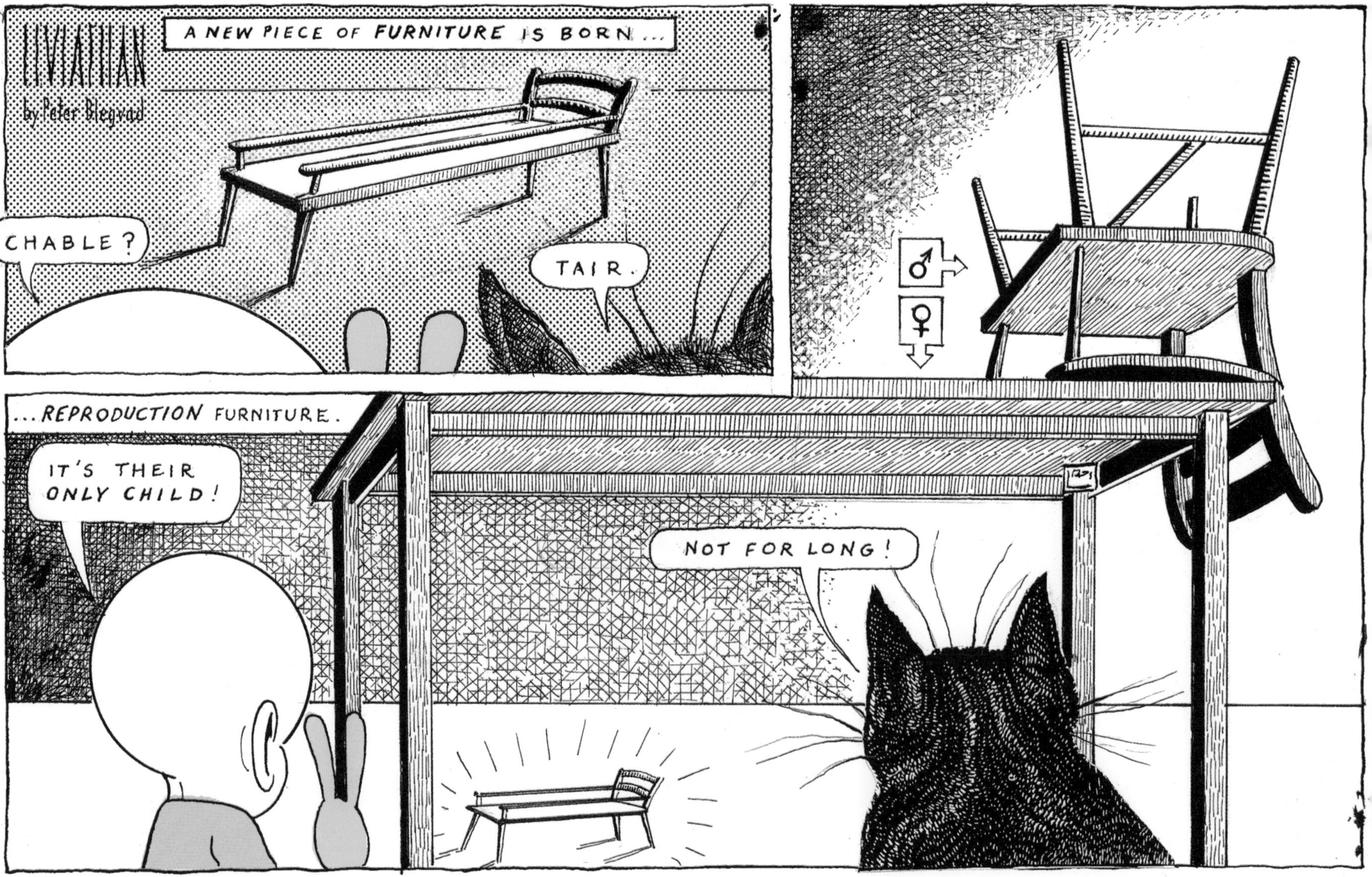
LEVIATHAN
by Peter Blegvad
A NEW PIECE OF FURNITURE IS BORN...
CHABLE?
TAIR.
...REPRODUCTION FURNITURE.
IT'S THEIR ONLY CHILD!
NOT FOR LONG!

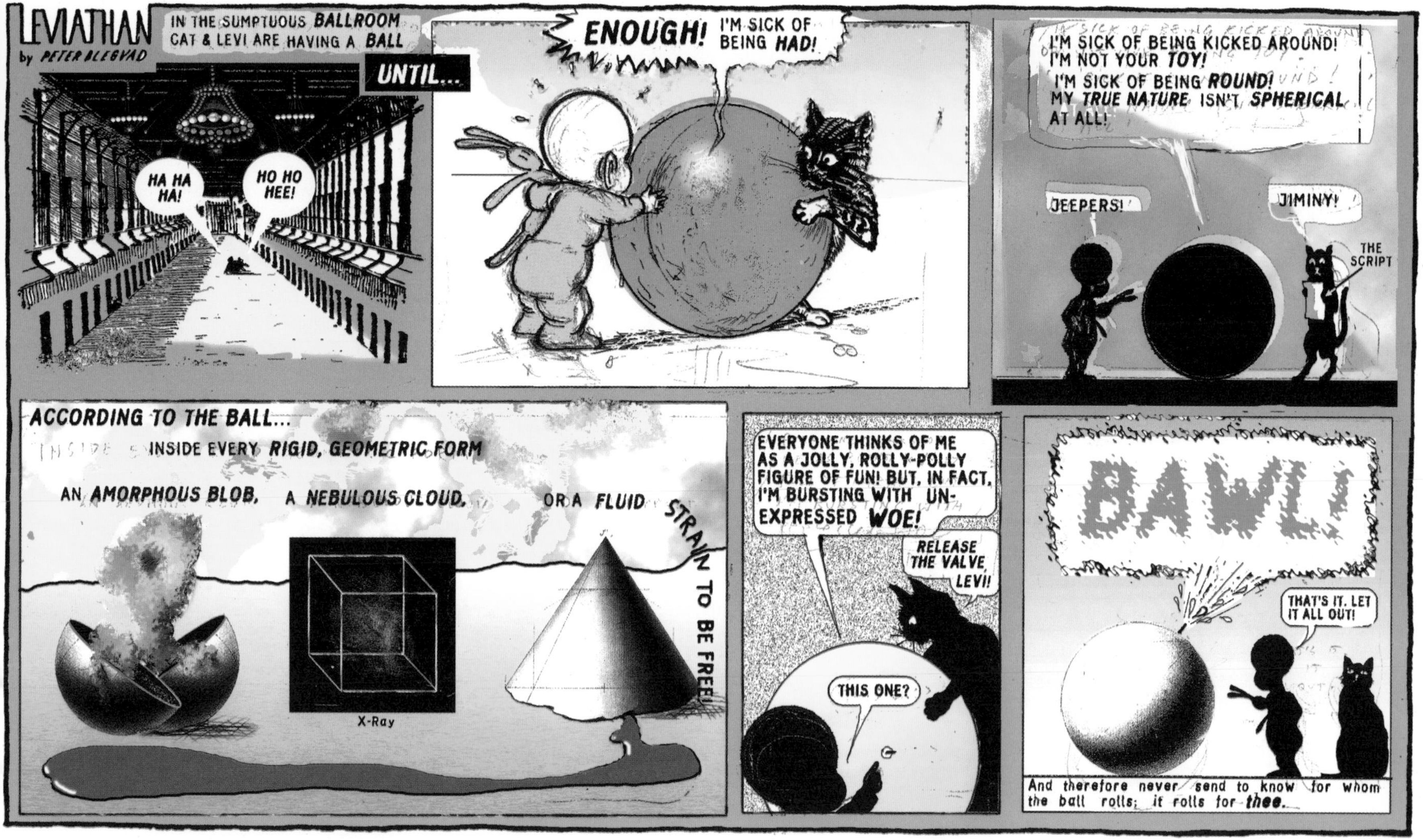

LEVIATHAN
by PETER BLEGVAD
IN THE SUMPTUOUS BALLROOM CAT & LEVI ARE HAVING A BALL
UNTIL...
HA HA HA!
HO HO HEE!
ENOUGH! I'M SICK OF BEING HAD!
I'M SICK OF BEING KICKED AROUND! I'M NOT YOUR TOY! I'M SICK OF BEING ROUND! MY TRUE NATURE ISN'T SPHERICAL AT ALL!
JEEPERS!
JIMINY!
THE SCRIPT
ACCORDING TO THE BALL...
INSIDE EVERY RIGID, GEOMETRIC FORM
AN AMORPHOUS BLOB, A NEBULOUS CLOUD, OR A FLUID STRAIN TO BE FREE!
X-Ray
EVERYONE THINKS OF ME AS A JOLLY, ROLLY-POLLY FIGURE OF FUN! BUT, IN FACT, I'M BURSTING WITH UN-EXPRESSED WOE!
RELEASE THE VALVE LEVI!
THIS ONE?
BAWL!
THAT'S IT. LET IT ALL OUT!
And therefore never send to know for whom the ball rolls; it rolls for thee.

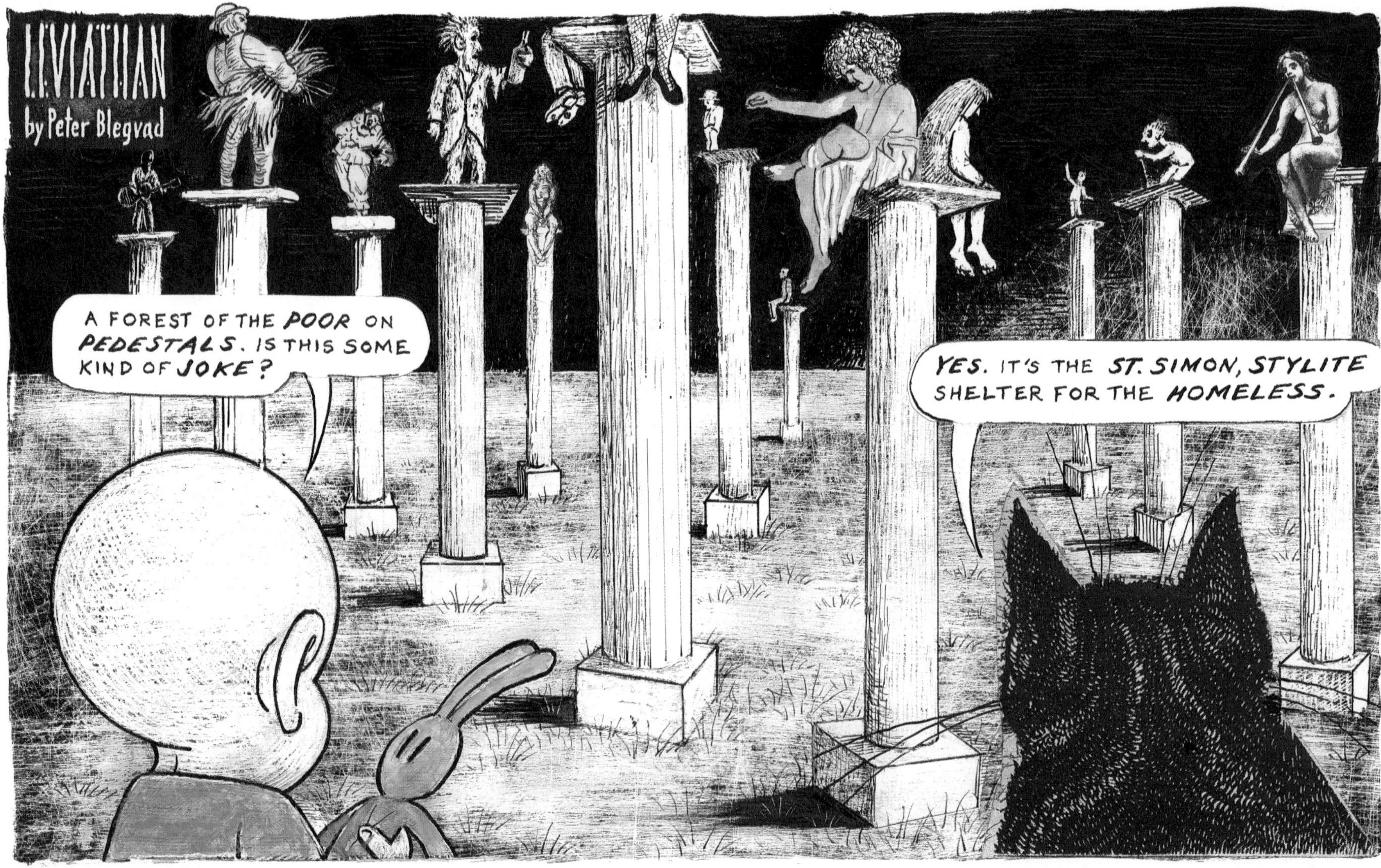
LEVIATHAN
by Peter Blegvad
A FOREST OF THE POOR ON PEDESTALS. IS THIS SOME KIND OF JOKE?
YES. IT'S THE ST. SIMON, STYLITE SHELTER FOR THE HOMELESS.

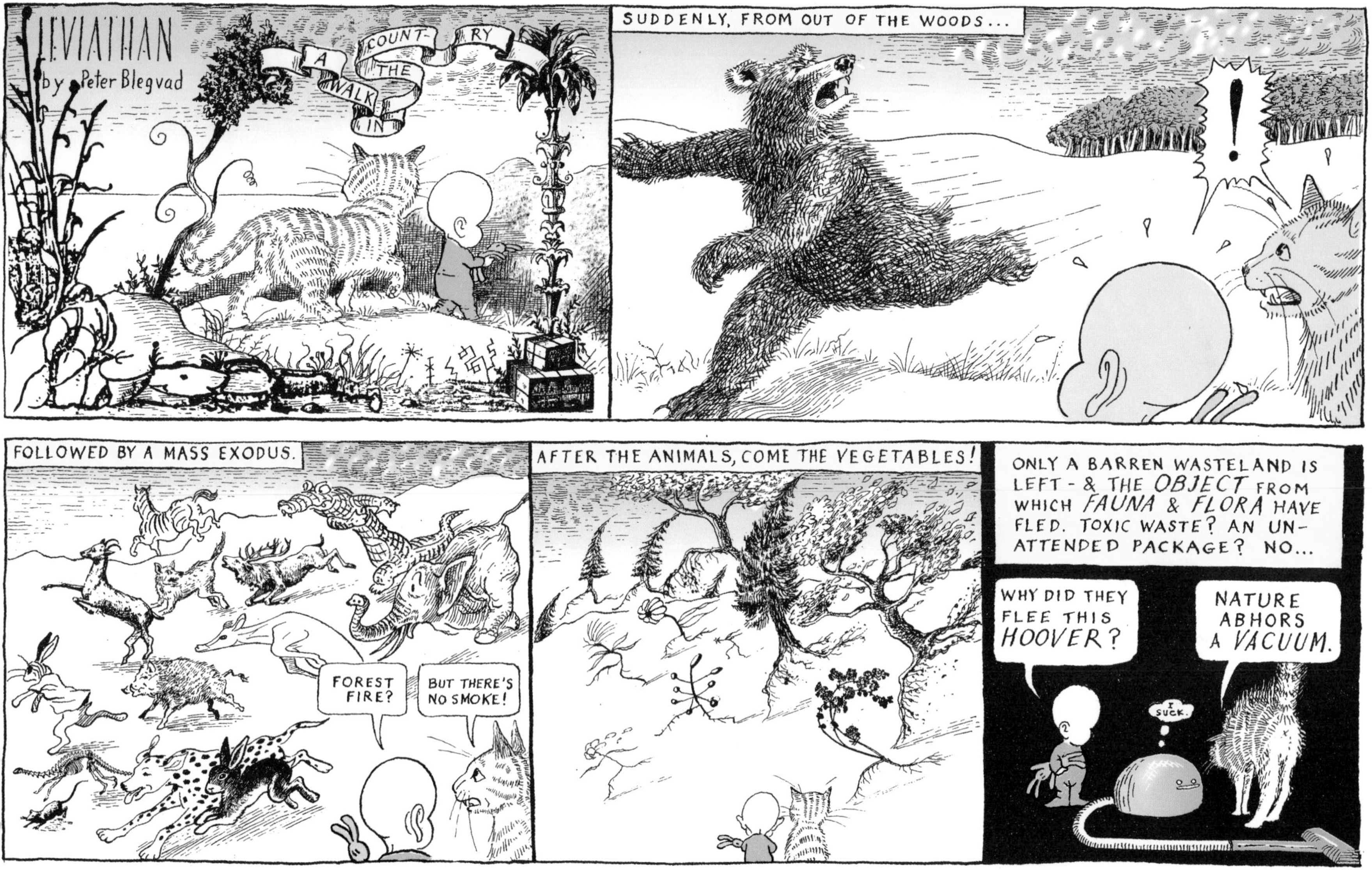
LEVIATHAN
by Peter Blegvad
A WALK IN THE COUNT- RY
SUDDENLY, FROM OUT OF THE WOODS...
!
FOLLOWED BY A MASS EXODUS.
FOREST FIRE?
BUT THERE'S NO SMOKE!
AFTER THE ANIMALS, COME THE VEGETABLES!
ONLY A BARREN WASTELAND IS LEFT - & THE OBJECT FROM WHICH FAUNA & FLORA HAVE FLED. TOXIC WASTE? AN UN-ATTENDED PACKAGE? NO...
WHY DID THEY FLEE THIS HOOVER?
NATURE ABHORS A VACUUM.
I SUCK.

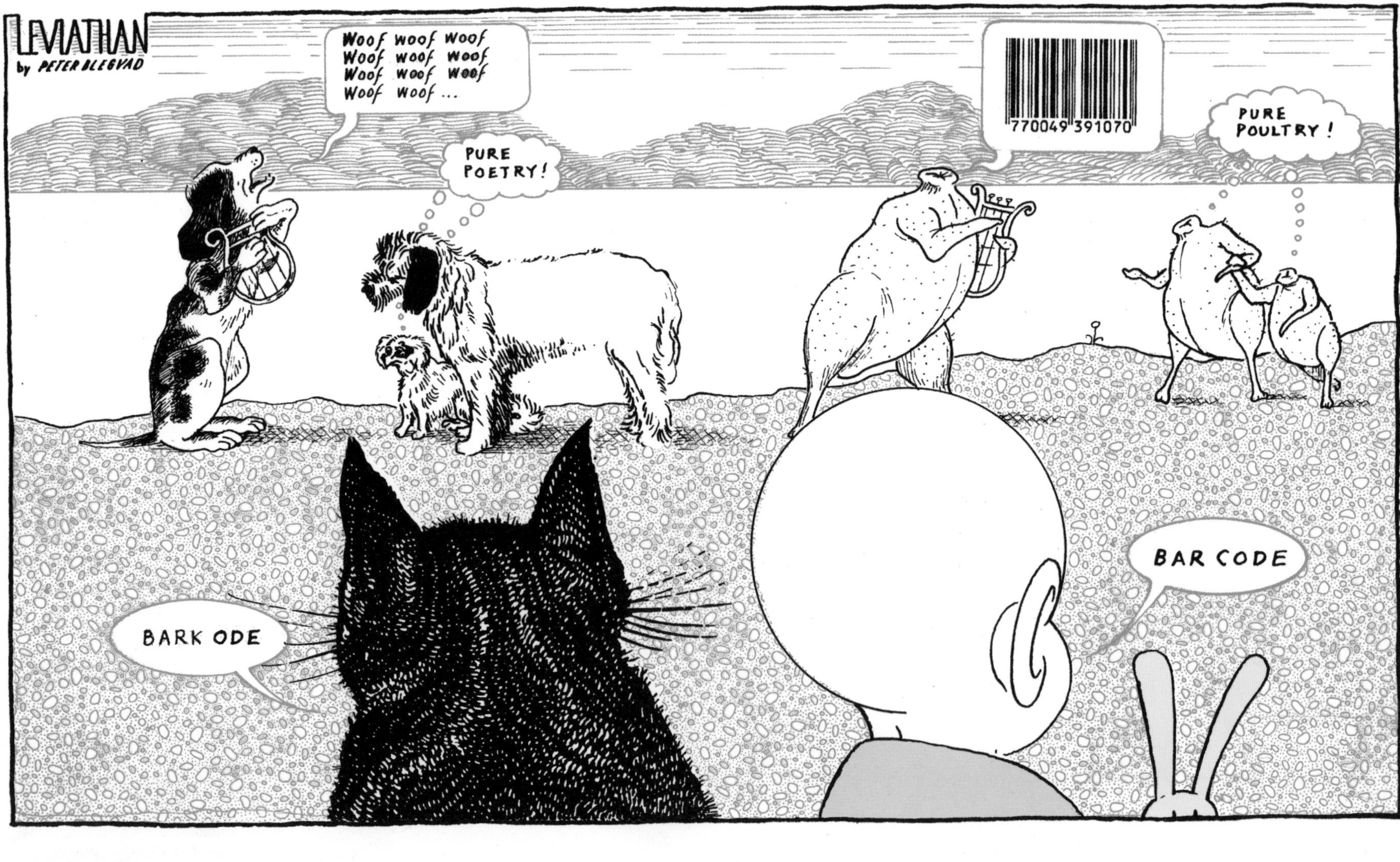
LEVIATHAN
by PETER BLEGVAD
Woof woof woof Woof woof woof Woof woof woof Woof woof ...
PURE POETRY!
770049 391070
PURE POULTRY!
BARK ODE
BAR CODE

# V. TERRA INCOGNITA

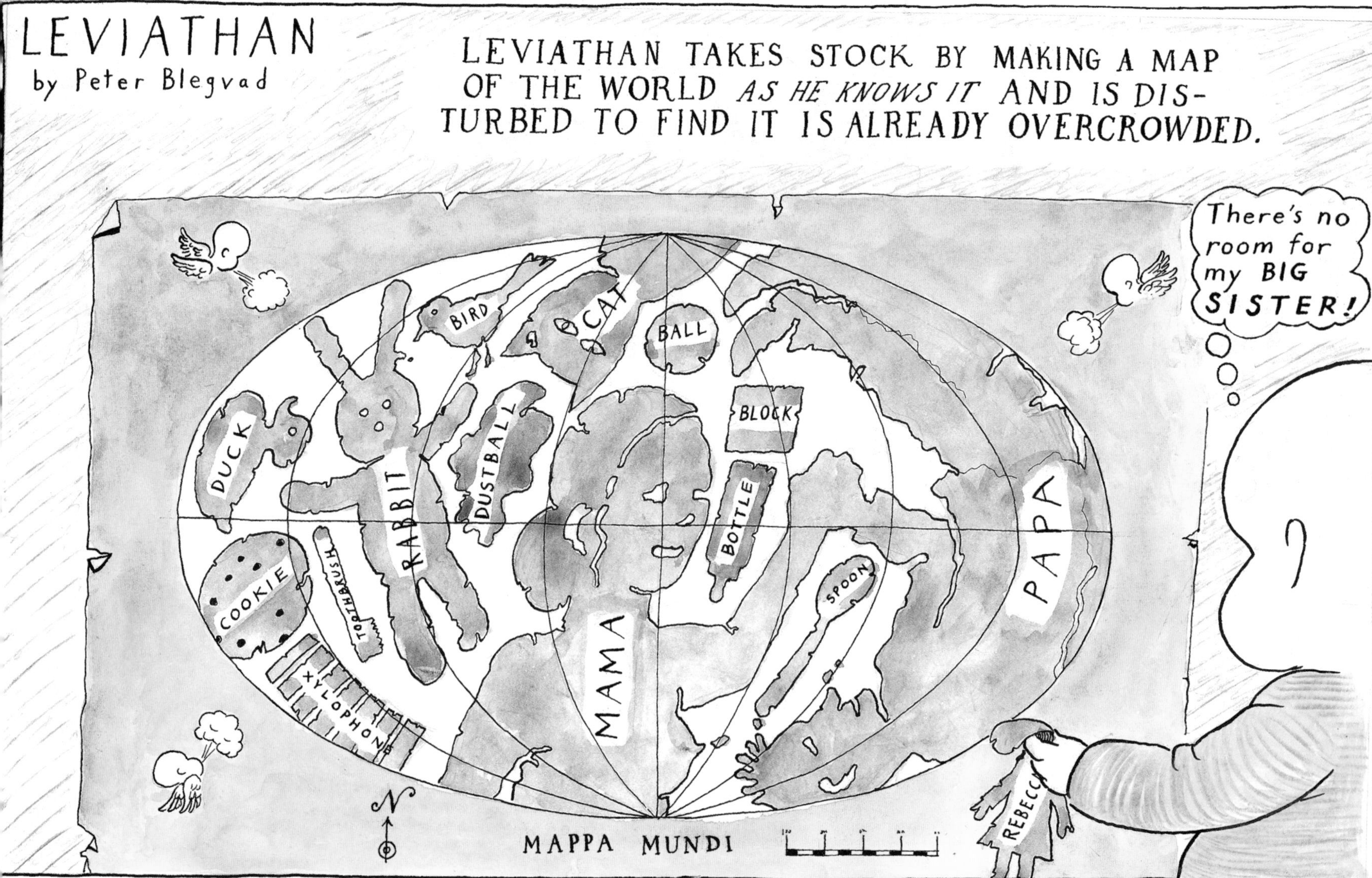
LEVIATHAN
by Peter Blegvad
LEVIATHAN TAKES STOCK BY MAKING A MAP OF THE WORLD *AS HE KNOWS IT* AND IS DISTURBED TO FIND IT IS ALREADY OVERCROWDED.
BIRD
CAT
BALL
DUCK
RABBIT
DUSTBALL
BLOCK
BOTTLE
COOKIE
TOOTHBRUSH
XYLOPHONE
MAMA
SPOON
PAPA
REBECCA
N
MAPPA MUNDI
There's no room for my **BIG SISTER!**

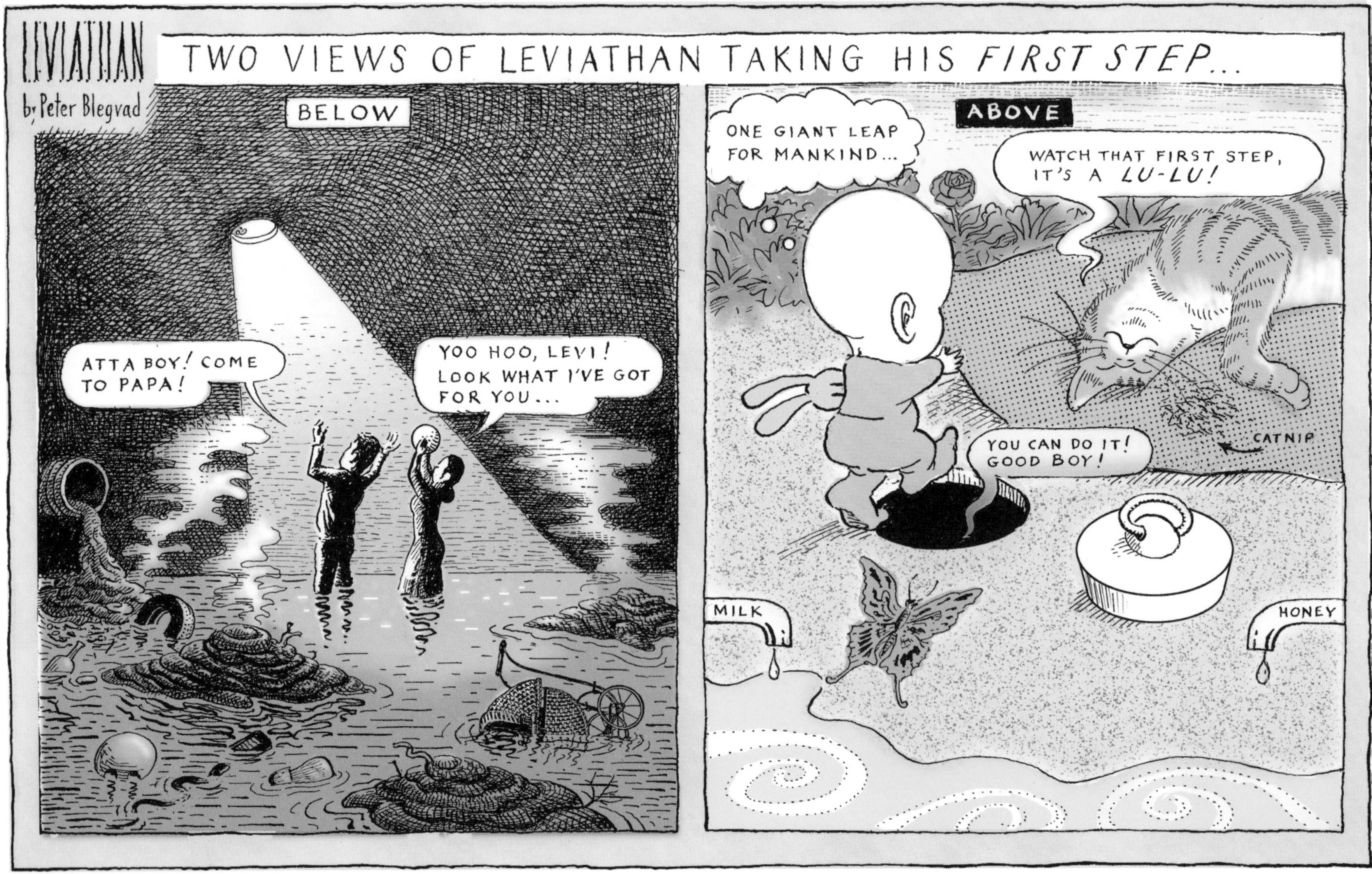
LEVIATHAN
by Peter Blegvad
TWO VIEWS OF LEVIATHAN TAKING HIS FIRST STEP...
BELOW
ATTA BOY! COME TO PAPA!
YOO HOO, LEVI! LOOK WHAT I'VE GOT FOR YOU...
ABOVE
ONE GIANT LEAP FOR MANKIND...
WATCH THAT FIRST STEP, IT'S A LU-LU!
YOU CAN DO IT! GOOD BOY!
CATNIP
MILK
HONEY

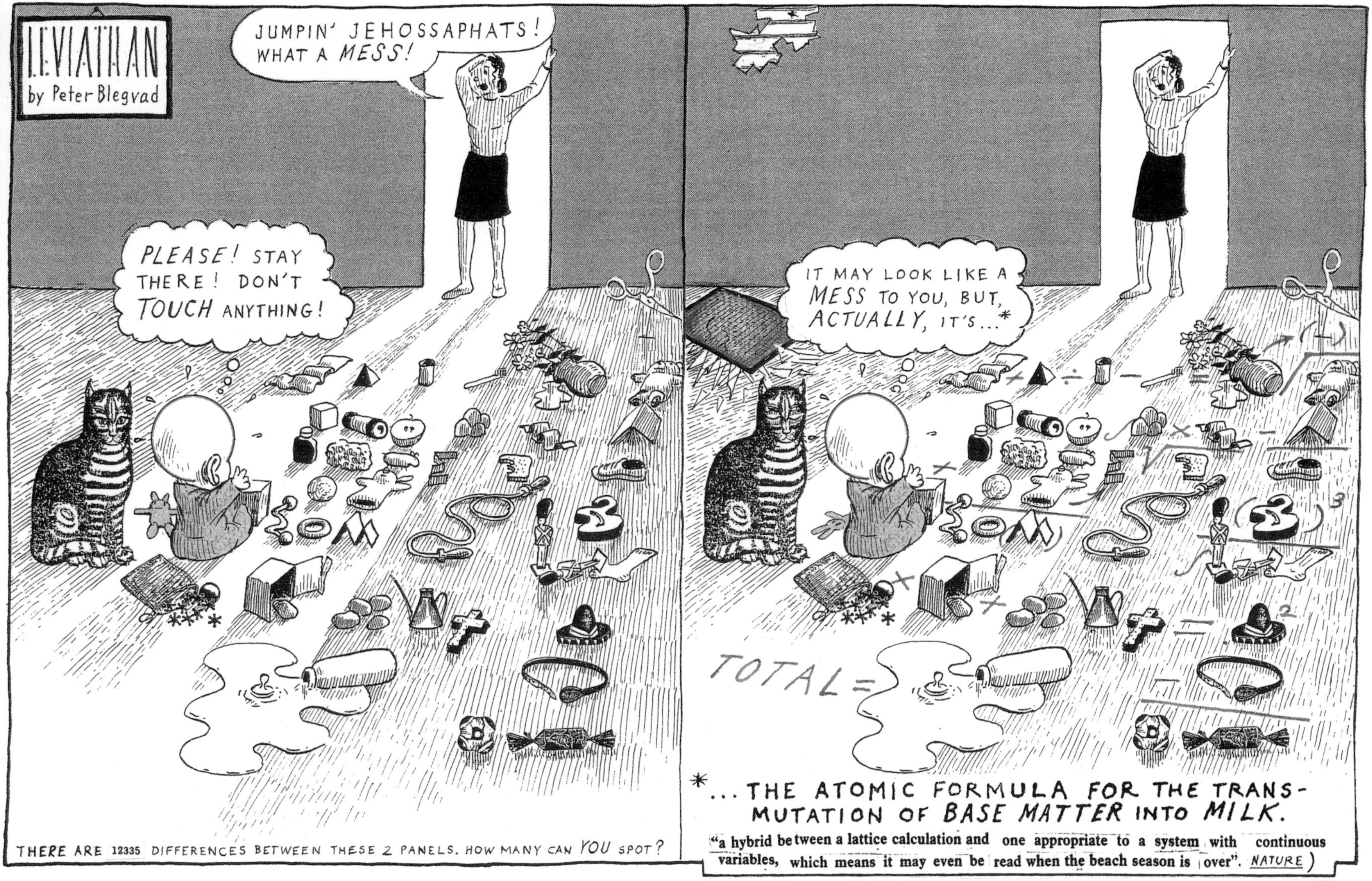
LEVIATHAN
by Peter Blegvad
JUMPIN' JEHOSSAPHATS! WHAT A MESS!
PLEASE! STAY THERE! DON'T TOUCH ANYTHING!
THERE ARE 12335 DIFFERENCES BETWEEN THESE 2 PANELS. HOW MANY CAN YOU SPOT?
IT MAY LOOK LIKE A MESS TO YOU, BUT, ACTUALLY, IT'S...*
TOTAL =
* ...THE ATOMIC FORMULA FOR THE TRANSMUTATION OF BASE MATTER INTO MILK.
("a hybrid between a lattice calculation and one appropriate to a system with continuous variables, which means it may even be read when the beach season is over". NATURE)

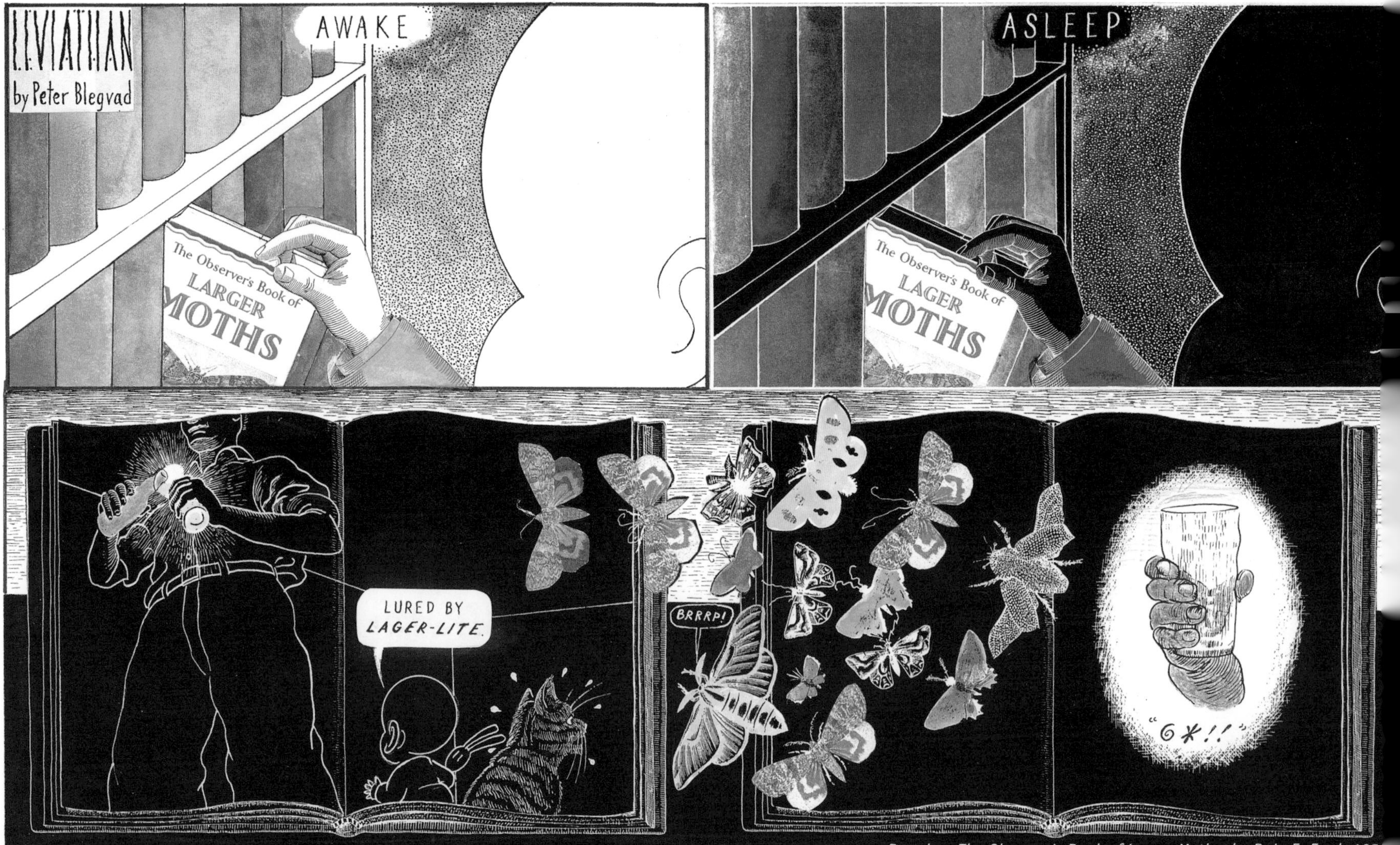

LEVIATHAN
by Peter Blegvad
AWAKE
The Observer's Book of LARGER MOTHS
ASLEEP
The Observer's Book of LAGER MOTHS
LURED BY LAGER-LITE.
BRRRP!
"G*!!"


Based on The Observer's Book of Larger Moths, by R. L. E. Ford, 195

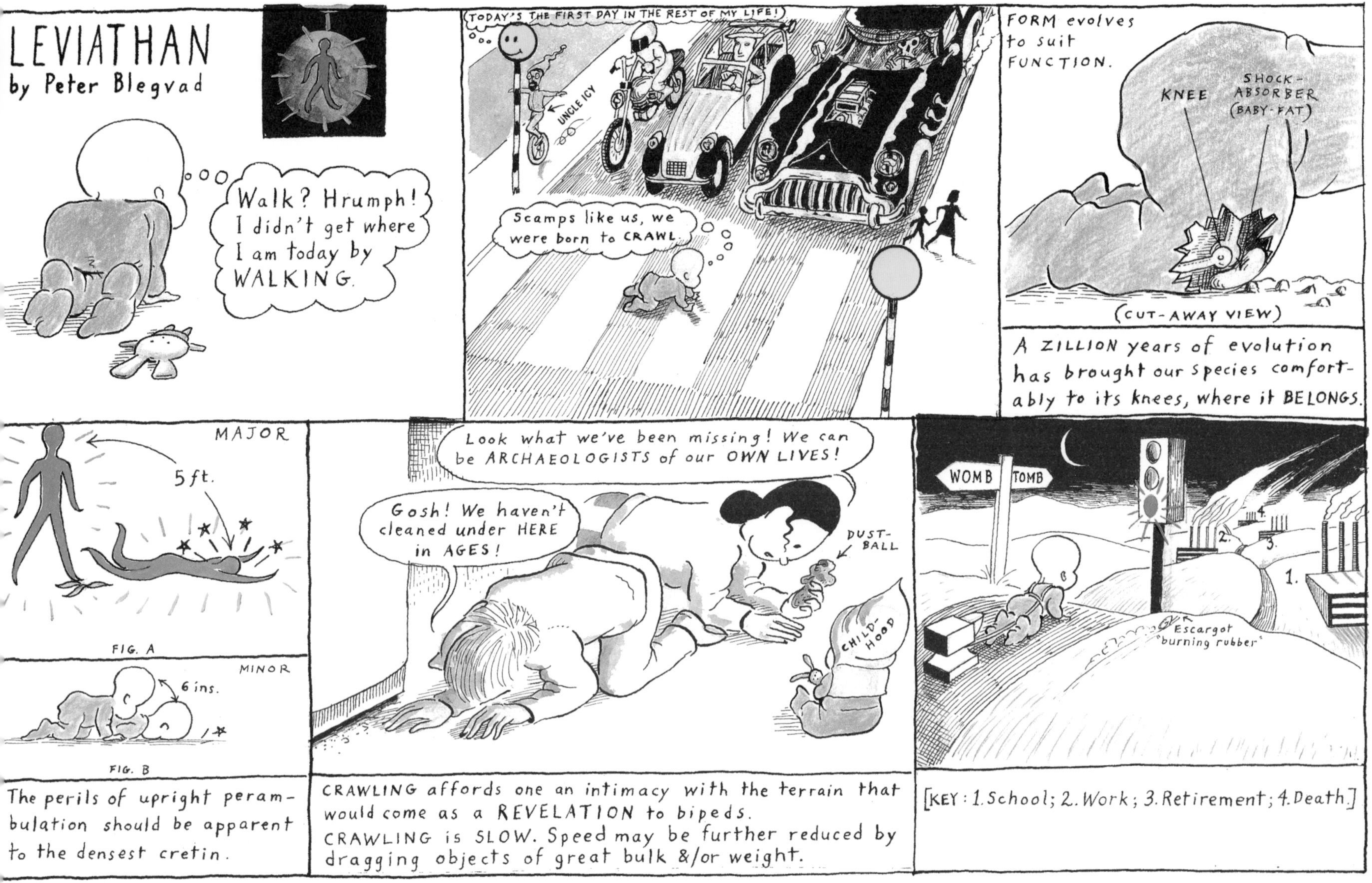

LEVIATHAN
by Peter Blegvad
Walk? Hrumph! I didn't get where I am today by WALKING.
TODAY'S THE FIRST DAY IN THE REST OF MY LIFE!
UNCLE ICY
Scamps like us, we were born to CRAWL.
FORM evolves to suit FUNCTION.
KNEE
SHOCK-ABSORBER (BABY-FAT)
(CUT-AWAY VIEW)
A ZILLION years of evolution has brought our species comfortably to its knees, where it BELONGS.
MAJOR
5 ft.
FIG. A
MINOR
6 ins.
FIG. B
The perils of upright perambulation should be apparent to the densest cretin.
Look what we've been missing! We can be ARCHAEOLOGISTS of our OWN LIVES!
Gosh! We haven't cleaned under HERE in AGES!
DUST-BALL
CHILD-HOOD
CRAWLING affords one an intimacy with the terrain that would come as a REVELATION to bipeds.
CRAWLING is SLOW. Speed may be further reduced by dragging objects of great bulk &/or weight.
WOMB
TOMB
1.
2.
3.
4.
Escargot "burning rubber"
[KEY: 1. School; 2. Work; 3. Retirement; 4. Death]

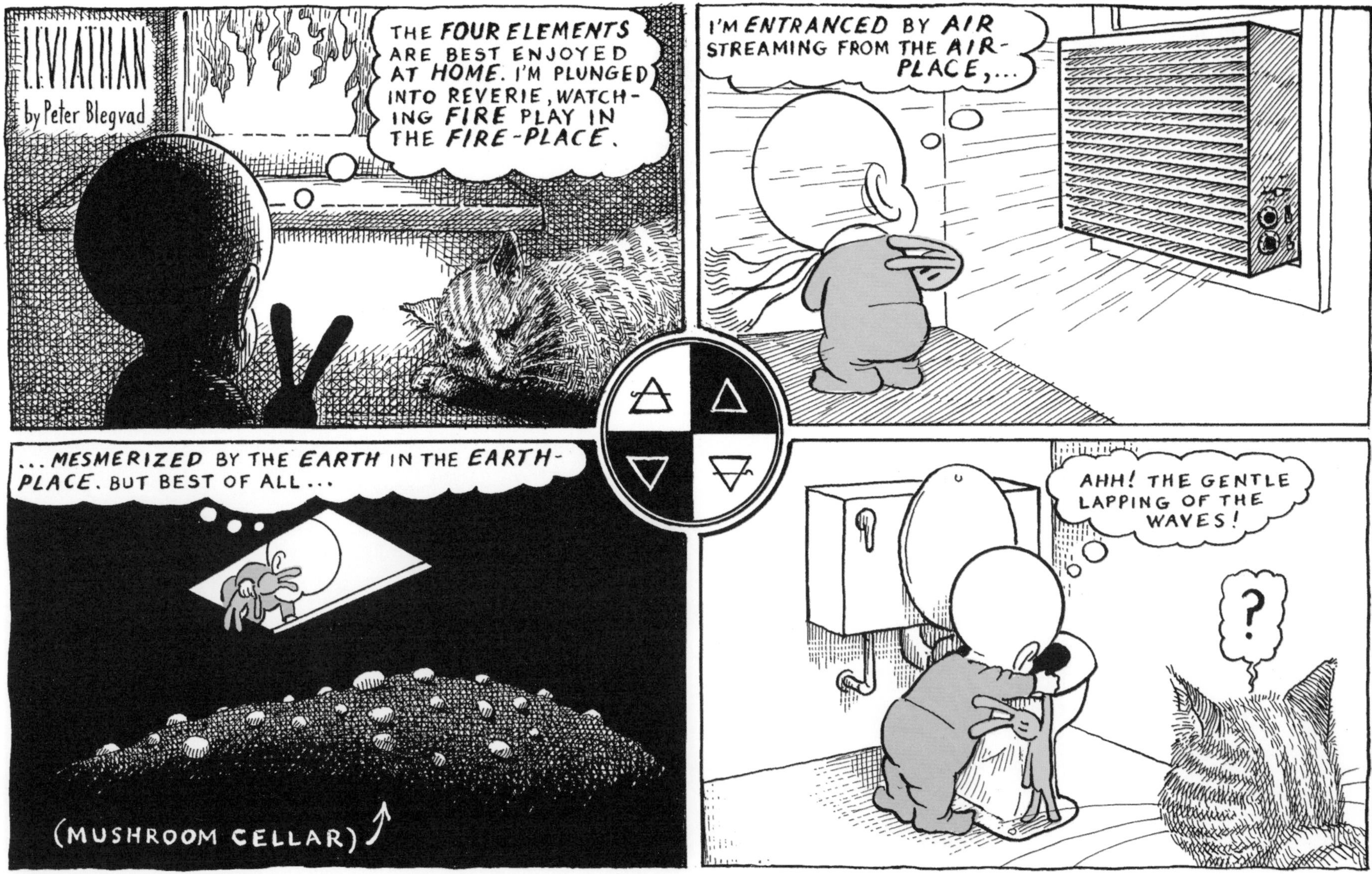
LEVIATHAN
by Peter Blegvad
THE FOUR ELEMENTS ARE BEST ENJOYED AT HOME. I'M PLUNGED INTO REVERIE, WATCHING FIRE PLAY IN THE FIRE-PLACE.
I'M ENTRANCED BY AIR STREAMING FROM THE AIR-PLACE,...
...MESMERIZED BY THE EARTH IN THE EARTH-PLACE. BUT BEST OF ALL...
(MUSHROOM CELLAR)
AHH! THE GENTLE LAPPING OF THE WAVES!
?

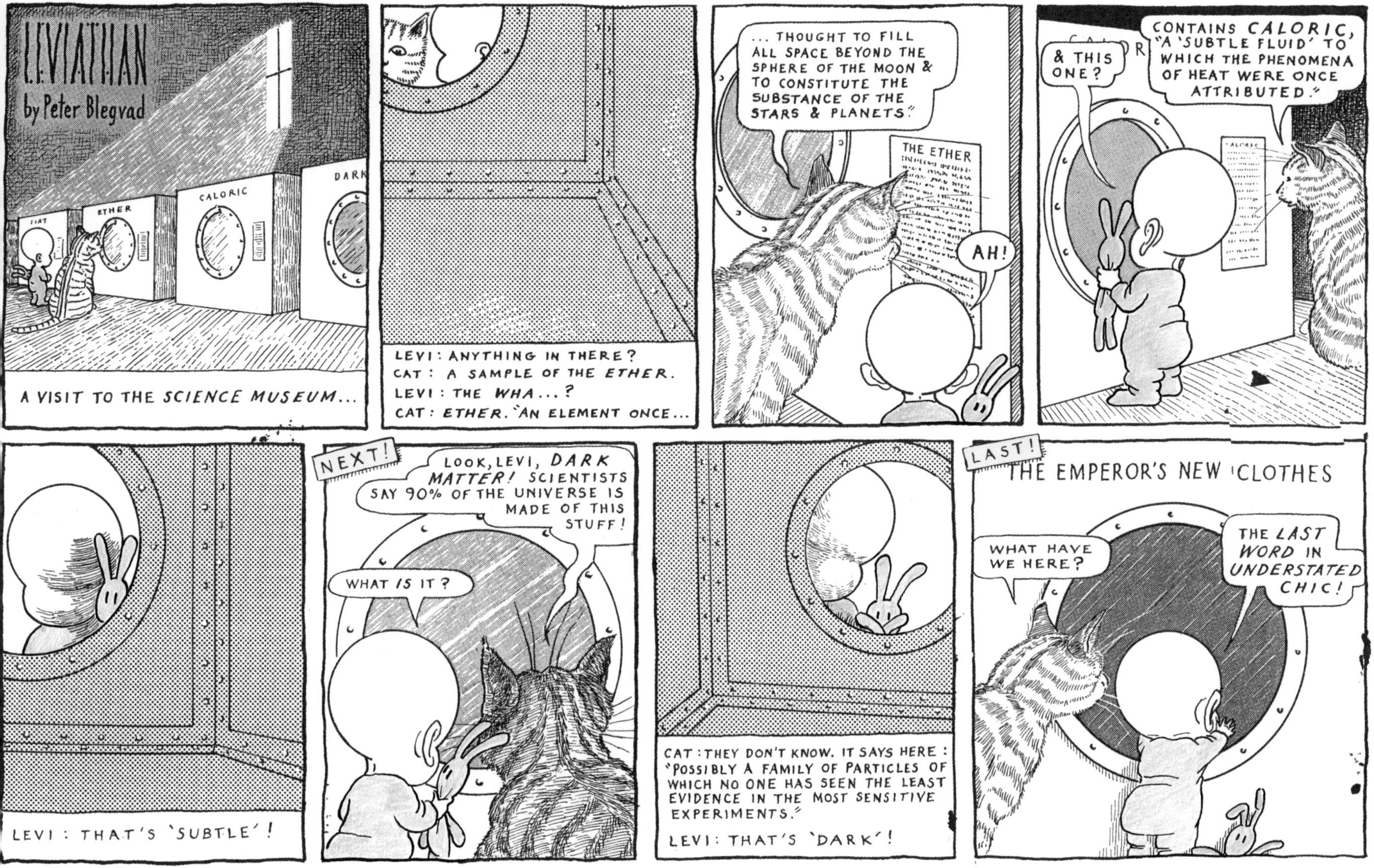
LEVIATHAN
by Peter Blegvad
THAT
ETHER
CALORIC
DARK
A VISIT TO THE *SCIENCE MUSEUM*...
LEVI: ANYTHING IN THERE?
CAT: A SAMPLE OF THE *ETHER*.
LEVI: THE *WHA*...?
CAT: *ETHER*. "AN ELEMENT ONCE...
... THOUGHT TO FILL ALL SPACE BEYOND THE SPHERE OF THE MOON & TO CONSTITUTE THE SUBSTANCE OF THE STARS & PLANETS."
THE ETHER
AH!
& THIS ONE?
CONTAINS *CALORIC*, "A 'SUBTLE FLUID' TO WHICH THE PHENOMENA OF HEAT WERE ONCE ATTRIBUTED."
LEVI: THAT'S 'SUBTLE'!
NEXT!
LOOK, LEVI, *DARK MATTER!* SCIENTISTS SAY 90% OF THE UNIVERSE IS MADE OF THIS STUFF!
WHAT *IS* IT?
CAT: THEY DON'T KNOW. IT SAYS HERE: "POSSIBLY A FAMILY OF PARTICLES OF WHICH NO ONE HAS SEEN THE LEAST EVIDENCE IN THE MOST SENSITIVE EXPERIMENTS."
LEVI: THAT'S 'DARK'!
LAST!
THE EMPEROR'S NEW CLOTHES
WHAT HAVE WE HERE?
THE *LAST WORD* IN *UNDERSTATED CHIC*!

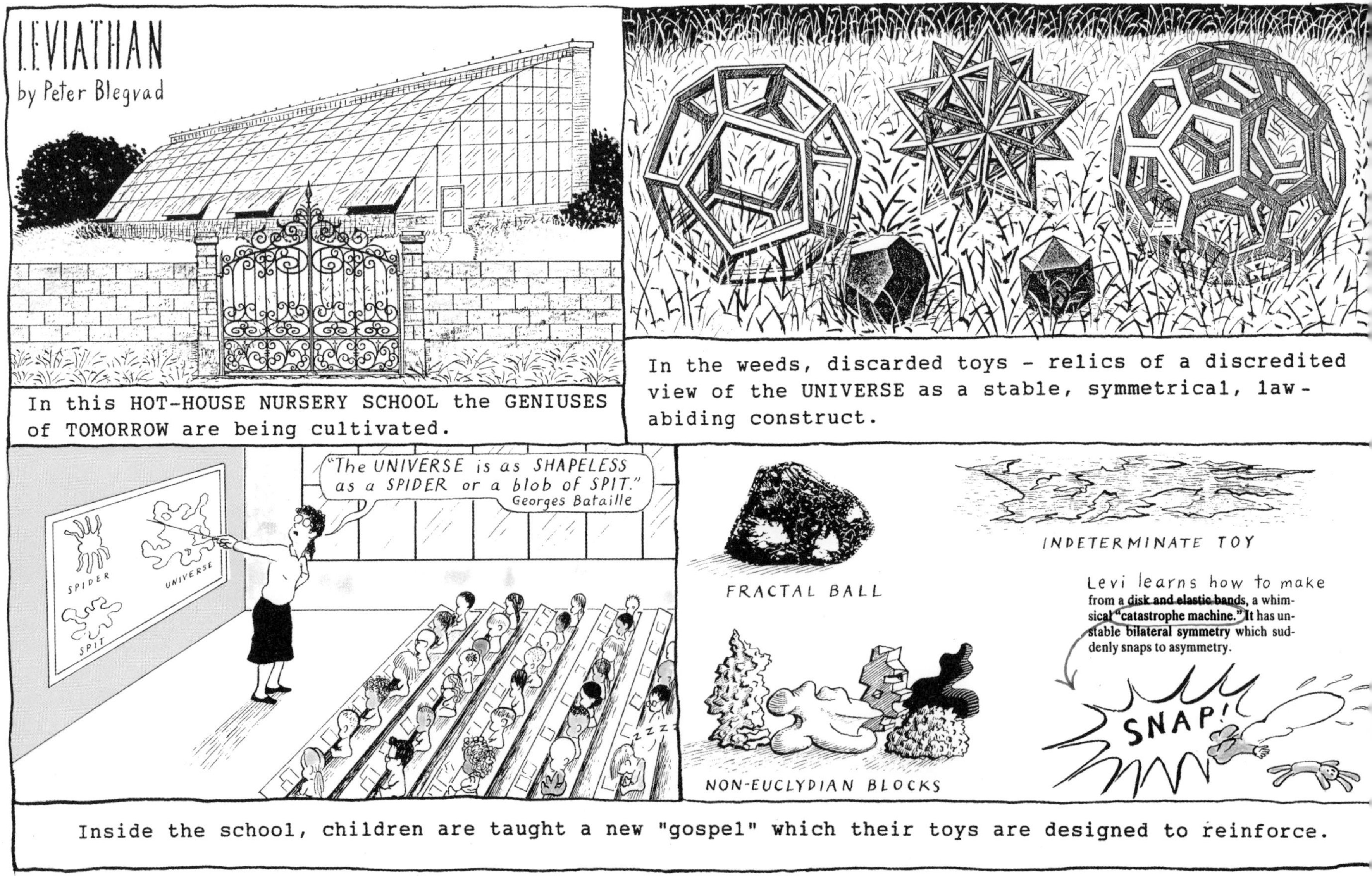
LEVIATHAN
by Peter Blegvad
In this HOT-HOUSE NURSERY SCHOOL the GENIUSES of TOMORROW are being cultivated.
In the weeds, discarded toys - relics of a discredited view of the UNIVERSE as a stable, symmetrical, law-abiding construct.
"The UNIVERSE is as SHAPELESS as a SPIDER or a blob of SPIT." Georges Bataille
SPIDER
UNIVERSE
SPIT
FRACTAL BALL
INDETERMINATE TOY
Levi learns how to make from a disk and elastic bands, a whimsical "catastrophe machine." It has unstable bilateral symmetry which suddenly snaps to asymmetry.
SNAP!
NON-EUCLYDIAN BLOCKS
Inside the school, children are taught a new "gospel" which their toys are designed to reinforce.

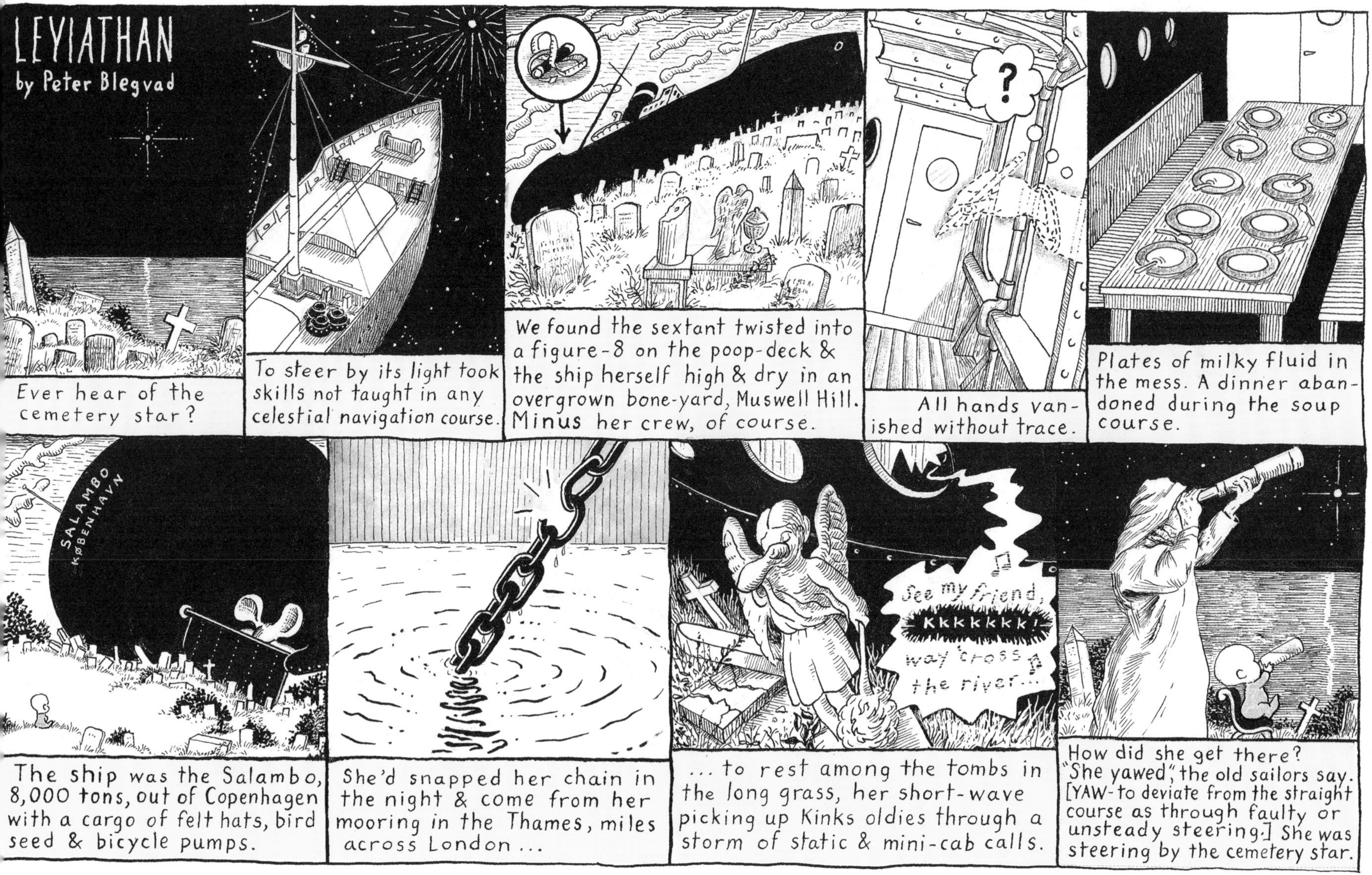
LEVIATHAN
by Peter Blegvad
Ever hear of the cemetery star?
To steer by its light took skills not taught in any celestial navigation course.
We found the sextant twisted into a figure-8 on the poop-deck & the ship herself high & dry in an overgrown bone-yard, Muswell Hill. Minus her crew, of course.
?
All hands vanished without trace.
Plates of milky fluid in the mess. A dinner abandoned during the soup course.
SALAMBO
KØBENHAVN
The ship was the Salambo, 8,000 tons, out of Copenhagen with a cargo of felt hats, bird seed & bicycle pumps.
She'd snapped her chain in the night & come from her mooring in the Thames, miles across London ...
See my friend,
KKKKKKK!
way 'cross the river...
... to rest among the tombs in the long grass, her short-wave picking up Kinks oldies through a storm of static & mini-cab calls.
How did she get there? "She yawed," the old sailors say. [YAW-to deviate from the straight course as through faulty or unsteady steering.] She was steering by the cemetery star.

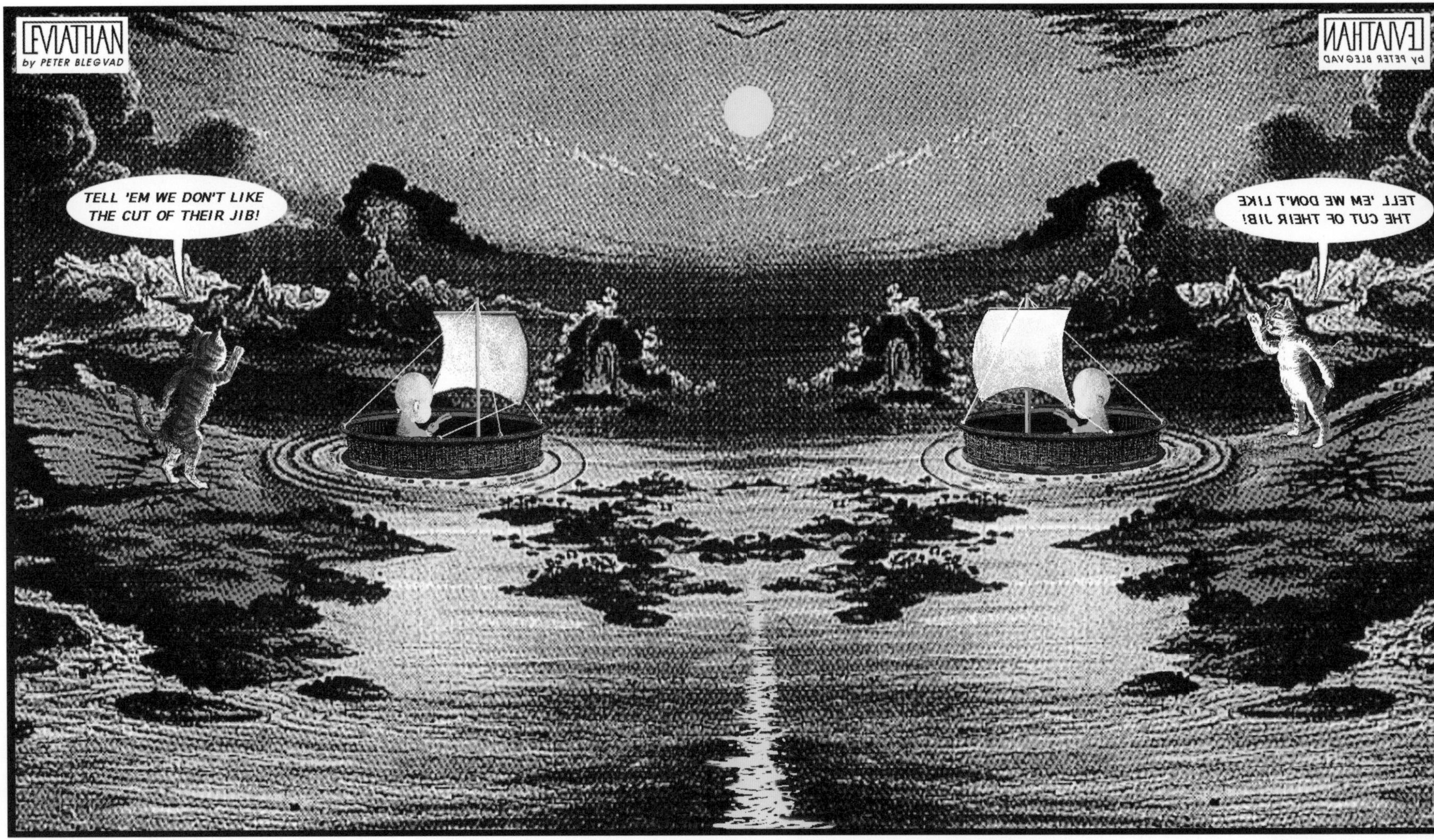

LEVIATHAN
by PETER BLEGVAD
TELL 'EM WE DON'T LIKE THE CUT OF THEIR JIB!

# VI. SCHEMA
# THINGS

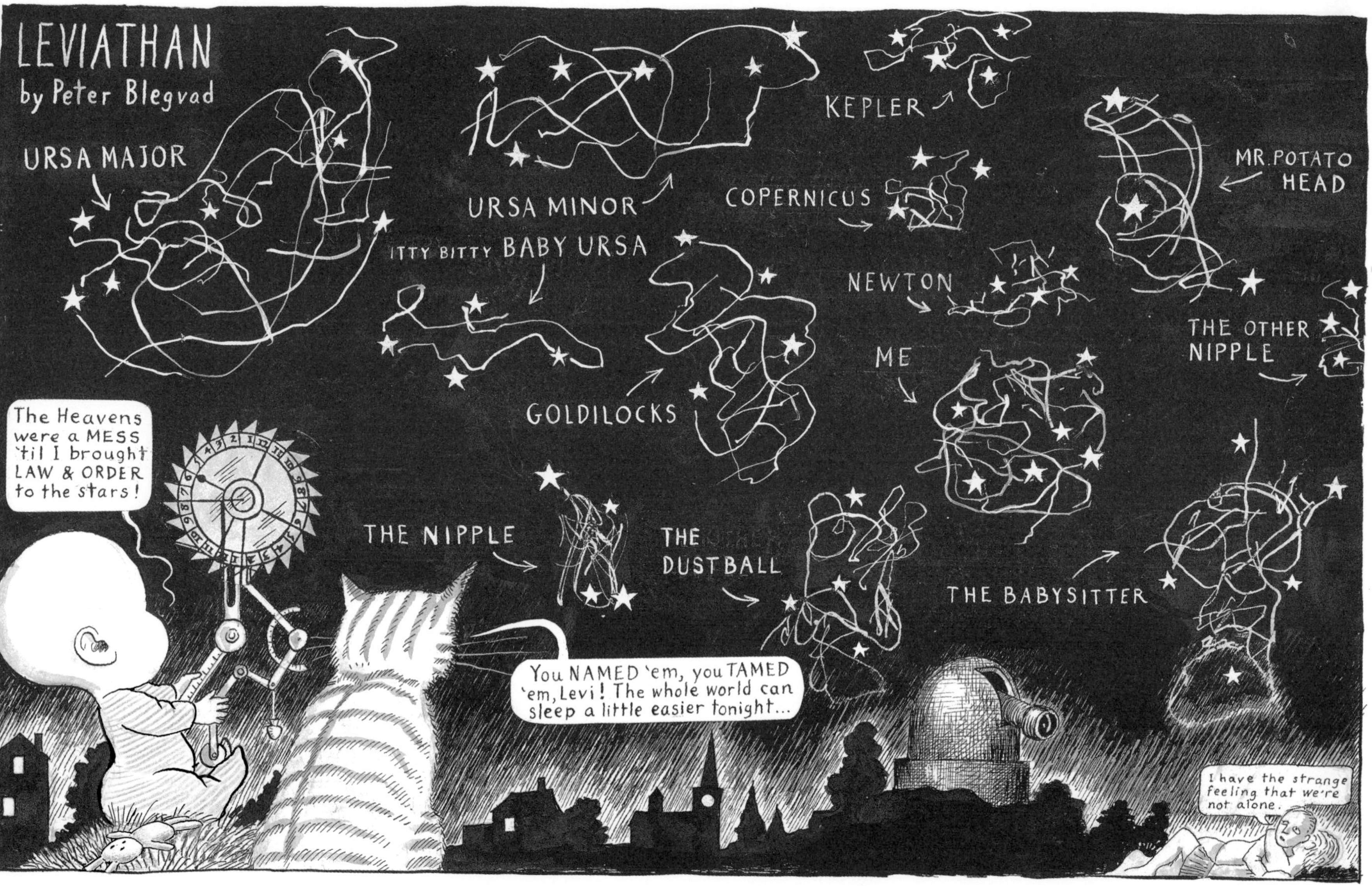

LEVIATHAN
by Peter Blegvad
URSA MAJOR
URSA MINOR
KEPLER
COPERNICUS
MR. POTATO HEAD
ITTY BITTY BABY URSA
NEWTON
THE OTHER NIPPLE
ME
GOLDILOCKS
The Heavens were a MESS 'til I brought LAW & ORDER to the stars!
THE NIPPLE
THE DUSTBALL
THE BABYSITTER
You NAMED 'em, you TAMED 'em, Levi! The whole world can sleep a little easier tonight...
I have the strange feeling that we're not alone.

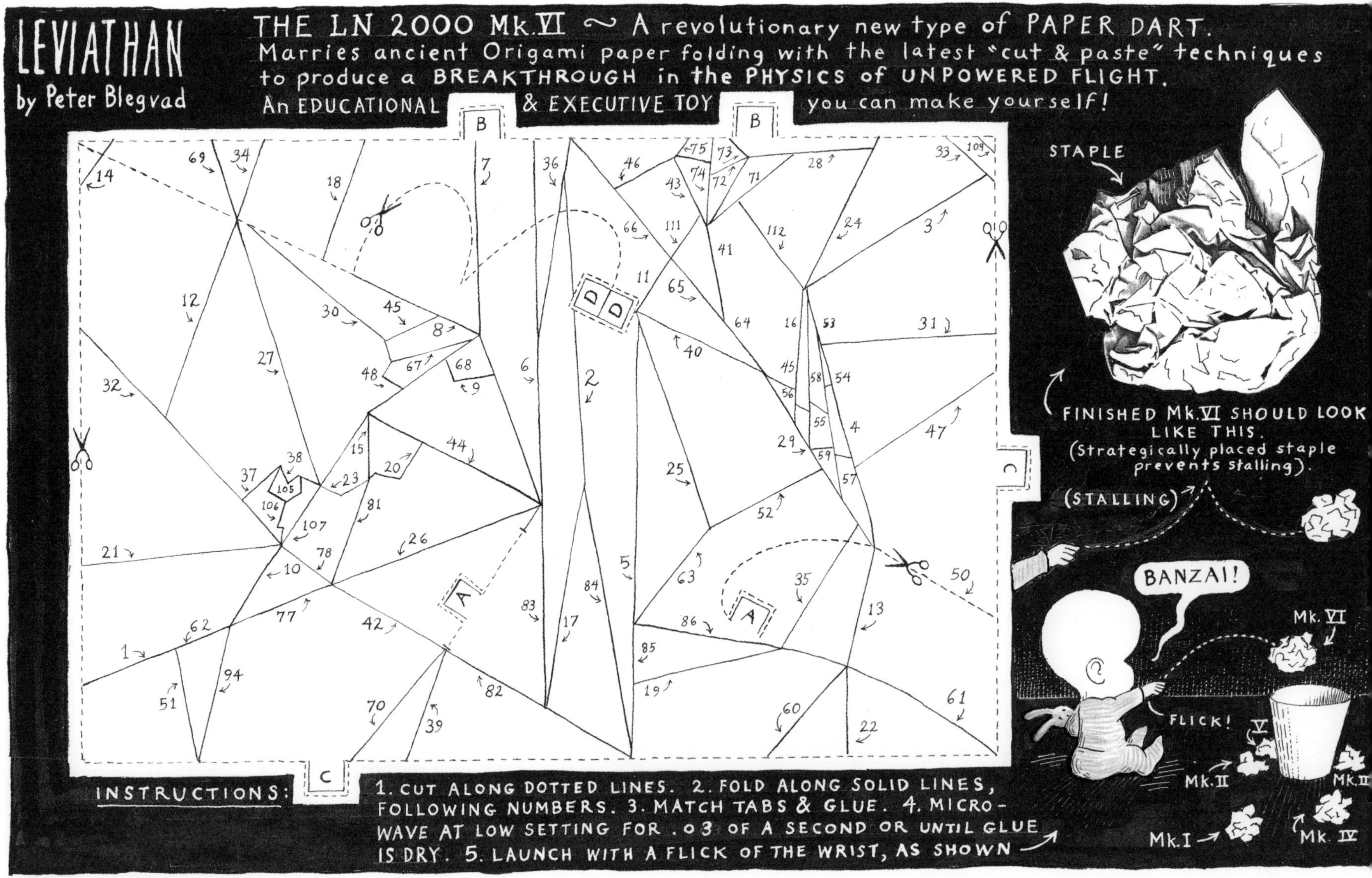
LEVIATHAN
by Peter Blegvad
THE LN 2000 Mk.VI ~ A revolutionary new type of PAPER DART.
Marries ancient Origami paper folding with the latest "cut & paste" techniques to produce a BREAKTHROUGH in the PHYSICS of UNPOWERED FLIGHT.
An EDUCATIONAL & EXECUTIVE TOY you can make yourself!
STAPLE
FINISHED Mk.VI SHOULD LOOK LIKE THIS.
(Strategically placed staple prevents stalling).
(STALLING)
BANZAI!
Mk.VI
FLICK!
V
Mk.II
Mk.III
Mk.I
Mk.IV
INSTRUCTIONS:
1. CUT ALONG DOTTED LINES. 2. FOLD ALONG SOLID LINES, FOLLOWING NUMBERS. 3. MATCH TABS & GLUE. 4. MICRO-WAVE AT LOW SETTING FOR .03 OF A SECOND OR UNTIL GLUE IS DRY. 5. LAUNCH WITH A FLICK OF THE WRIST, AS SHOWN

# LEVIATHAN
## by Peter Blegvad

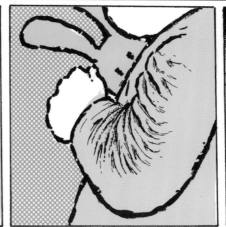

BUS ROUTES

WRINKLES WRULE!

ALL DAY, LEVI "FLEXES" HIS ARM IN ORDER TO STUDY THE INTRICATE WRINKLE SYSTEMS. THIS CAUSES IN HIS SLEEVE. HE'S RAPT, READING HIS FORTUNE IN THE FOLDS. IT DOESN'T ESCAPE HIM THAT

WRINKLES "RHYME" WITH OTHER FORMS IN NATURE.

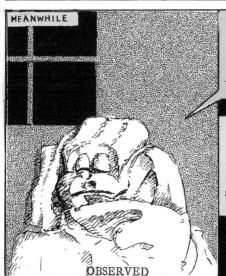

MEANWHILE

OBSERVED

## BELIEVE IT OR NOT

IN 1984, WELSH COMPOSER JOHN GREAVES CASUALLY TOSSED HIS JACKET ONTO A CHAIR SO THAT THE WRINKLES FORMED THIS FACE!

ARTIST BURNE HOGARTH, AUTHOR OF "DYNAMIC WRINKLES AND DRAPERY" (Watson-Guptill, 1992), HAS DEFINED THE KINETIC FORCES WHICH GIVE "RISE TO CATEGORICAL SYSTEMS OF WRINKLES AND FOLDS" IN CLOTHING!

**ABOVE:** *Not unlike a research scientist, Hogarth uses diagrams to illustrate his wrinkle theories.*

SWIPED FROM *THE COMICS JOURNAL* (Fantagraphics)

STONED OUT OF HIS MIND, ALDOUS HUXLEY CLAIMED TO HAVE SEEN "THE ABSOLUTE IN THE FOLDS OF A PAIR OF FLANNEL TROUSERS."

STREUTH!

**LEVIATHAN**
by Peter Blegvad

ZZZZ

**L**EVI'S BEDROOM, 5:14 A.M.

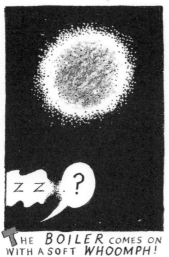

ZZ ?

**T**HE **BOILER** COMES ON WITH A SOFT **WHOOMPH!**

YAWN!

**O**UTSIDE, A **TWIG** SNAPS, & A **DOG** BARKS.

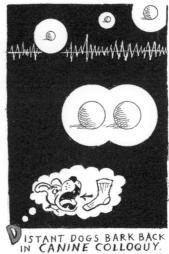

**D**ISTANT DOGS BARK BACK IN **CANINE COLLOQUY.**

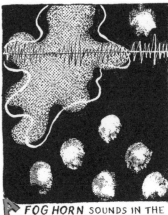

**A FOG HORN** SOUNDS IN THE BAY. THOSE THUDS ARE LEVI'S **HEARTBEATS.** THAT HIGH-PITCHED WHINE, HIS **NERVOUS SYSTEM!**

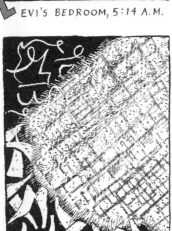
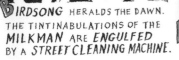

**B**IRDSONG HERALDS THE DAWN. THE TINTINABULATIONS OF THE **MILKMAN** ARE **ENGULFED** BY A **STREET CLEANING MACHINE.**

!

**A**N **ARGUMENT** BREAKS OUT BENEATH LEVI'S WINDOW...

!

**I**T GROWS INTO A **BRAWL**— CURSES, SCUFFLING, BLOWS!

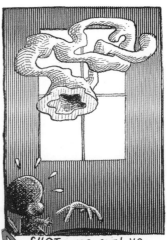

**A SHOT** RINGS OUT! NO, IT'S JUST A **CAR** BACKFIRING.

SCREECH CRASH TINKLE HONK VROOOM BLAM TWEET Nee-nu Nee-nu Nee-nu KA-BLOOIE SNAP CRACKLE ZA-BLOOIE DRRING DRRRING OINK ZZZZZ WOOF

**I**N THE **CLEAR LIGHT** OF DAY, LEVI'S **SYNESTHESIA** ABATES.

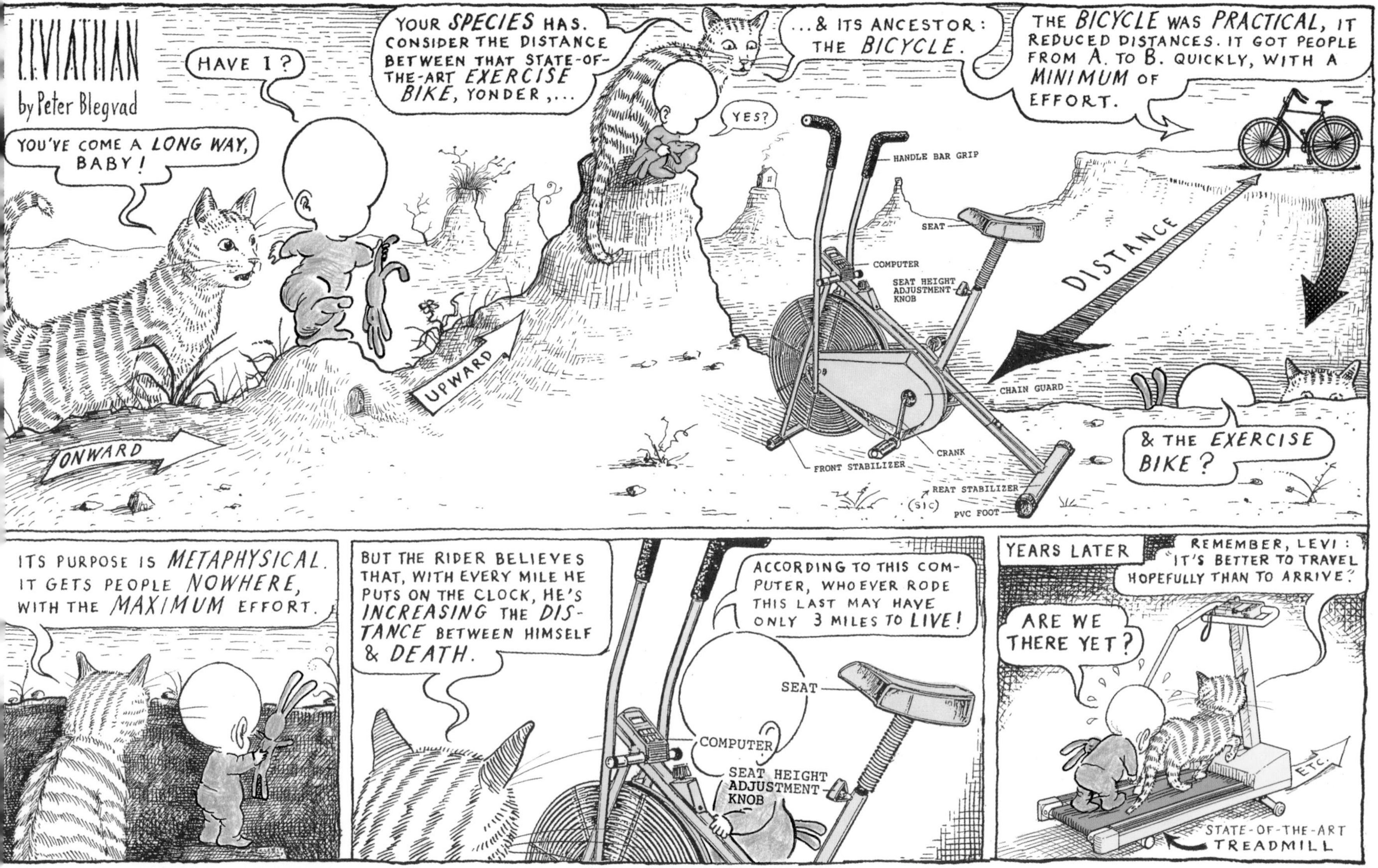

LEVIATHAN
by Peter Blegvad
YOU'VE COME A LONG WAY, BABY!
HAVE I?
YOUR SPECIES HAS. CONSIDER THE DISTANCE BETWEEN THAT STATE-OF-THE-ART EXERCISE BIKE, YONDER,...
YES?
...& ITS ANCESTOR: THE BICYCLE.
THE BICYCLE WAS PRACTICAL, IT REDUCED DISTANCES. IT GOT PEOPLE FROM A. TO B. QUICKLY, WITH A MINIMUM OF EFFORT.
ONWARD
UPWARD
HANDLE BAR GRIP
SEAT
COMPUTER
SEAT HEIGHT ADJUSTMENT KNOB
CHAIN GUARD
CRANK
FRONT STABILIZER
REAT STABILIZER
(SIC)
PVC FOOT
DISTANCE
& THE EXERCISE BIKE?
ITS PURPOSE IS METAPHYSICAL. IT GETS PEOPLE NOWHERE, WITH THE MAXIMUM EFFORT.
BUT THE RIDER BELIEVES THAT, WITH EVERY MILE HE PUTS ON THE CLOCK, HE'S INCREASING THE DISTANCE BETWEEN HIMSELF & DEATH.
ACCORDING TO THIS COMPUTER, WHOEVER RODE THIS LAST MAY HAVE ONLY 3 MILES TO LIVE!
SEAT
COMPUTER
SEAT HEIGHT ADJUSTMENT KNOB
YEARS LATER
REMEMBER, LEVI: "IT'S BETTER TO TRAVEL HOPEFULLY THAN TO ARRIVE."
ARE WE THERE YET?
ETC.
STATE-OF-THE-ART TREADMILL

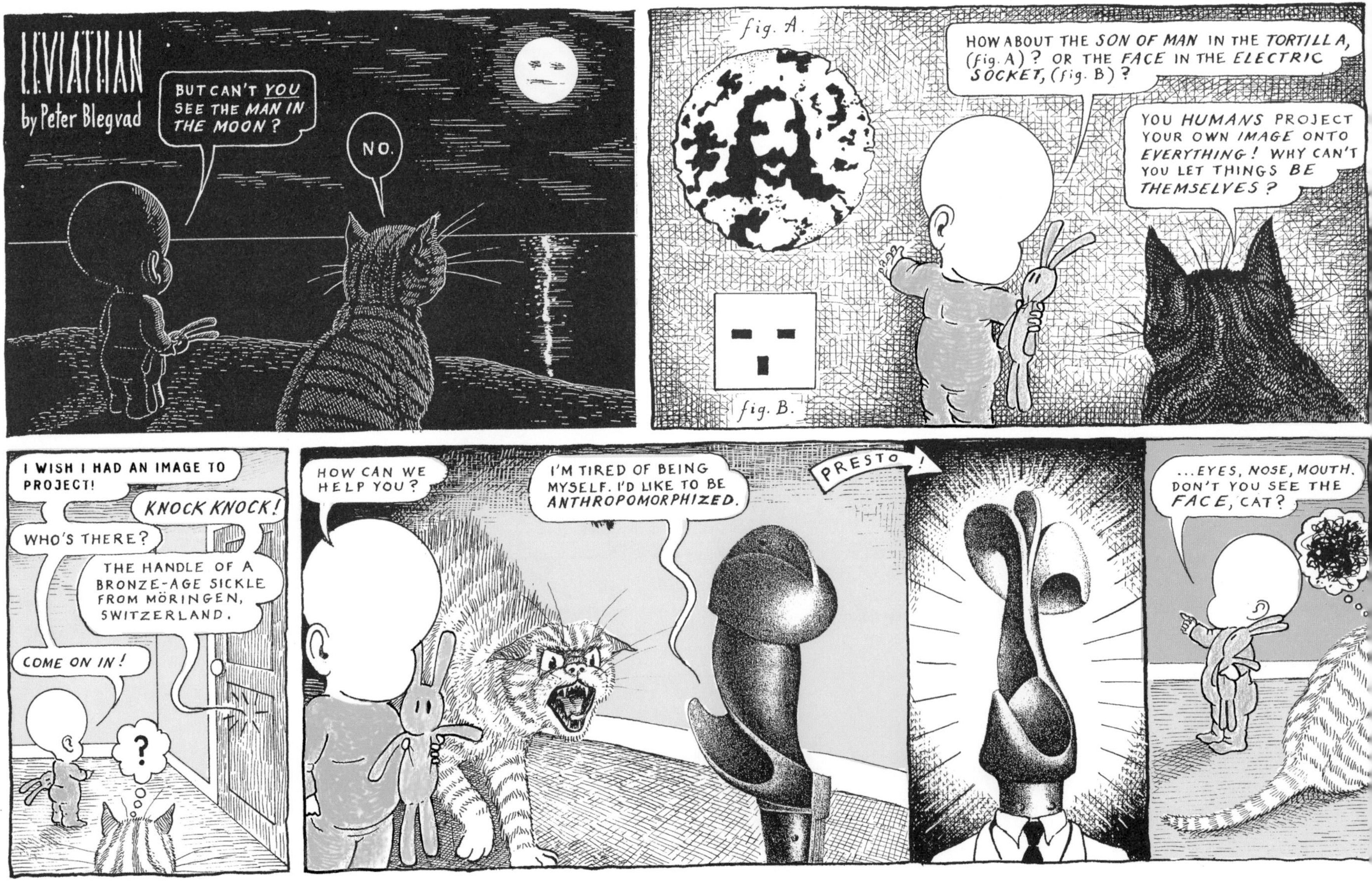
LEVIATHAN
by Peter Blegvad
BUT CAN'T YOU SEE THE MAN IN THE MOON?
NO.
fig. A.
HOW ABOUT THE SON OF MAN IN THE TORTILLA, (fig. A)? OR THE FACE IN THE ELECTRIC SOCKET, (fig. B)?
YOU HUMANS PROJECT YOUR OWN IMAGE ONTO EVERYTHING! WHY CAN'T YOU LET THINGS BE THEMSELVES?
fig. B.
I WISH I HAD AN IMAGE TO PROJECT!
KNOCK KNOCK!
WHO'S THERE?
THE HANDLE OF A BRONZE-AGE SICKLE FROM MÖRINGEN, SWITZERLAND.
COME ON IN!
?
HOW CAN WE HELP YOU?
I'M TIRED OF BEING MYSELF. I'D LIKE TO BE ANTHROPOMORPHIZED.
PRESTO!
...EYES, NOSE, MOUTH. DON'T YOU SEE THE FACE, CAT?

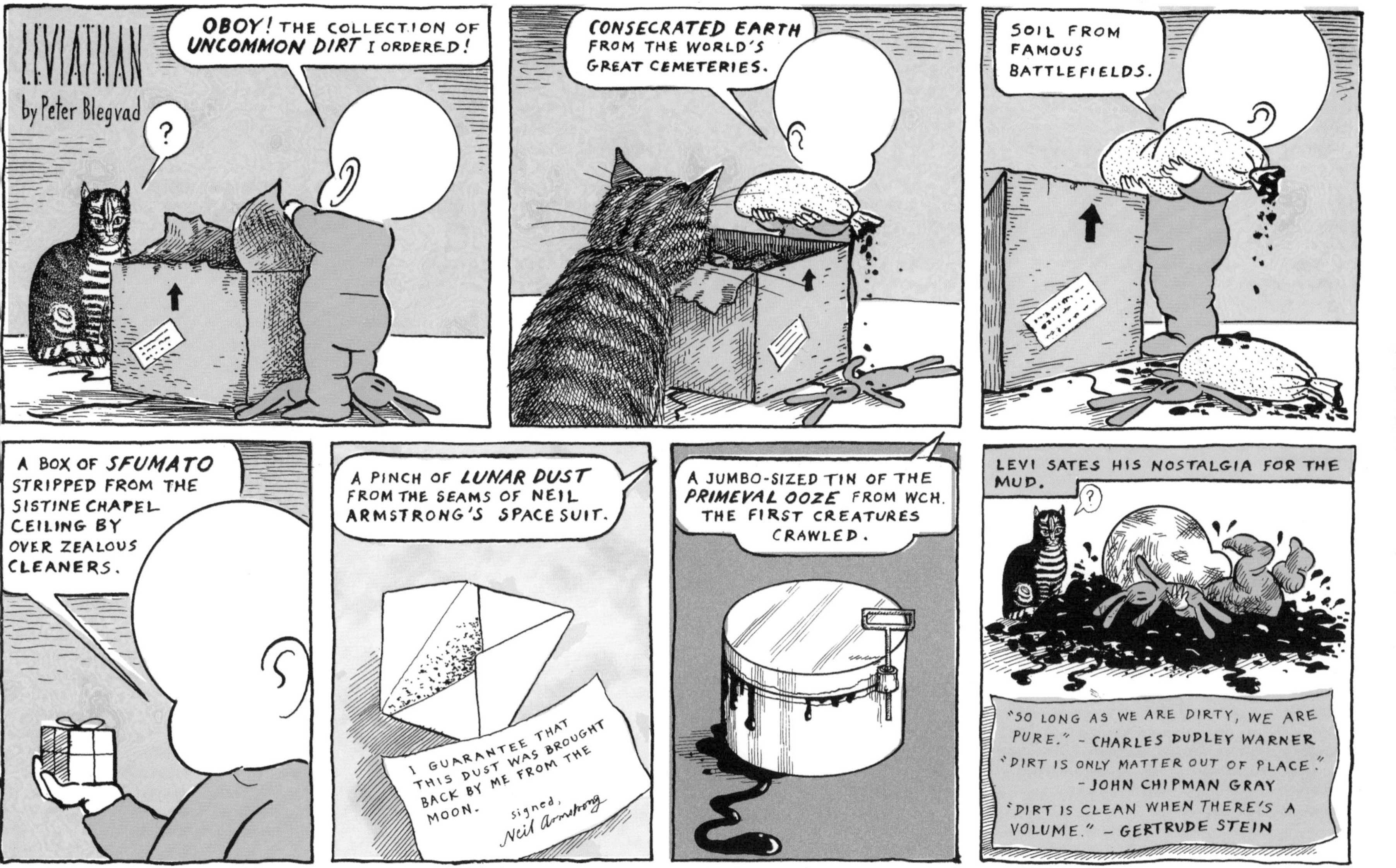
LEVIATHAN
by Peter Blegvad
OBOY! THE COLLECTION OF UNCOMMON DIRT I ORDERED!
?
CONSECRATED EARTH FROM THE WORLD'S GREAT CEMETERIES.
SOIL FROM FAMOUS BATTLEFIELDS.
A BOX OF SFUMATO STRIPPED FROM THE SISTINE CHAPEL CEILING BY OVER ZEALOUS CLEANERS.
A PINCH OF LUNAR DUST FROM THE SEAMS OF NEIL ARMSTRONG'S SPACE SUIT.
I GUARANTEE THAT THIS DUST WAS BROUGHT BACK BY ME FROM THE MOON.
signed, Neil Armstrong
A JUMBO-SIZED TIN OF THE PRIMEVAL OOZE FROM WCH. THE FIRST CREATURES CRAWLED.
LEVI SATES HIS NOSTALGIA FOR THE MUD.
?
"SO LONG AS WE ARE DIRTY, WE ARE PURE." - CHARLES DUDLEY WARNER
"DIRT IS ONLY MATTER OUT OF PLACE." - JOHN CHIPMAN GRAY
"DIRT IS CLEAN WHEN THERE'S A VOLUME." - GERTRUDE STEIN

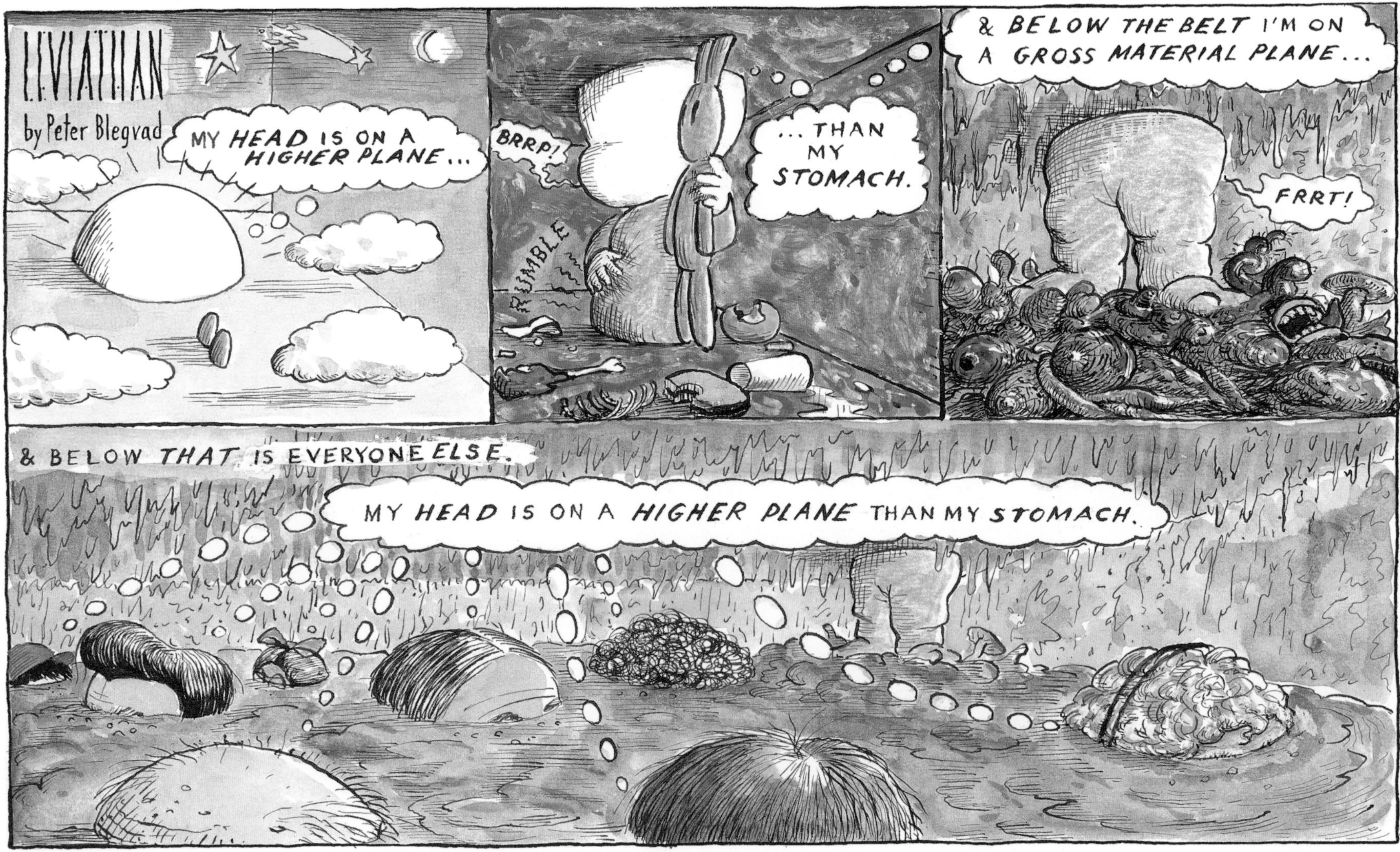
LEVIATHAN
by Peter Blegvad
MY HEAD IS ON A HIGHER PLANE...
BRRP!
RUMBLE
... THAN MY STOMACH.
& BELOW THE BELT I'M ON A GROSS MATERIAL PLANE...
FRRT!
& BELOW THAT IS EVERYONE ELSE.
MY HEAD IS ON A HIGHER PLANE THAN MY STOMACH.

# VII. NAMELESS DREAD

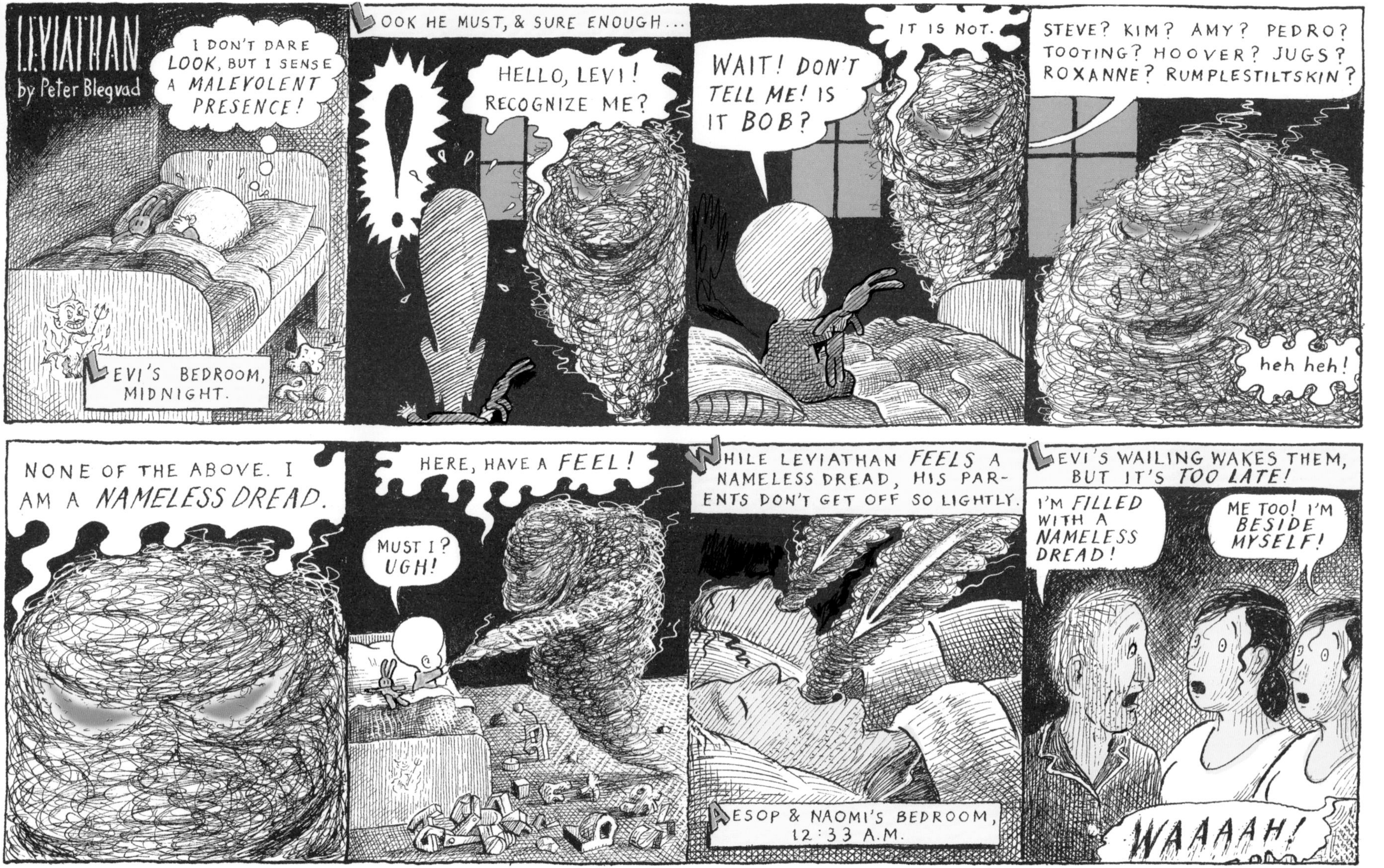
LEVIATHAN
by Peter Blegvad
I DON'T DARE LOOK, BUT I SENSE A MALEVOLENT PRESENCE!
LEVI'S BEDROOM, MIDNIGHT.
LOOK HE MUST, & SURE ENOUGH...
!
HELLO, LEVI! RECOGNIZE ME?
WAIT! DON'T TELL ME! IS IT BOB?
IT IS NOT.
STEVE? KIM? AMY? PEDRO? TOOTING? HOOVER? JUGS? ROXANNE? RUMPLESTILTSKIN?
heh heh!
NONE OF THE ABOVE. I AM A NAMELESS DREAD.
HERE, HAVE A FEEL!
MUST I? UGH!
WHILE LEVIATHAN FEELS A NAMELESS DREAD, HIS PARENTS DON'T GET OFF SO LIGHTLY.
AESOP & NAOMI'S BEDROOM, 12:33 A.M.
LEVI'S WAILING WAKES THEM, BUT IT'S TOO LATE!
I'M FILLED WITH A NAMELESS DREAD!
ME TOO! I'M BESIDE MYSELF!
WAAAAH!

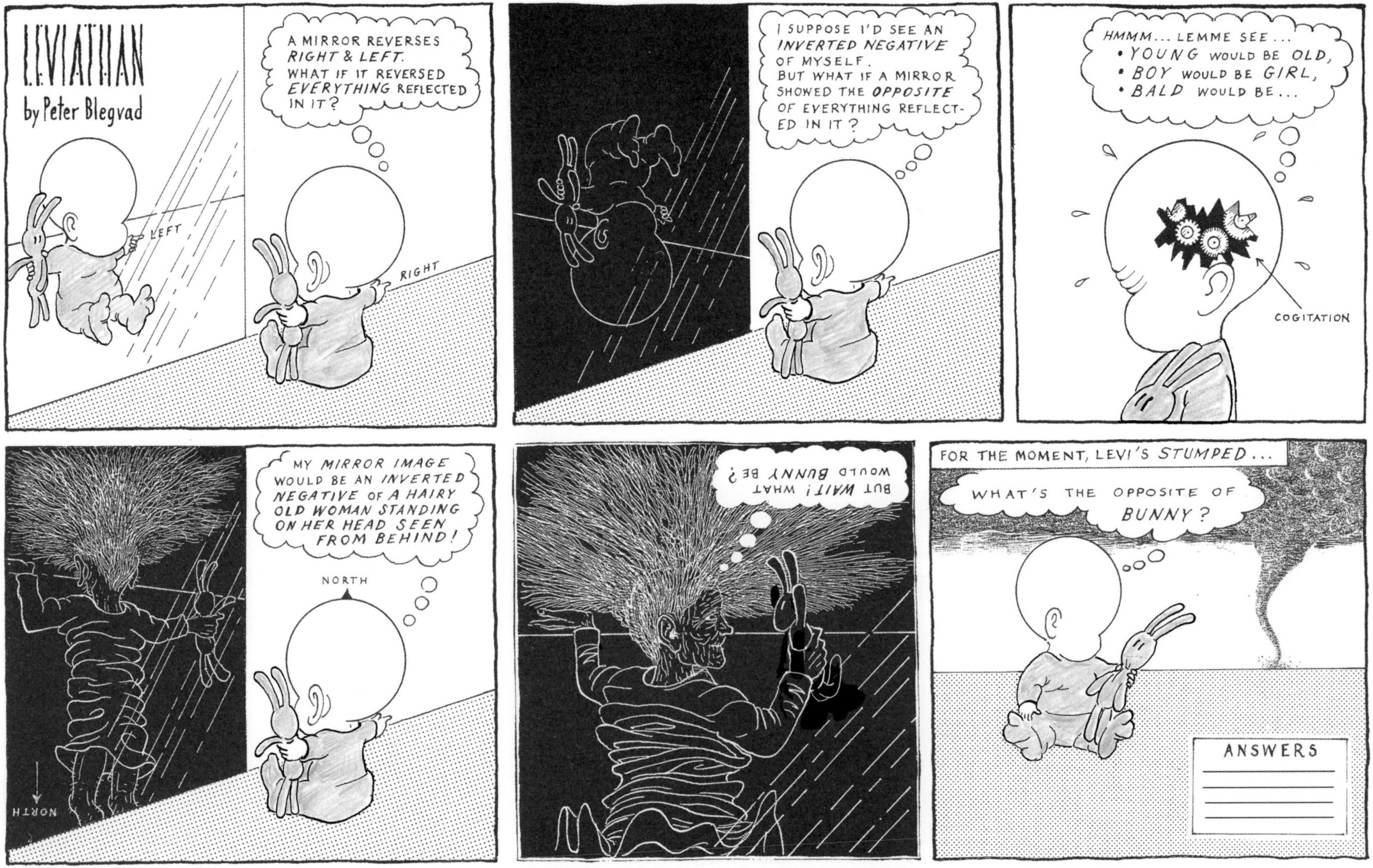
LEVIATHAN
by Peter Blegvad
LEFT
A MIRROR REVERSES RIGHT & LEFT. WHAT IF IT REVERSED EVERYTHING REFLECTED IN IT?
RIGHT
I SUPPOSE I'D SEE AN INVERTED NEGATIVE OF MYSELF. BUT WHAT IF A MIRROR SHOWED THE OPPOSITE OF EVERYTHING REFLECTED IN IT?
HMMM... LEMME SEE... • YOUNG WOULD BE OLD, • BOY WOULD BE GIRL, • BALD WOULD BE...
COGITATION
NORTH
MY MIRROR IMAGE WOULD BE AN INVERTED NEGATIVE OF A HAIRY OLD WOMAN STANDING ON HER HEAD SEEN FROM BEHIND!
NORTH
BUT WAIT! WHAT WOULD BUNNY BE?
FOR THE MOMENT, LEVI'S STUMPED...
WHAT'S THE OPPOSITE OF BUNNY?
ANSWERS

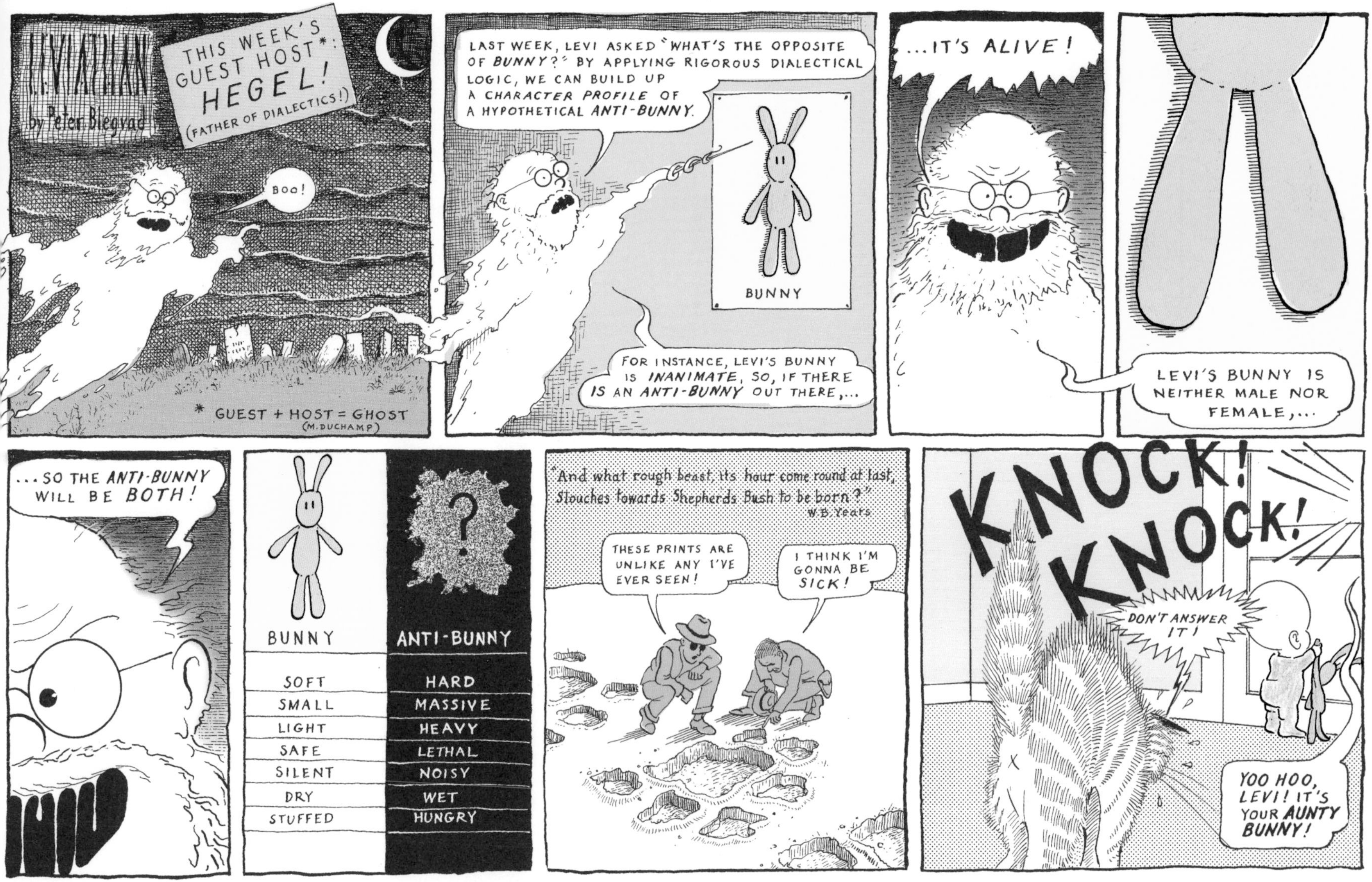
LEVIATHAN
by Peter Blegvad
THIS WEEK'S GUEST HOST*: HEGEL! (FATHER OF DIALECTICS!)
BOO!
* GUEST + HOST = GHOST (M. DUCHAMP)
LAST WEEK, LEVI ASKED "WHAT'S THE OPPOSITE OF BUNNY?" BY APPLYING RIGOROUS DIALECTICAL LOGIC, WE CAN BUILD UP A CHARACTER PROFILE OF A HYPOTHETICAL ANTI-BUNNY.
BUNNY
FOR INSTANCE, LEVI'S BUNNY IS INANIMATE, SO, IF THERE IS AN ANTI-BUNNY OUT THERE,...
...IT'S ALIVE!
LEVI'S BUNNY IS NEITHER MALE NOR FEMALE,...
...SO THE ANTI-BUNNY WILL BE BOTH!
BUNNY
ANTI-BUNNY
?
SOFT
HARD
SMALL
MASSIVE
LIGHT
HEAVY
SAFE
LETHAL
SILENT
NOISY
DRY
WET
STUFFED
HUNGRY
"And what rough beast, its hour come round at last, Slouches towards Shepherds Bush to be born?" W.B. Yeats
THESE PRINTS ARE UNLIKE ANY I'VE EVER SEEN!
I THINK I'M GONNA BE SICK!
KNOCK! KNOCK!
DON'T ANSWER IT!
?
YOO HOO, LEVI! IT'S YOUR AUNTY BUNNY!

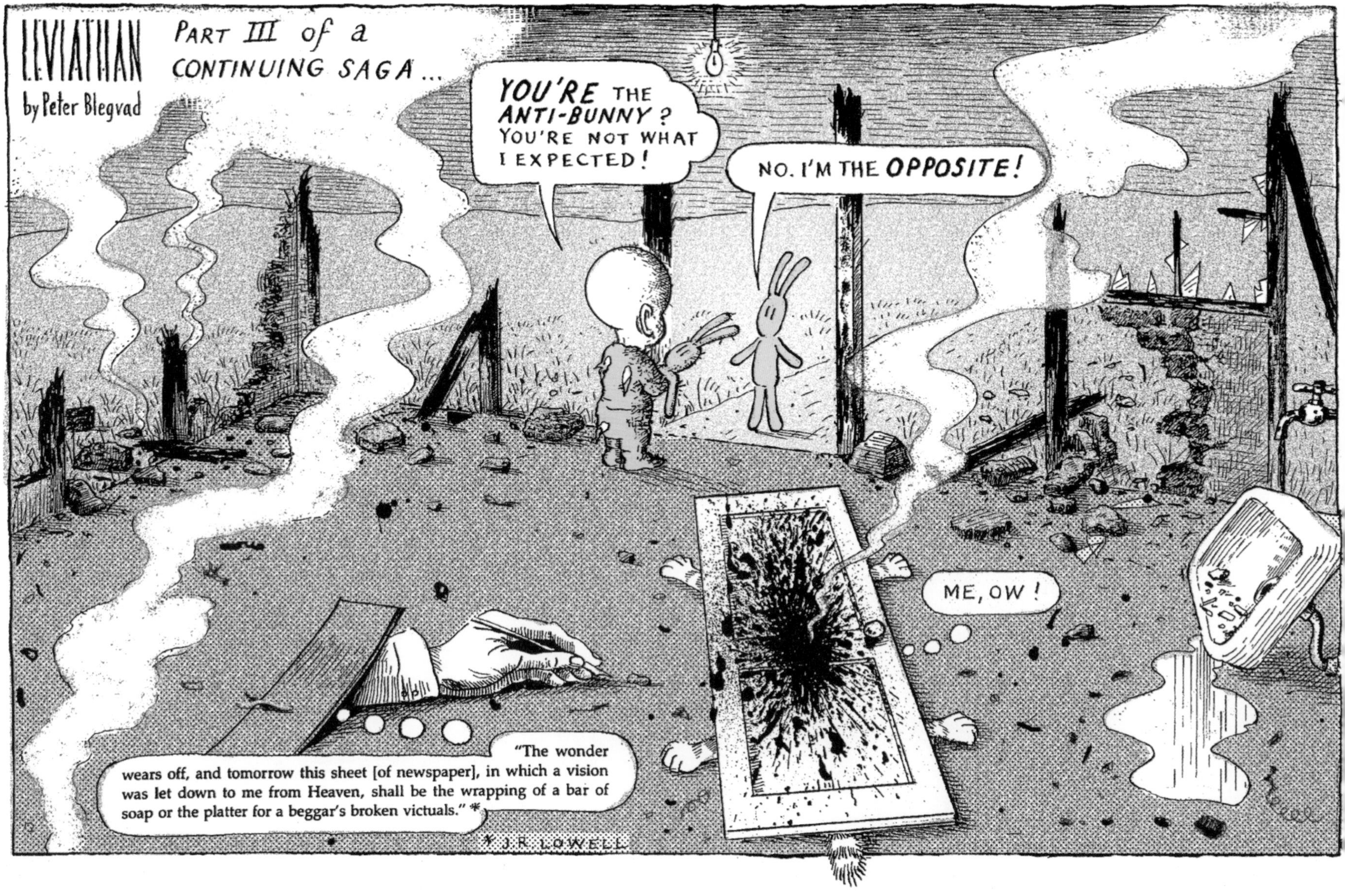
LEVIATHAN
by Peter Blegvad
PART III of a CONTINUING SAGA...
YOU'RE THE ANTI-BUNNY? YOU'RE NOT WHAT I EXPECTED!
NO. I'M THE OPPOSITE!
ME, OW!
"The wonder wears off, and tomorrow this sheet [of newspaper], in which a vision was let down to me from Heaven, shall be the wrapping of a bar of soap or the platter for a beggar's broken victuals." *
* J.R. LOWELL

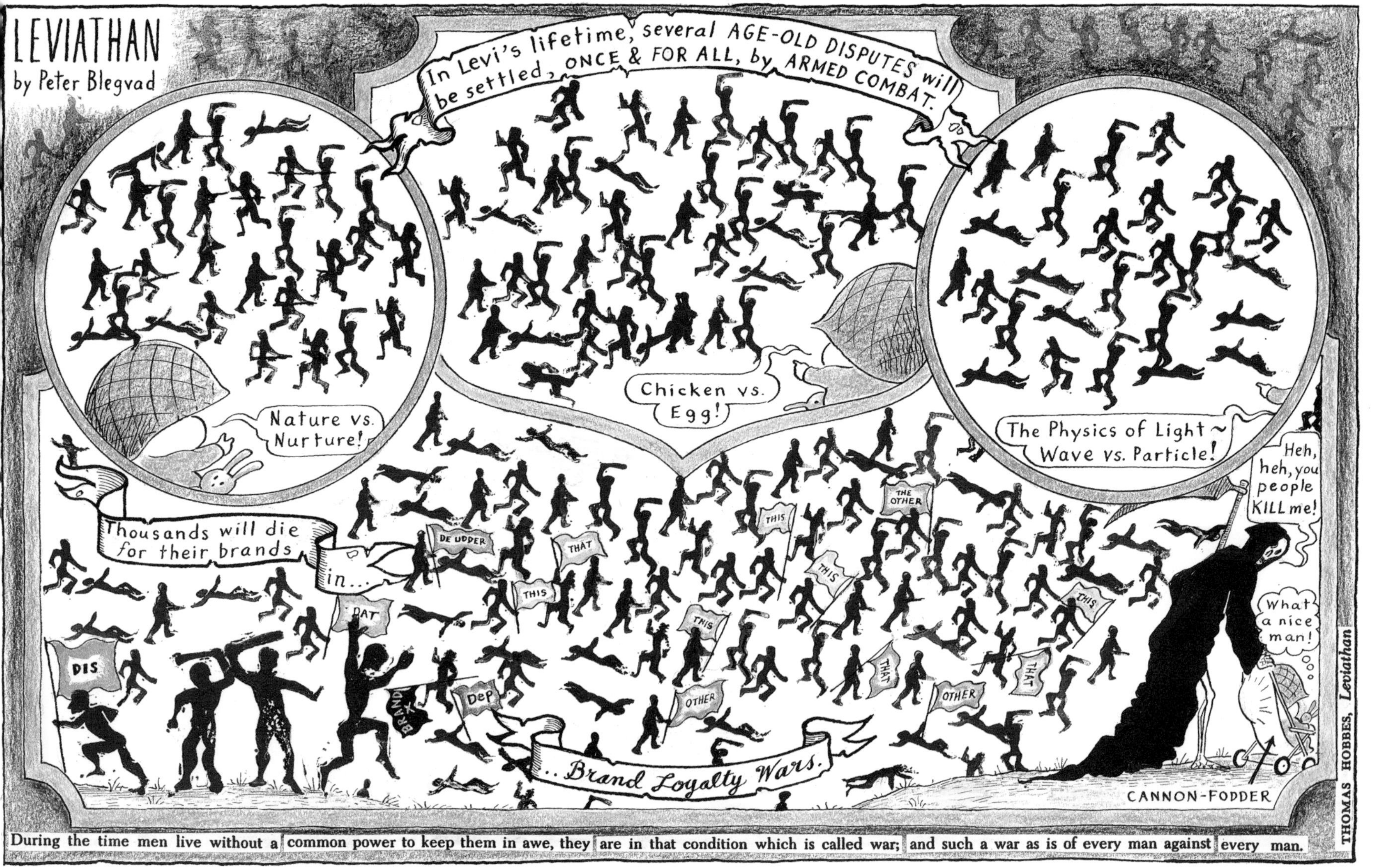
LEVIATHAN
by Peter Blegvad
In Levi's lifetime, several AGE-OLD DISPUTES will be settled, ONCE & FOR ALL, by ARMED COMBAT.
Nature vs. Nurture!
Chicken vs. Egg!
The Physics of Light ~ Wave vs. Particle!
Thousands will die for their brands
in...
...Brand Loyalty Wars.
DE UDDER
THAT
THIS
THE OTHER
THIS
THIS
THIS
DAT
THIS
DIS
BRAND X
Dep
OTHER
THAT
OTHER
THAT
Heh, heh, you people KILL me!
What a nice man!
CANNON-FODDER
During the time men live without a common power to keep them in awe, they are in that condition which is called war; and such a war as is of every man against every man.
THOMAS HOBBES, Leviathan

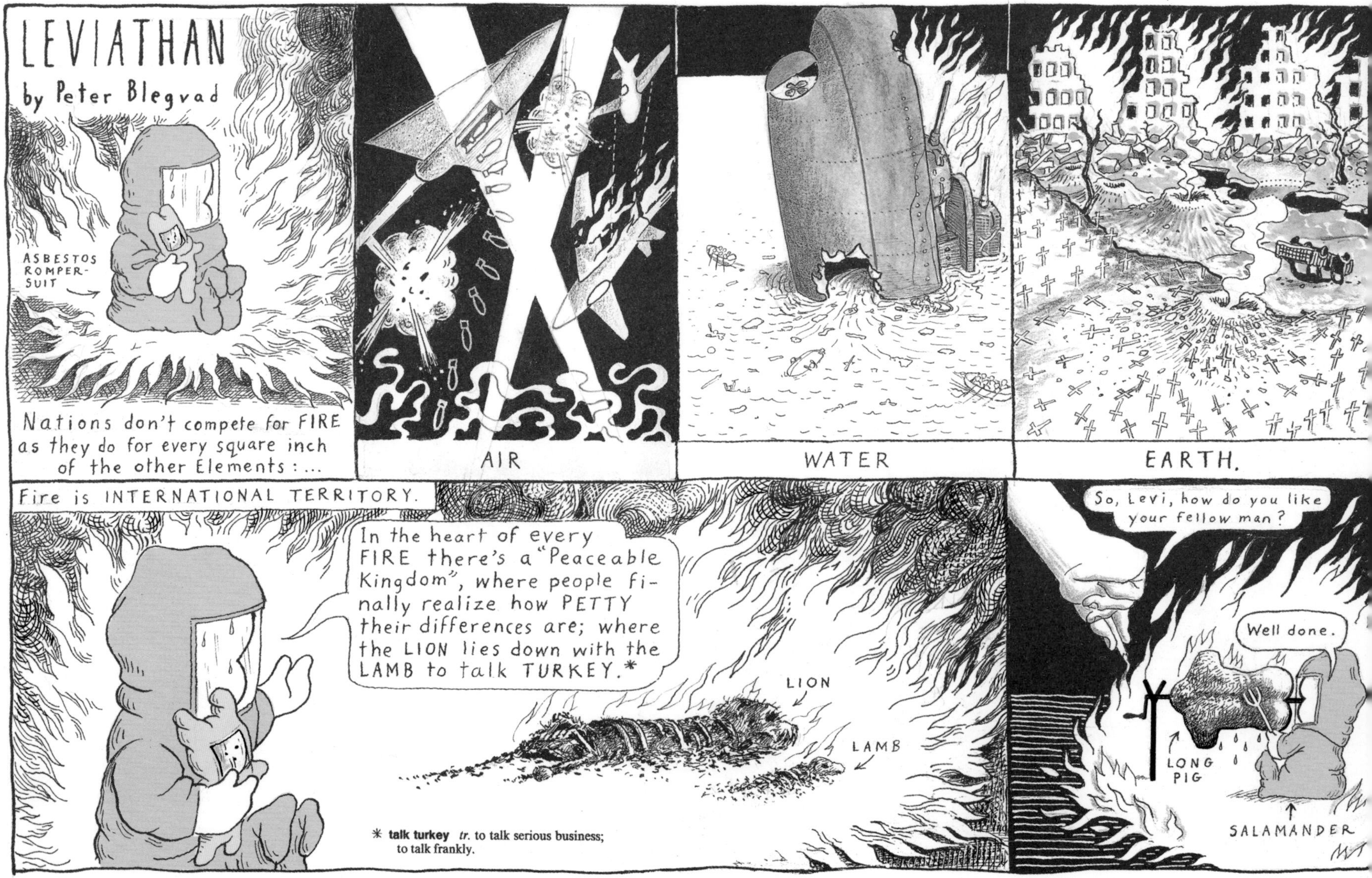
LEVIATHAN
by Peter Blegvad
ASBESTOS ROMPER-SUIT
Nations don't compete for FIRE as they do for every square inch of the other Elements: ...
AIR
WATER
EARTH.
Fire is INTERNATIONAL TERRITORY.
In the heart of every FIRE there's a "Peaceable Kingdom", where people finally realize how PETTY their differences are; where the LION lies down with the LAMB to talk TURKEY.*
LION
LAMB
* talk turkey tr. to talk serious business; to talk frankly.
So, Levi, how do you like your fellow man?
Well done.
LONG PIG
SALAMANDER

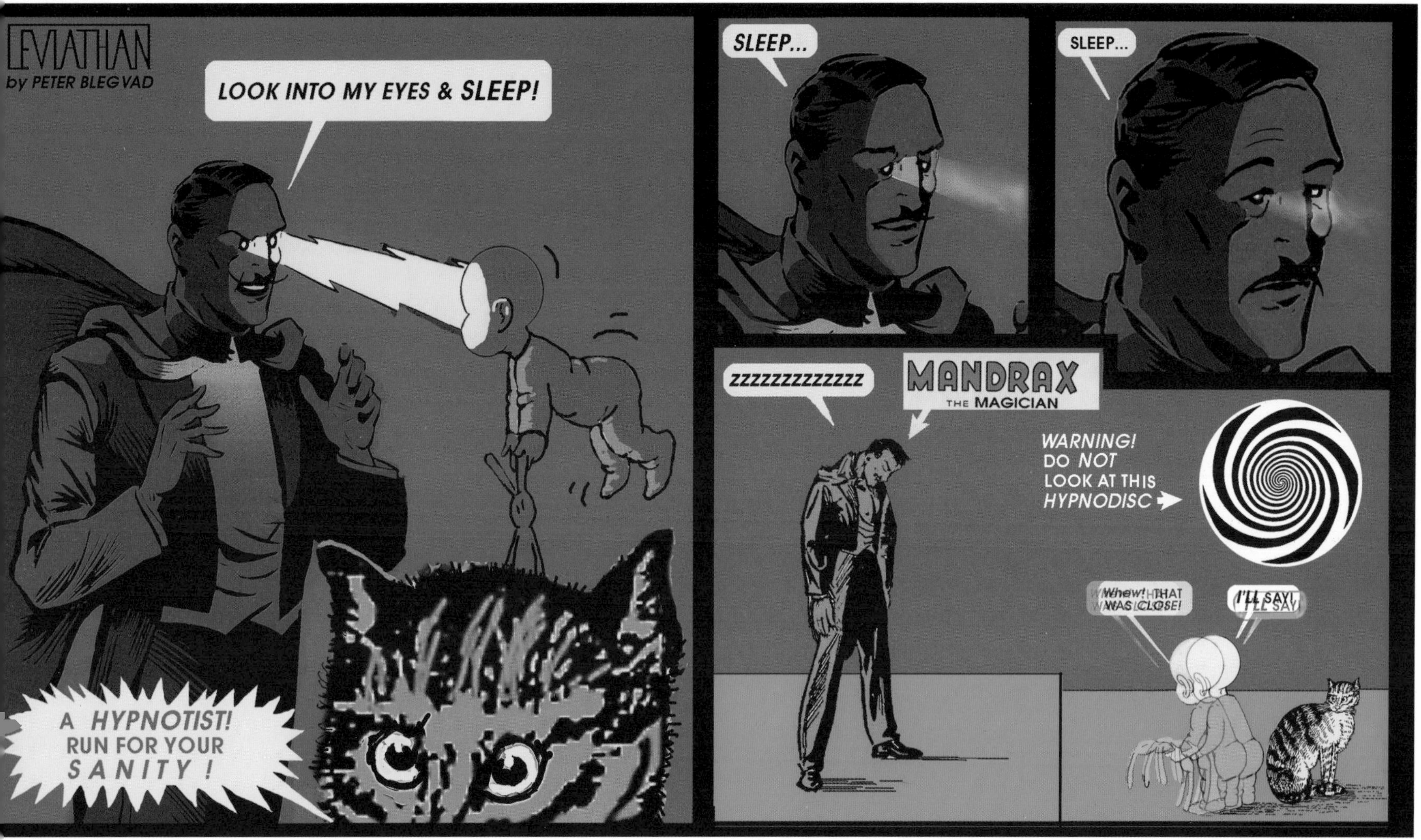

LEVIATHAN
by PETER BLEGVAD
LOOK INTO MY EYES & SLEEP!
A HYPNOTIST! RUN FOR YOUR SANITY!
SLEEP...
SLEEP...
ZZZZZZZZZZZZZ
MANDRAX THE MAGICIAN
WARNING! DO NOT LOOK AT THIS HYPNODISC
Whew! THAT WAS CLOSE!
I'LL SAY!

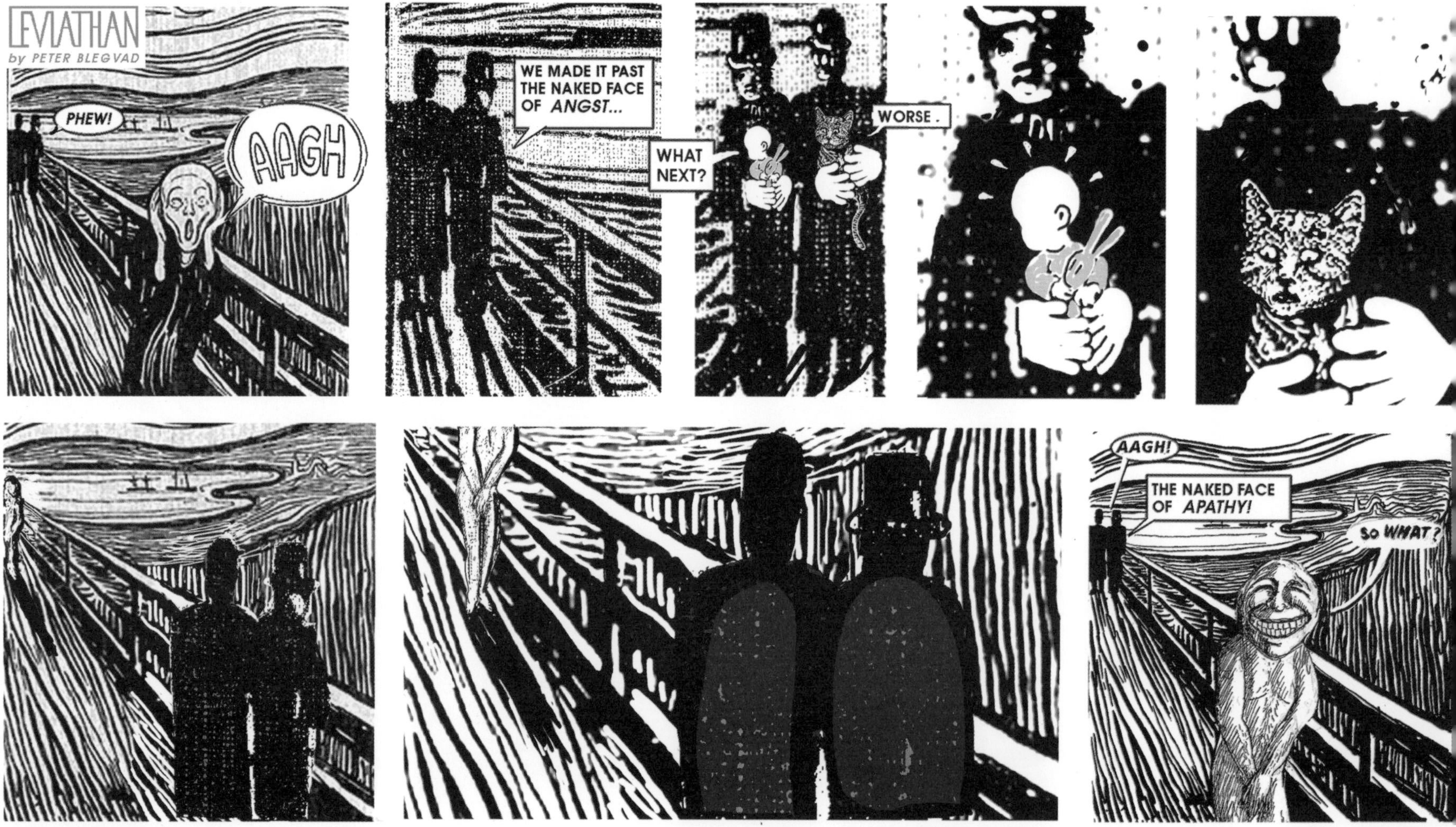
LEVIATHAN
by PETER BLEGVAD
PHEW!
AAGH
WE MADE IT PAST THE NAKED FACE OF ANGST...
WHAT NEXT?
WORSE.
AAGH!
THE NAKED FACE OF APATHY!
So WHAT?

# VIII. WORDS ENOUGH & TIME

Z
A

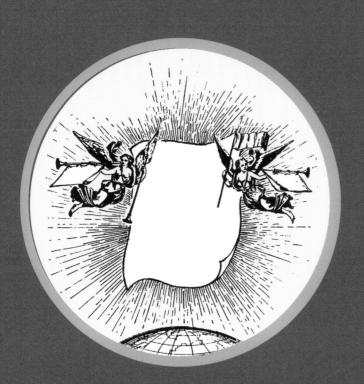

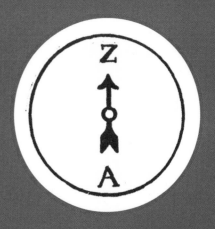

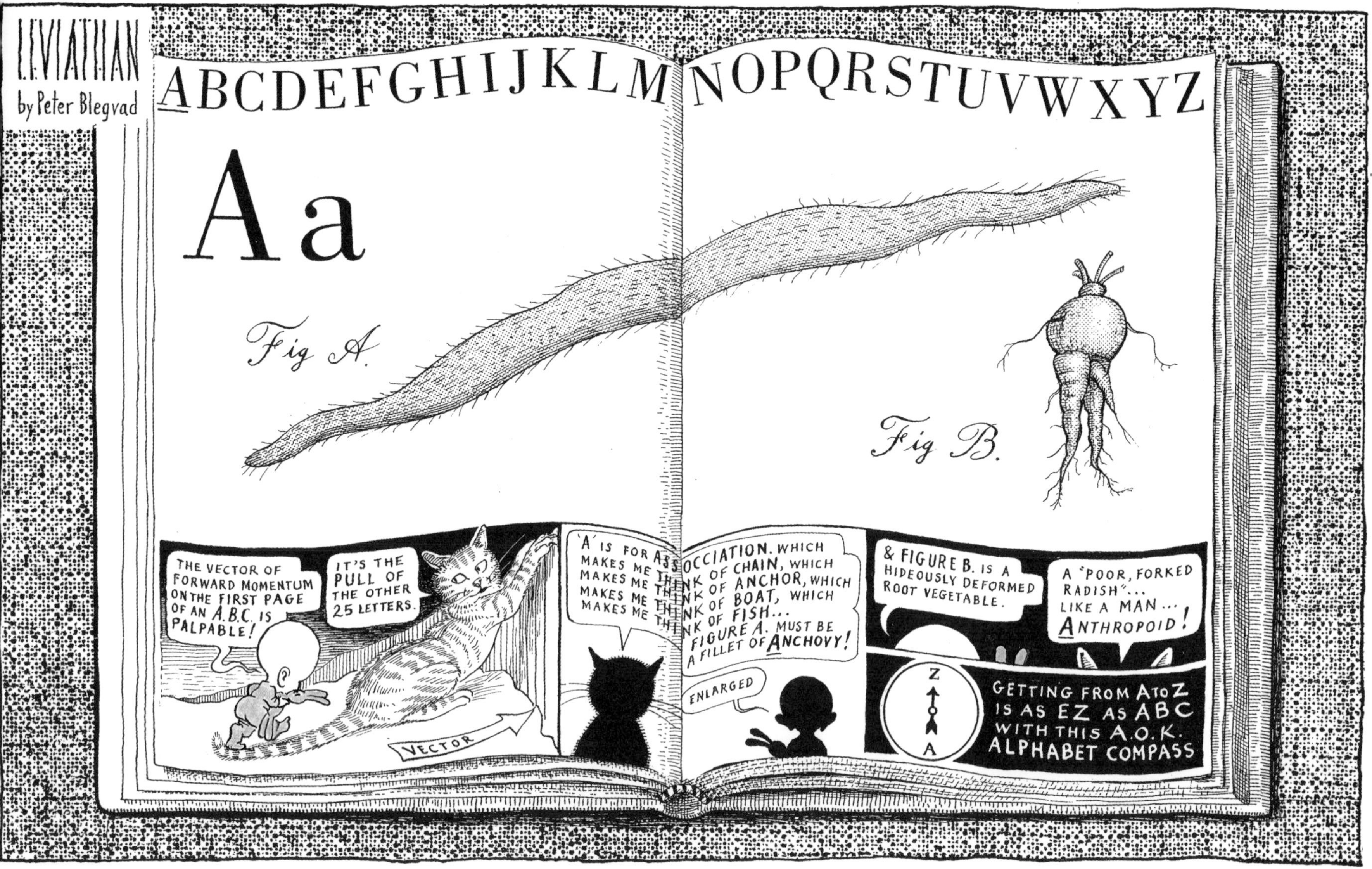

LEVIATHAN
by Peter Blegvad
ABCDEFGHIJKLM NOPQRSTUVWXYZ
Aa
Fig A.
Fig B.
THE VECTOR OF FORWARD MOMENTUM ON THE FIRST PAGE OF AN A.B.C. IS PALPABLE!
IT'S THE PULL OF THE OTHER 25 LETTERS.
VECTOR
'A' IS FOR ASSOCIATION. WHICH MAKES ME THINK OF CHAIN, WHICH MAKES ME THINK OF ANCHOR, WHICH MAKES ME THINK OF BOAT, WHICH MAKES ME THINK OF FISH... FIGURE A. MUST BE A FILLET OF ANCHOVY!
ENLARGED
& FIGURE B. IS A HIDEOUSLY DEFORMED ROOT VEGETABLE.
A "POOR, FORKED RADISH"... LIKE A MAN... ANTHROPOID!
Z
A
GETTING FROM A to Z IS AS EZ AS ABC WITH THIS A.O.K. ALPHABET COMPASS

**LEVIATHAN** by Peter Blegvad

AUTHOR, JAMES KELMAN, WON THE 1994 BOOKER PRIZE FOR HIS NOVEL, "HOW LATE IT WAS, HOW LATE." IN HIS ACCEPTANCE SPEECH HE SAID:

"IF WE WANT THE BLANK PAGE TO STAY BLANK," THEN LET IT STAY BLANK." BRAVO! HIS WORDS INSPIRE ME TO PROPOSE A *PRIZE* FOR THE BEST *BLANK PAGE* IN LITERATURE...

THE PRIZE - A BLANK CHEQUE

STILL WITH ME? THEN *LET'S MEET THE CONTESTANTS!*

The Life and Opinions — CHAPTER XVIII

Of Tristram Shandy — CHAPTER XIX

1. THE *SMART MONEY'S* ON THE TWO *BLANK* "CHAPTERS" IN LAURENCE STERNE'S "*TRISTRAM SHANDY*". STERNE SAYS: "I LOOK UPON A CHAPTER WHICH HAS *ONLY NOTHING IN IT* WITH RESPECT; AND CONSIDERING WHAT WORSE THINGS ARE IN THE WORLD..." HE ALSO WISHES THAT "... IT MAY BE A LESSON TO THE WORLD, '*TO LET PEOPLE TELL THEIR STORIES THEIR OWN WAY*.'"

2. "RIDICULOUS!" SCOFFS *ORPHÉE* IN JEAN COCTEAU'S FILM, WHEN SHOWN A COPY OF *NUDISME*, A LITERARY MAGAZINE COMPRISED ENTIRELY OF *BLANK PAGES*...

NUDISME

"IT WOULD BE MORE RIDICULOUS IF IT CONTAINED RIDICULOUS TEXTS." REPLIES HIS COMPANION.

3. PAINTING OF BROTHER BARNABUS "WALKING THROUGH A SNOWSTORM FROM BADEN-BADEN TO CARLSBAD, CLAD IN WHITE PYJAMAS, FOLLOWED BY A FLOCK OF WHITE PONIES. OVERHEAD, AS IF LEADING THE WAY, IS A MYSTIC WHITE GUILLEMOT." FLANN O'BRIEN, *Comhthrom Féinne* III, 1.

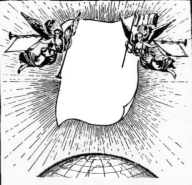

4. NO ONE HAS WRITTEN *ABOUT* THE BLANK PAGE WITH MORE PASSIONATE DEVOTION THAN STÉPHANE MALLARMÉ. ACCORDING TO CHARLES MAURON: "WHITENESS, SILENCE, EMPTINESS... OF THE 'VIRGIN PAPER'... ARE TRANSFORMED TO THE HIGHEST IDEAL."

EVERYTHING COLONEL PARKER TAUGHT ME — by ELVIS A. PRESLEY

5. *BLANK BOOK* ELVIS HAD MADE UP TO AMUSE FRIENDS. RECENTLY AUCTIONED BY SOTHEBY'S.

(LEVI & CAT ARE IN HELL)

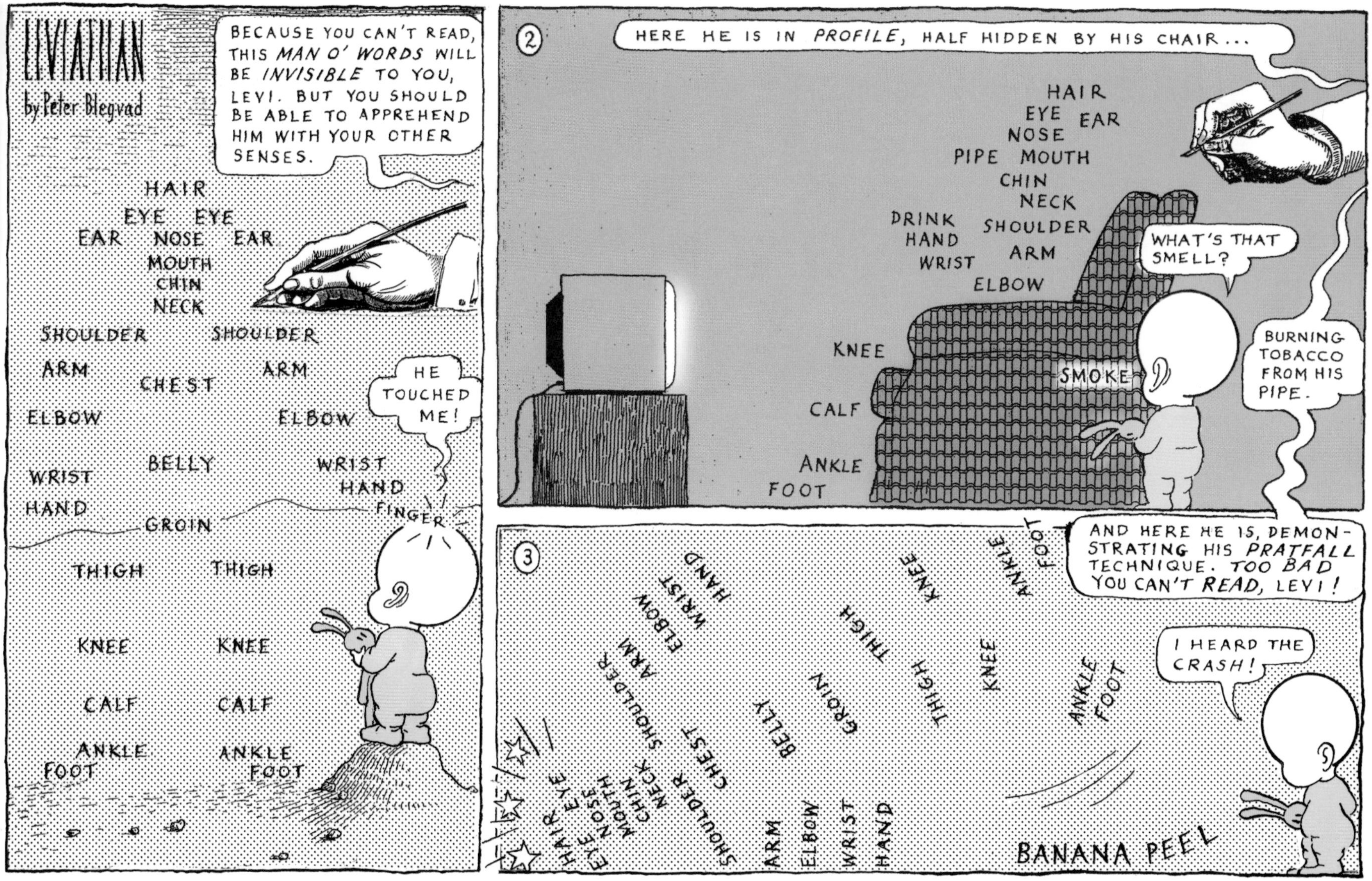
LEVIATHAN
by Peter Blegvad
BECAUSE YOU CAN'T READ, THIS MAN O' WORDS WILL BE INVISIBLE TO YOU, LEVI. BUT YOU SHOULD BE ABLE TO APPREHEND HIM WITH YOUR OTHER SENSES.
HAIR
EYE EYE
EAR NOSE EAR
MOUTH
CHIN
NECK
SHOULDER SHOULDER
ARM CHEST ARM
ELBOW ELBOW
BELLY
WRIST WRIST
HAND HAND
FINGER
GROIN
THIGH THIGH
KNEE KNEE
CALF CALF
ANKLE ANKLE
FOOT FOOT
HE TOUCHED ME!
2
HERE HE IS IN PROFILE, HALF HIDDEN BY HIS CHAIR...
HAIR
EYE EAR
NOSE
PIPE MOUTH
CHIN
NECK
DRINK
HAND
WRIST
SHOULDER
ARM
ELBOW
KNEE
CALF
ANKLE
FOOT
SMOKE
WHAT'S THAT SMELL?
BURNING TOBACCO FROM HIS PIPE.
3
AND HERE HE IS, DEMONSTRATING HIS PRATFALL TECHNIQUE. TOO BAD YOU CAN'T READ, LEVI!
HAIR EYE EYE NOSE MOUTH CHIN NECK SHOULDER CHEST SHOULDER ARM ELBOW WRIST HAND
BELLY GROIN
ARM ELBOW WRIST HAND
THIGH KNEE ANKLE FOOT
THIGH KNEE ANKLE FOOT
BANANA PEEL
I HEARD THE CRASH!

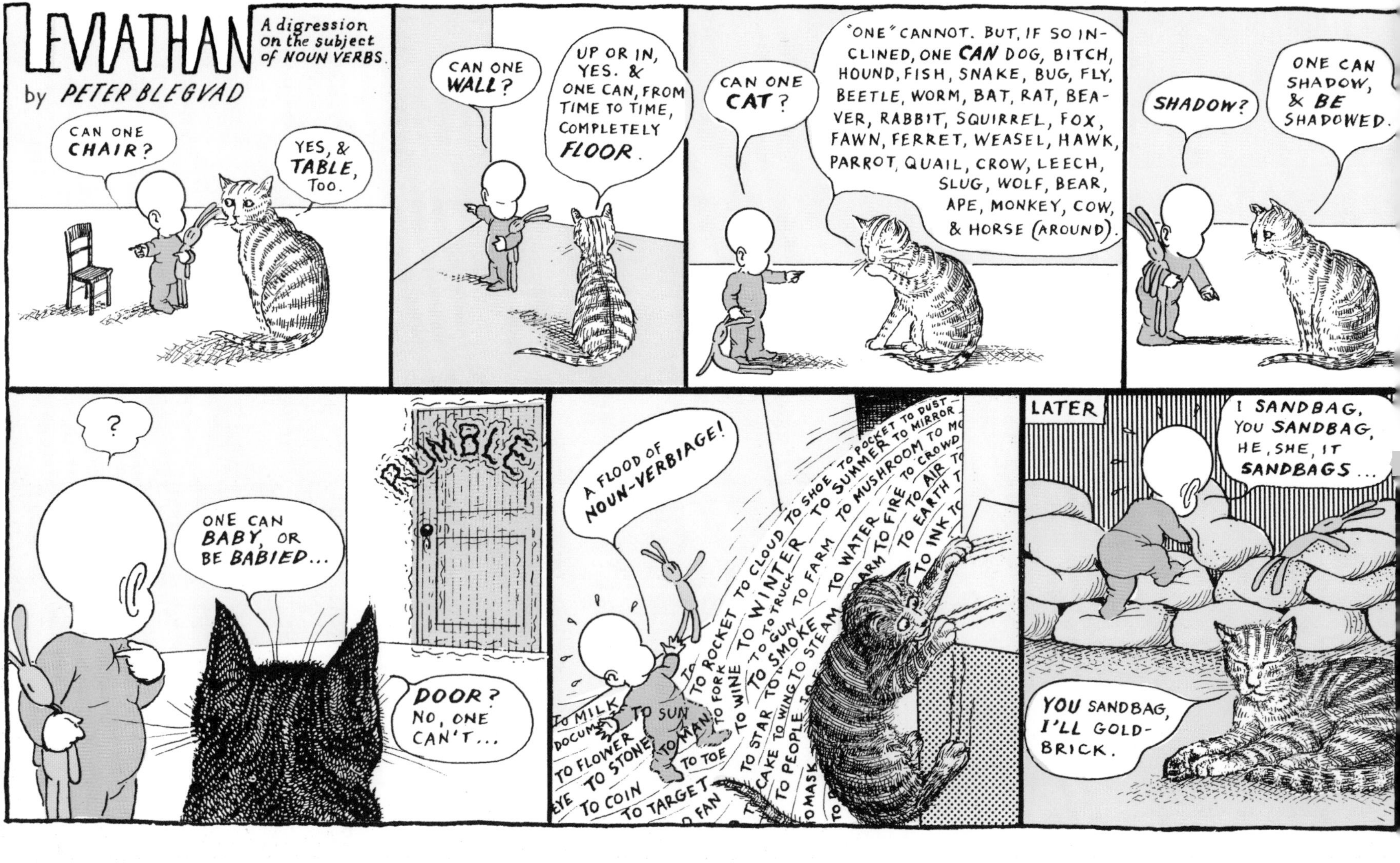

LEVIATHAN
A digression on the subject of NOUN VERBS.
by PETER BLEGVAD
CAN ONE CHAIR?
YES, & TABLE, TOO.
CAN ONE WALL?
UP OR IN, YES. & ONE CAN, FROM TIME TO TIME, COMPLETELY FLOOR.
CAN ONE CAT?
"ONE" CANNOT. BUT, IF SO INCLINED, ONE CAN DOG, BITCH, HOUND, FISH, SNAKE, BUG, FLY, BEETLE, WORM, BAT, RAT, BEAVER, RABBIT, SQUIRREL, FOX, FAWN, FERRET, WEASEL, HAWK, PARROT, QUAIL, CROW, LEECH, SLUG, WOLF, BEAR, APE, MONKEY, COW, & HORSE (AROUND).
SHADOW?
ONE CAN SHADOW, & BE SHADOWED.
?
ONE CAN BABY, OR BE BABIED...
RUMBLE
DOOR? NO, ONE CAN'T...
A FLOOD OF NOUN-VERBIAGE!
TO MILK TO SUN TO FLOWER TO STONE TO MAN TO TOE TO COIN TO TARGET TO FORK TO ROCKET TO CLOUD TO SHOE TO POCKET TO DUST TO WINE TO WINTER TO TRUCK TO GUN TO SMOKE TO STAR TO CAKE TO WING TO STEAM TO PEOPLE TO MASK TO SUMMER TO MIRROR TO FARM TO MUSHROOM TO CROWD TO WATER TO FIRE TO AIR TO EARTH TO INK
LATER
I SANDBAG, YOU SANDBAG, HE, SHE, IT SANDBAGS...
YOU SANDBAG, I'LL GOLD-BRICK.

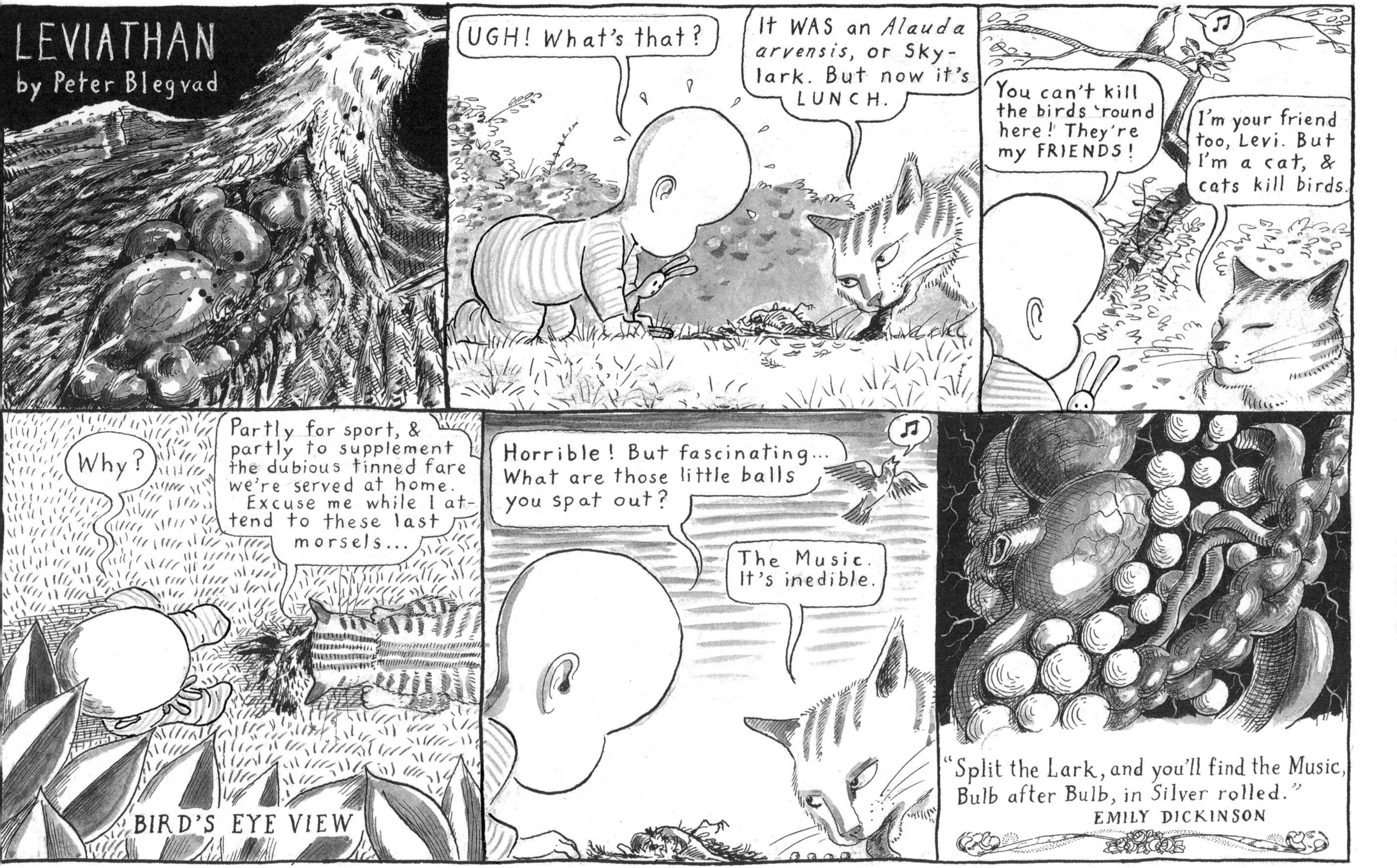
LEVIATHAN
by Peter Blegvad
UGH! What's that?
It WAS an *Alauda arvensis*, or Sky-lark. But now it's LUNCH.
You can't kill the birds 'round here! They're my FRIENDS!
I'm your friend too, Levi. But I'm a cat, & cats kill birds.
Why?
Partly for sport, & partly to supplement the dubious tinned fare we're served at home. Excuse me while I attend to these last morsels...
BIRD'S EYE VIEW
Horrible! But fascinating... What are those little balls you spat out?
The Music. It's inedible.
"Split the Lark, and you'll find the Music, Bulb after Bulb, in Silver rolled."
EMILY DICKINSON

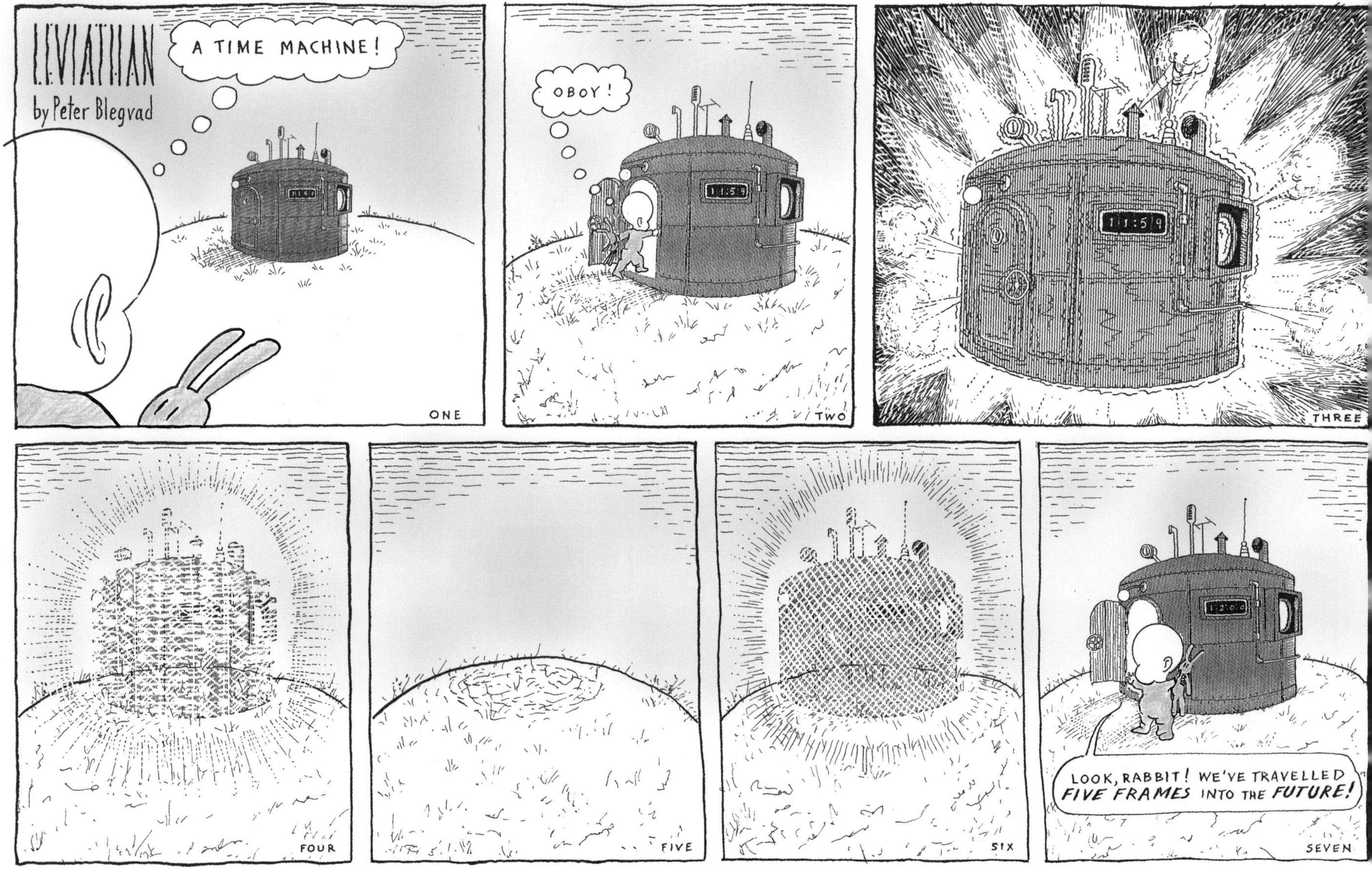
LEVIATHAN
by Peter Blegvad
A TIME MACHINE!
ONE
OBOY!
TWO
THREE
FOUR
FIVE
SIX
LOOK, RABBIT! WE'VE TRAVELLED FIVE FRAMES INTO THE FUTURE!
SEVEN

# IX. WILDS, WOODS, & GAS

GULP!

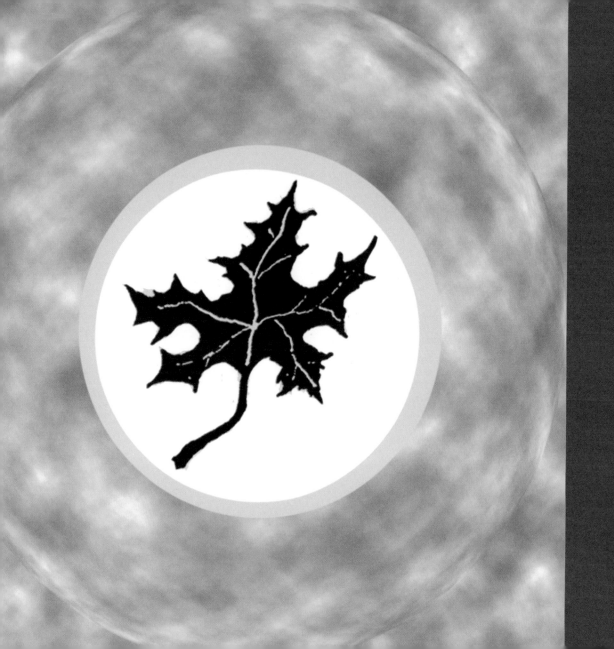

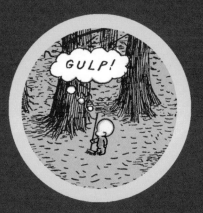

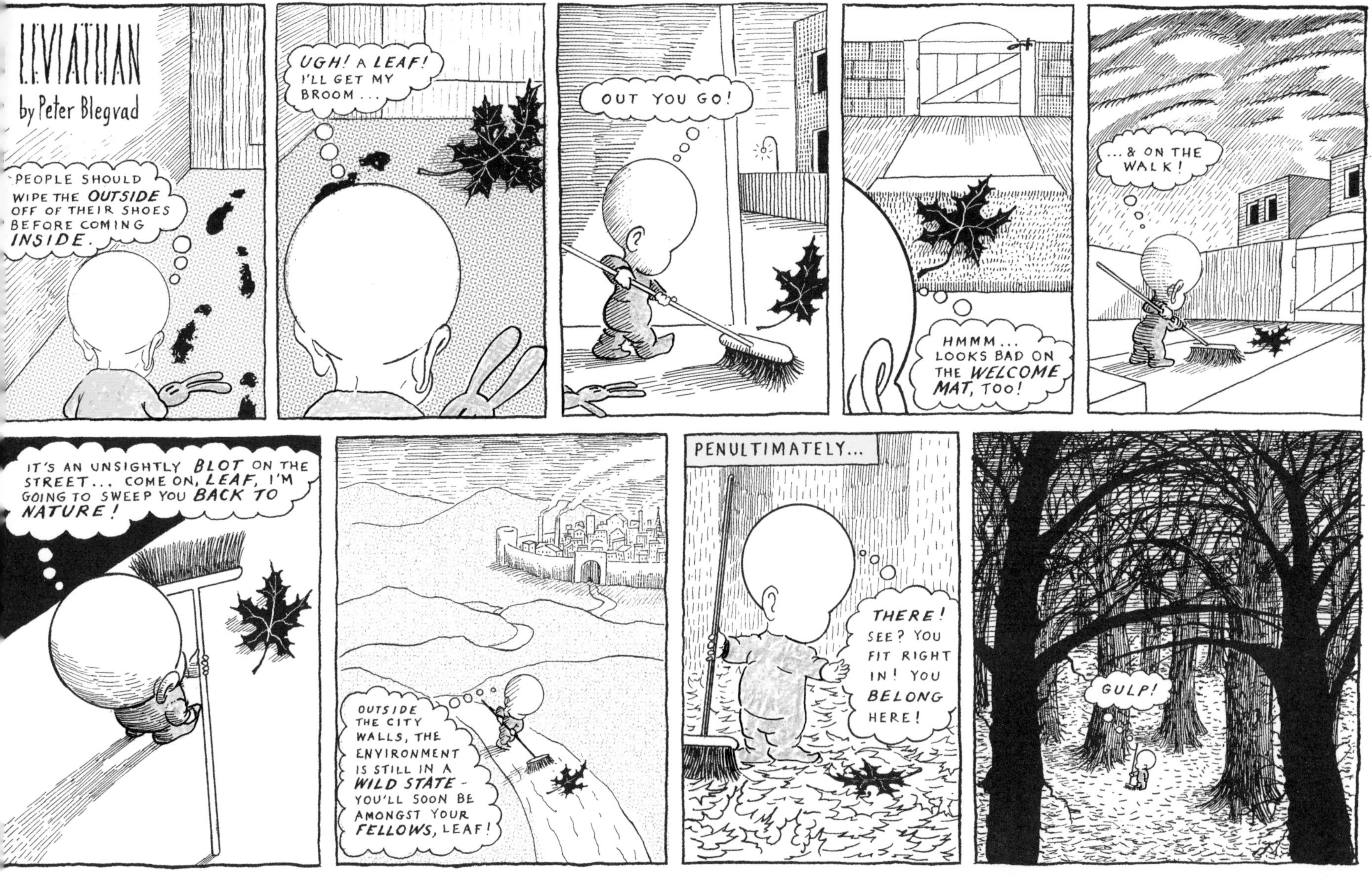
LEVIATHAN
by Peter Blegvad
PEOPLE SHOULD WIPE THE OUTSIDE OFF OF THEIR SHOES BEFORE COMING INSIDE.
UGH! A LEAF! I'LL GET MY BROOM...
OUT YOU GO!
HMMM... LOOKS BAD ON THE WELCOME MAT, TOO!
...& ON THE WALK!
IT'S AN UNSIGHTLY BLOT ON THE STREET... COME ON, LEAF, I'M GOING TO SWEEP YOU BACK TO NATURE!
OUTSIDE THE CITY WALLS, THE ENVIRONMENT IS STILL IN A WILD STATE - YOU'LL SOON BE AMONGST YOUR FELLOWS, LEAF!
PENULTIMATELY...
THERE! SEE? YOU FIT RIGHT IN! YOU BELONG HERE!
GULP!

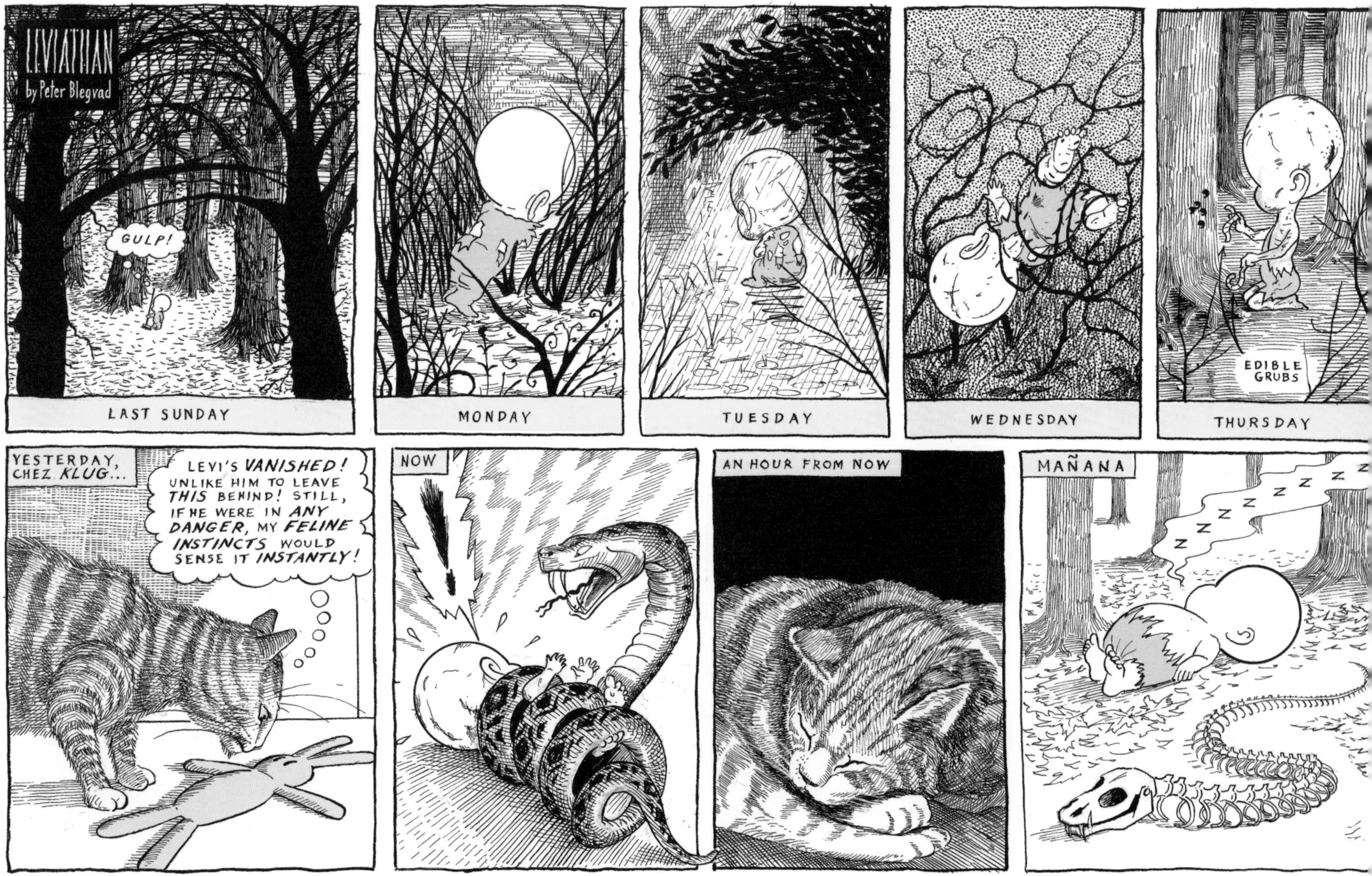
LEVIATHAN
by Peter Blegvad
GULP!
LAST SUNDAY
MONDAY
TUESDAY
WEDNESDAY
EDIBLE GRUBS
THURSDAY
YESTERDAY, CHEZ KLUG...
LEVI'S VANISHED! UNLIKE HIM TO LEAVE THIS BEHIND! STILL, IF HE WERE IN ANY DANGER, MY FELINE INSTINCTS WOULD SENSE IT INSTANTLY!
NOW
AN HOUR FROM NOW
MAÑANA
Z Z Z Z Z Z Z Z Z

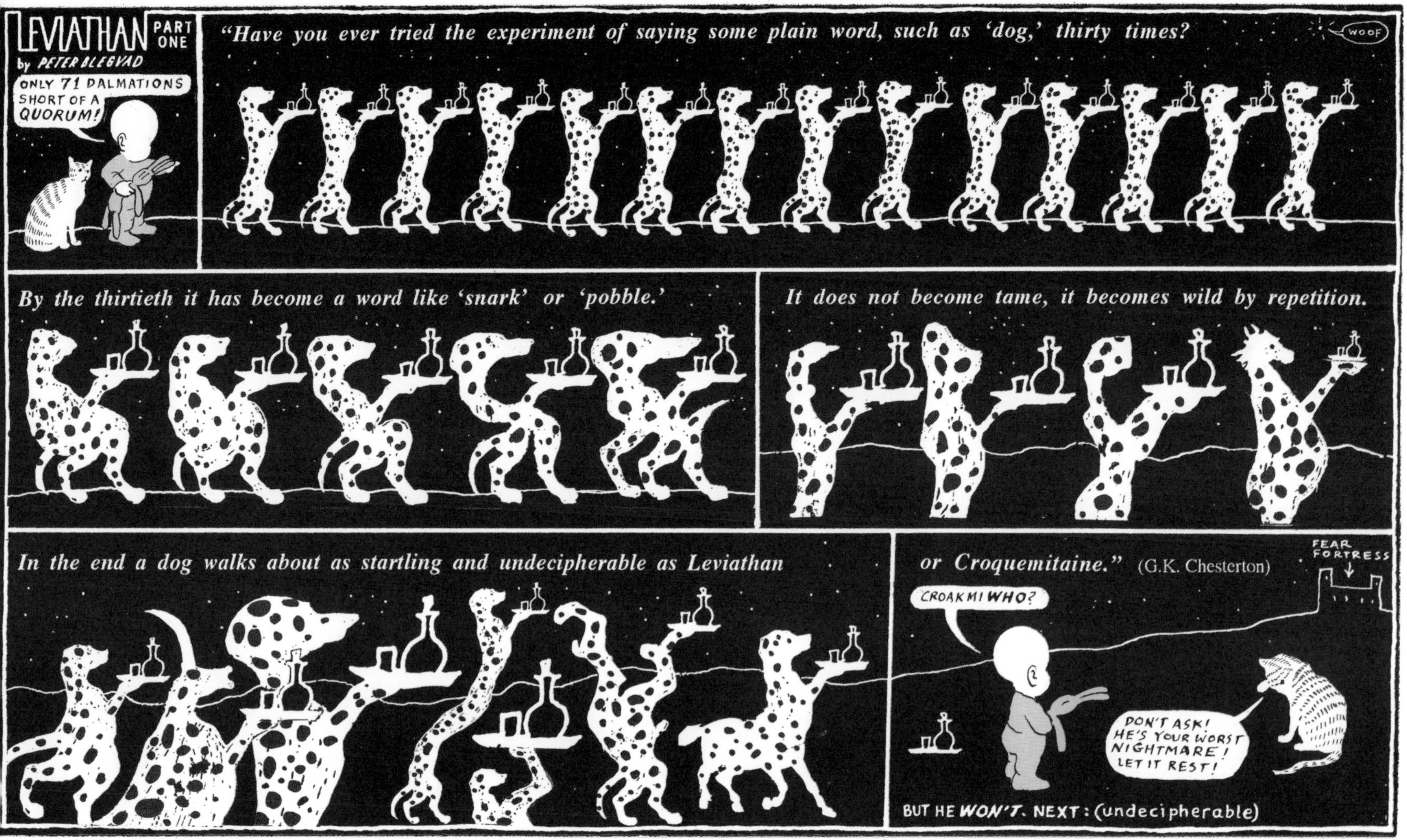
LEVIATHAN PART ONE
by PETER BLEGVAD
ONLY 71 DALMATIONS SHORT OF A QUORUM!
"Have you ever tried the experiment of saying some plain word, such as 'dog,' thirty times?
WOOF
By the thirtieth it has become a word like 'snark' or 'pobble.'
It does not become tame, it becomes wild by repetition.
In the end a dog walks about as startling and undecipherable as Leviathan
or Croquemitaine." (G.K. Chesterton)
FEAR FORTRESS
CROAKMI WHO?
DON'T ASK! HE'S YOUR WORST NIGHTMARE! LET IT REST!
BUT HE WON'T. NEXT: (undecipherable)

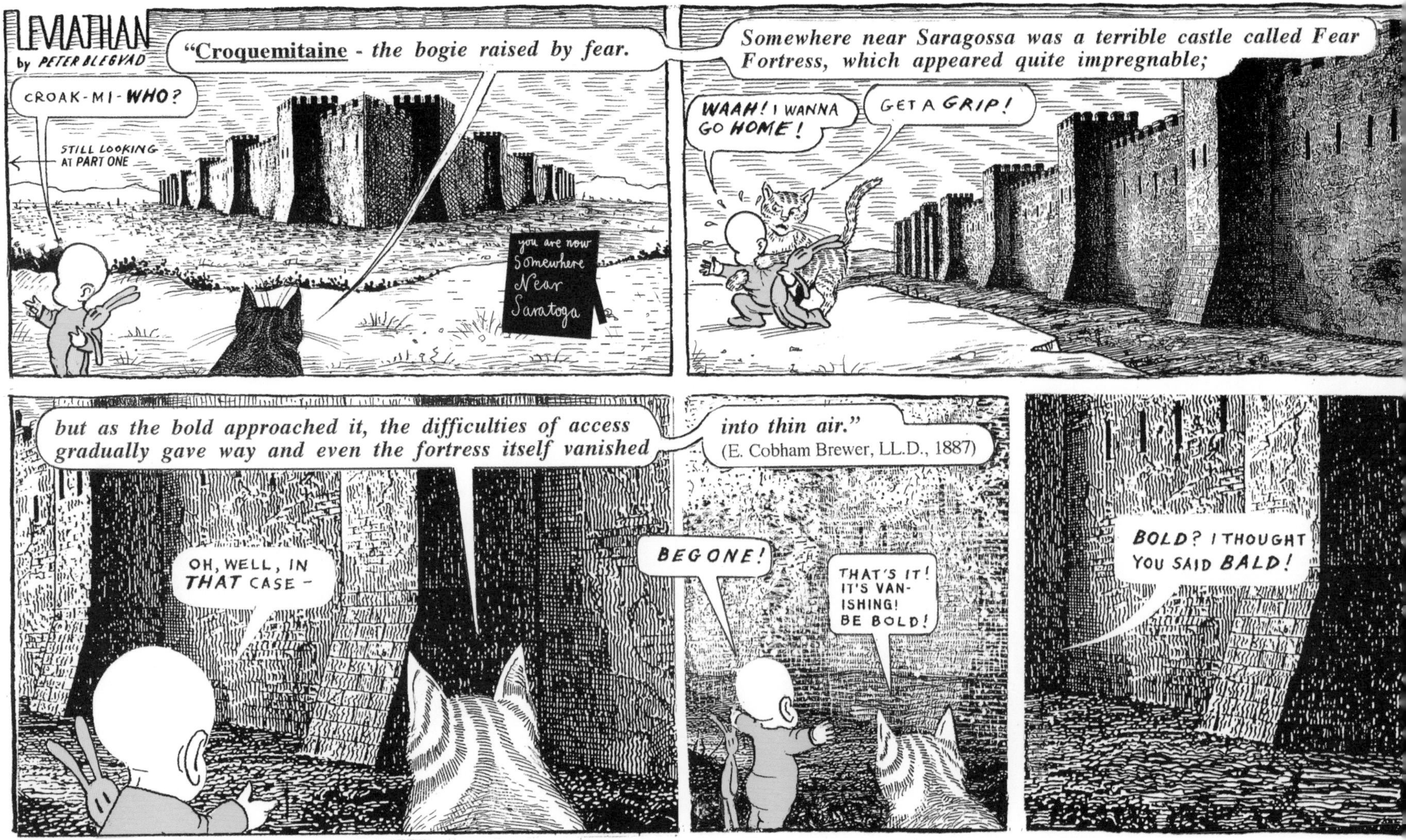
LEVIATHAN
by PETER BLEGVAD
"Croquemitaine - the bogie raised by fear.
CROAK-MI-WHO?
STILL LOOKING AT PART ONE
you are now Somewhere Near Saratoga
Somewhere near Saragossa was a terrible castle called Fear Fortress, which appeared quite impregnable;
WAAH! I WANNA GO HOME!
GET A GRIP!
but as the bold approached it, the difficulties of access gradually gave way and even the fortress itself vanished
OH, WELL, IN THAT CASE -
into thin air."
(E. Cobham Brewer, LL.D., 1887)
BEGONE!
THAT'S IT! IT'S VANISHING! BE BOLD!
BOLD? I THOUGHT YOU SAID BALD!

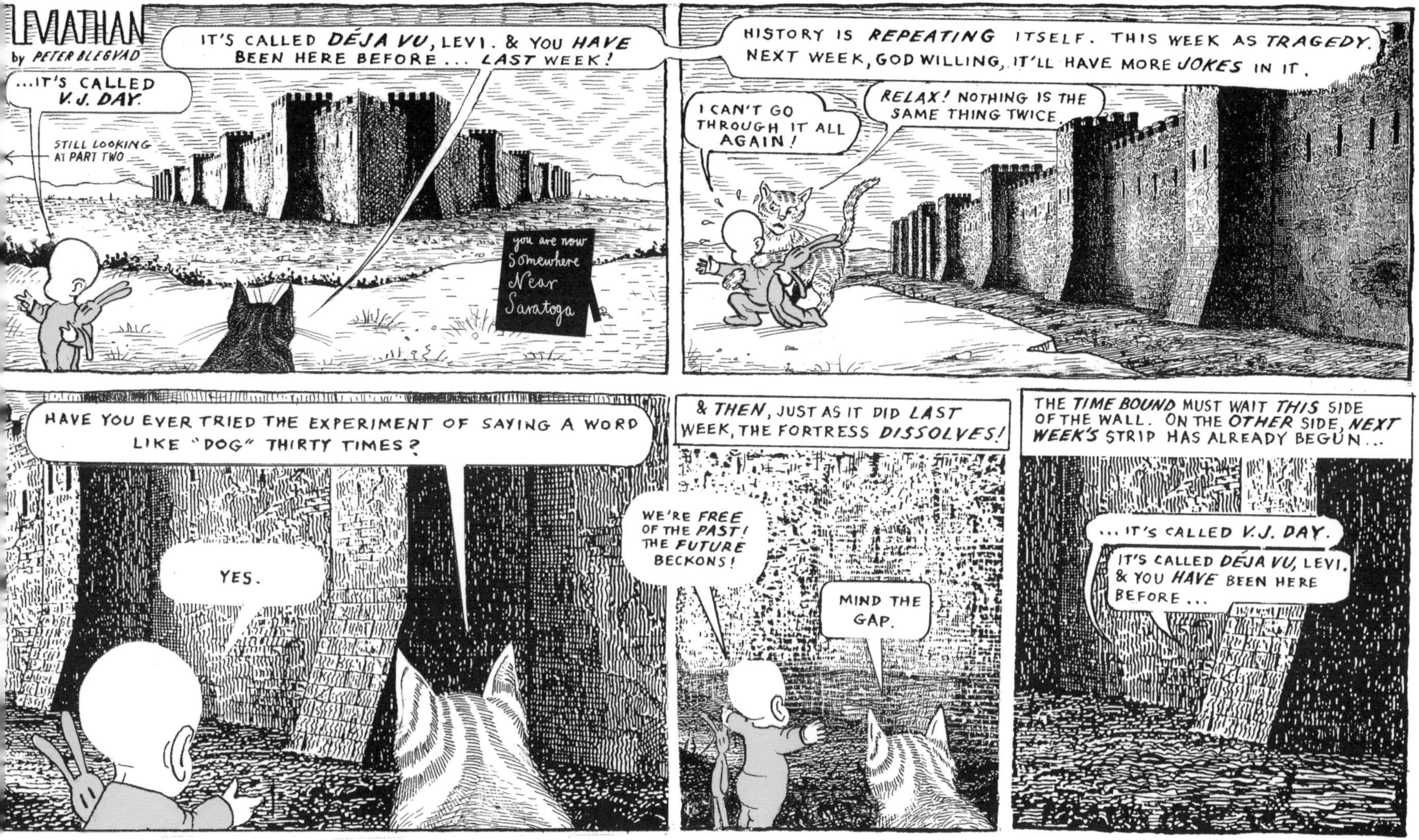
LEVIATHAN
by PETER BLEGVAD
...IT'S CALLED V. J. DAY.
IT'S CALLED DÉJA VU, LEVI. & YOU HAVE BEEN HERE BEFORE... LAST WEEK!
STILL LOOKING AT PART TWO
you are now Somewhere Near Saratoga
HISTORY IS REPEATING ITSELF. THIS WEEK AS TRAGEDY. NEXT WEEK, GOD WILLING, IT'LL HAVE MORE JOKES IN IT.
I CAN'T GO THROUGH IT ALL AGAIN!
RELAX! NOTHING IS THE SAME THING TWICE.
HAVE YOU EVER TRIED THE EXPERIMENT OF SAYING A WORD LIKE "DOG" THIRTY TIMES?
YES.
& THEN, JUST AS IT DID LAST WEEK, THE FORTRESS DISSOLVES!
WE'RE FREE OF THE PAST! THE FUTURE BECKONS!
MIND THE GAP.
THE TIME BOUND MUST WAIT THIS SIDE OF THE WALL. ON THE OTHER SIDE, NEXT WEEK'S STRIP HAS ALREADY BEGUN...
... IT'S CALLED V.J. DAY.
IT'S CALLED DÉJA VU, LEVI. & YOU HAVE BEEN HERE BEFORE...

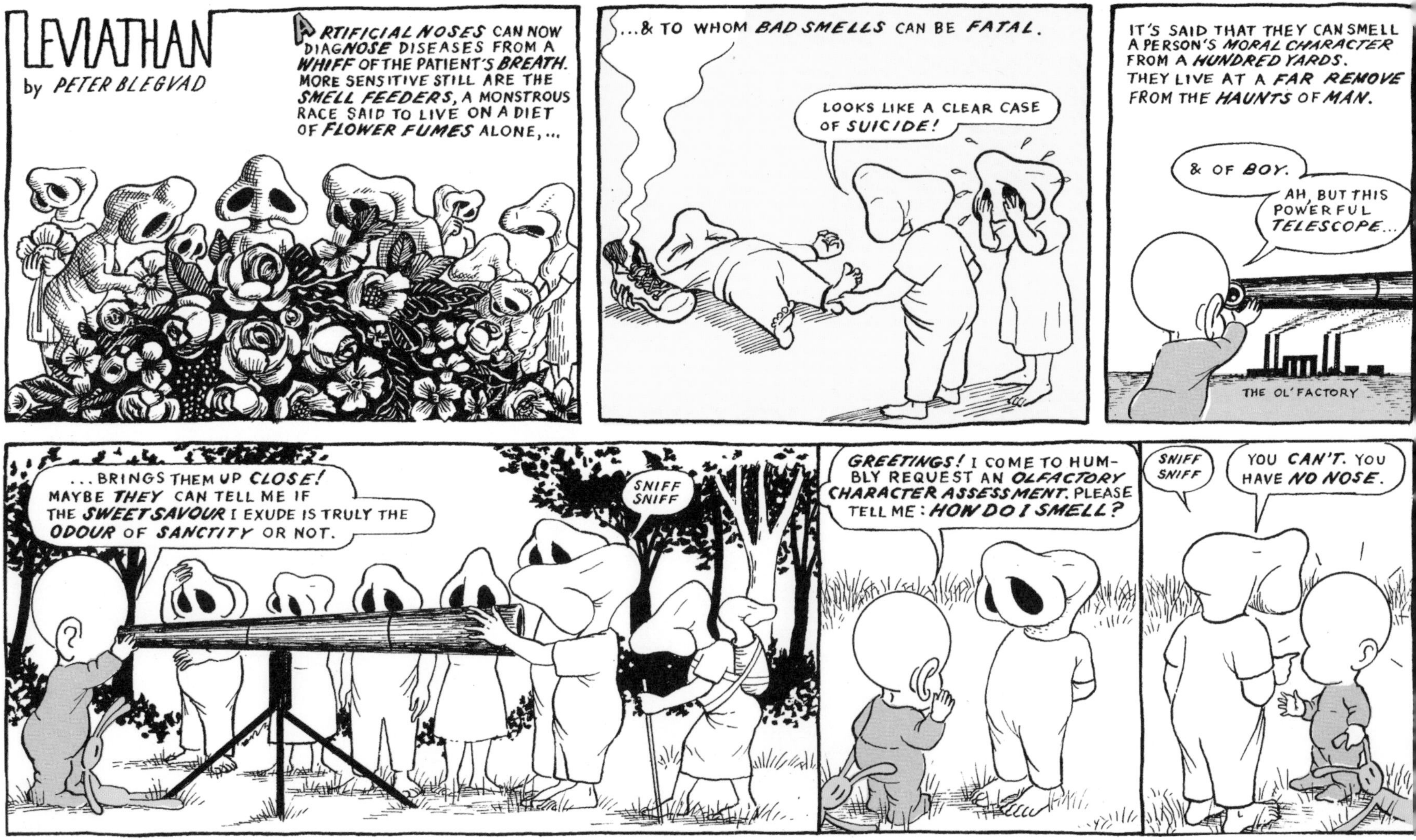
LEVIATHAN
by PETER BLEGVAD
ARTIFICIAL NOSES CAN NOW DIAGNOSE DISEASES FROM A WHIFF OF THE PATIENT'S BREATH. MORE SENSITIVE STILL ARE THE SMELL FEEDERS, A MONSTROUS RACE SAID TO LIVE ON A DIET OF FLOWER FUMES ALONE, ...
...& TO WHOM BAD SMELLS CAN BE FATAL.
LOOKS LIKE A CLEAR CASE OF SUICIDE!
IT'S SAID THAT THEY CAN SMELL A PERSON'S MORAL CHARACTER FROM A HUNDRED YARDS. THEY LIVE AT A FAR REMOVE FROM THE HAUNTS OF MAN.
& OF BOY.
AH, BUT THIS POWERFUL TELESCOPE...
THE OL' FACTORY
...BRINGS THEM UP CLOSE! MAYBE THEY CAN TELL ME IF THE SWEET SAVOUR I EXUDE IS TRULY THE ODOUR OF SANCTITY OR NOT.
SNIFF SNIFF
GREETINGS! I COME TO HUMBLY REQUEST AN OLFACTORY CHARACTER ASSESSMENT. PLEASE TELL ME: HOW DO I SMELL?
SNIFF SNIFF
YOU CAN'T. YOU HAVE NO NOSE.

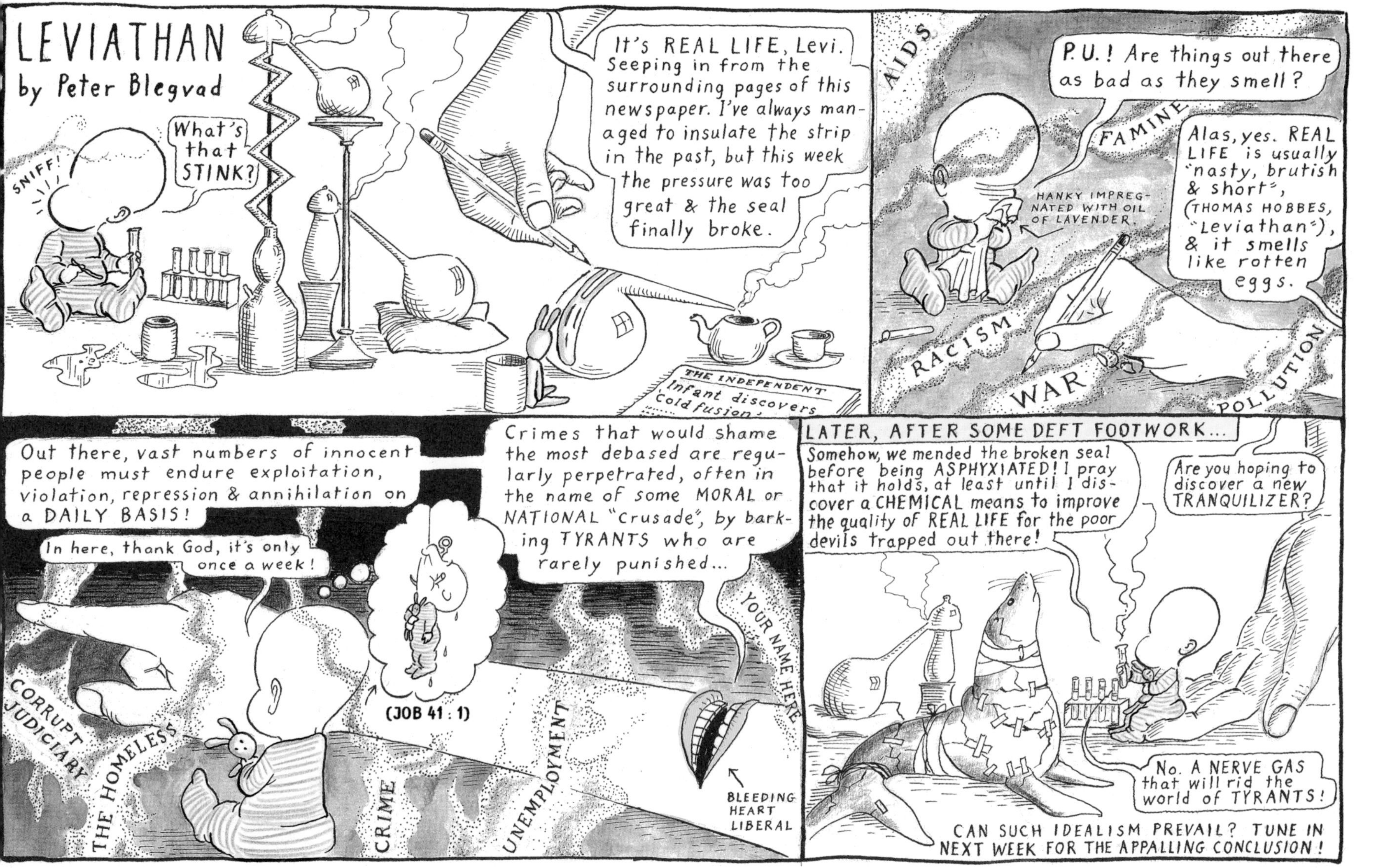
LEVIATHAN
by Peter Blegvad
SNIFF!
What's that STINK?
It's REAL LIFE, Levi. Seeping in from the surrounding pages of this newspaper. I've always managed to insulate the strip in the past, but this week the pressure was too great & the seal finally broke.
THE INDEPENDENT
Infant discovers Cold fusion
AIDS
FAMINE
RACISM
WAR
POLLUTION
P.U.! Are things out there as bad as they smell?
HANKY IMPREGNATED WITH OIL OF LAVENDER.
Alas, yes. REAL LIFE is usually "nasty, brutish & short", (THOMAS HOBBES, "Leviathan"), & it smells like rotten eggs.
Out there, vast numbers of innocent people must endure exploitation, violation, repression & annihilation on a DAILY BASIS!
In here, thank God, it's only once a week!
Crimes that would shame the most debased are regularly perpetrated, often in the name of some MORAL or NATIONAL "crusade", by barking TYRANTS who are rarely punished...
(JOB 41 : 1)
YOUR NAME HERE
CORRUPT JUDICIARY
THE HOMELESS
CRIME
UNEMPLOYMENT
BLEEDING HEART LIBERAL
LATER, AFTER SOME DEFT FOOTWORK...
Somehow, we mended the broken seal before being ASPHYXIATED! I pray that it holds, at least until I discover a CHEMICAL means to improve the quality of REAL LIFE for the poor devils trapped out there!
Are you hoping to discover a new TRANQUILIZER?
No. A NERVE GAS that will rid the world of TYRANTS!
CAN SUCH IDEALISM PREVAIL? TUNE IN NEXT WEEK FOR THE APPALLING CONCLUSION!

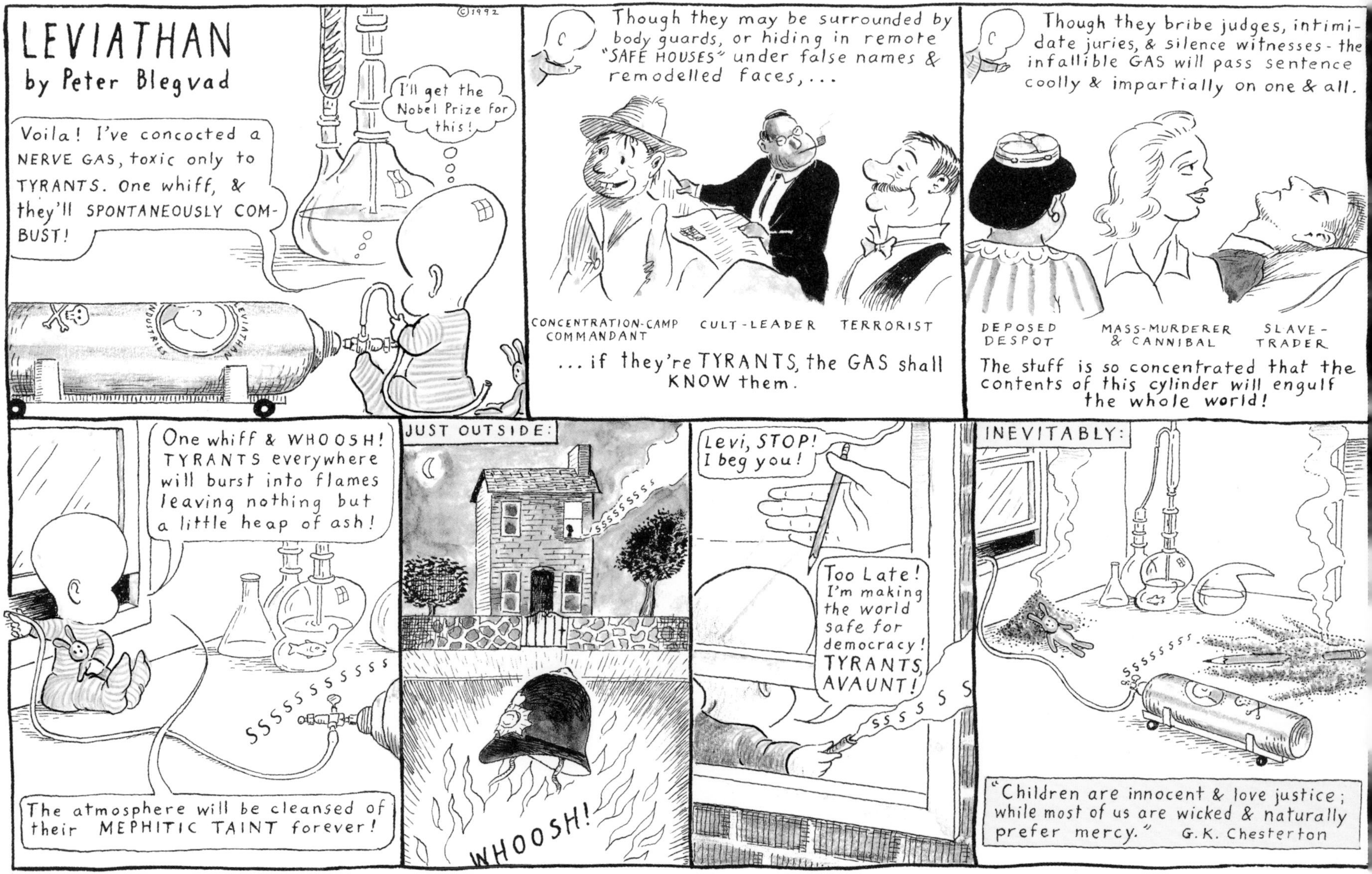
LEVIATHAN
by Peter Blegvad
©1992
I'll get the Nobel Prize for this!
Voila! I've concocted a NERVE GAS, toxic only to TYRANTS. One whiff, & they'll SPONTANEOUSLY COMBUST!
LEVIATHAN INDUSTRIES
Though they may be surrounded by body guards, or hiding in remote "SAFE HOUSES" under false names & remodelled faces, ...
CONCENTRATION-CAMP COMMANDANT
CULT-LEADER
TERRORIST
... if they're TYRANTS, the GAS shall KNOW them.
Though they bribe judges, intimidate juries, & silence witnesses - the infallible GAS will pass sentence coolly & impartially on one & all.
DEPOSED DESPOT
MASS-MURDERER & CANNIBAL
SLAVE-TRADER
The stuff is so concentrated that the contents of this cylinder will engulf the whole world!
One whiff & WHOOSH! TYRANTS everywhere will burst into flames leaving nothing but a little heap of ash!
SSSSSSSSSSS
The atmosphere will be cleansed of their MEPHITIC TAINT forever!
JUST OUTSIDE:
SSSSSSSSS
WHOOSH!
Levi, STOP! I beg you!
Too Late! I'm making the world safe for democracy! TYRANTS, AVAUNT!
SSSSSS
INEVITABLY:
SSSSSSSS
"Children are innocent & love justice; while most of us are wicked & naturally prefer mercy." G.K. Chesterton

# X. I GOT A MILLION OF 'EM

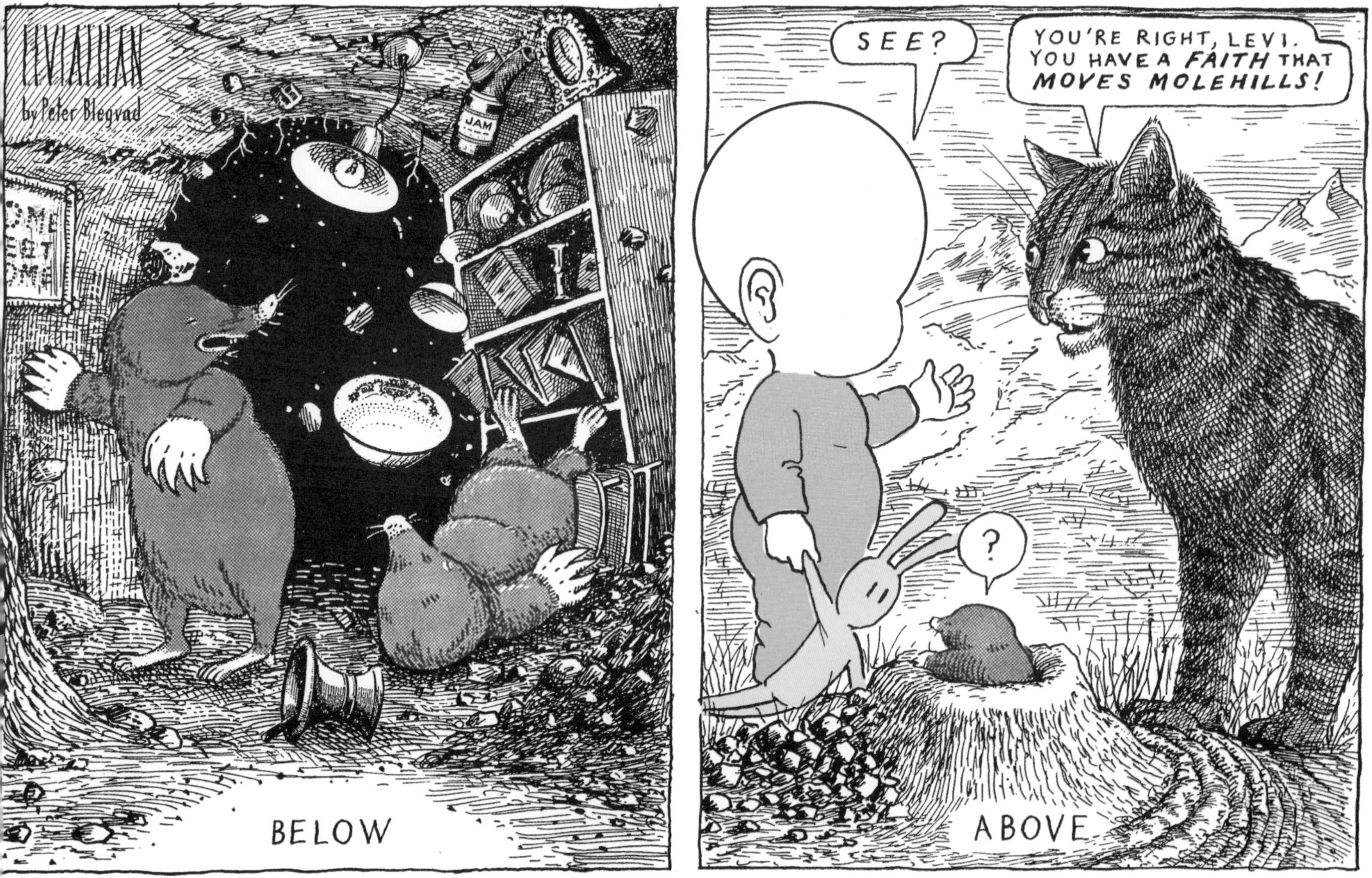
LEVIATHAN
by Peter Blegvad
JAM
BELOW
SEE?
YOU'RE RIGHT, LEVI. YOU HAVE A FAITH THAT MOVES MOLEHILLS!
?
ABOVE

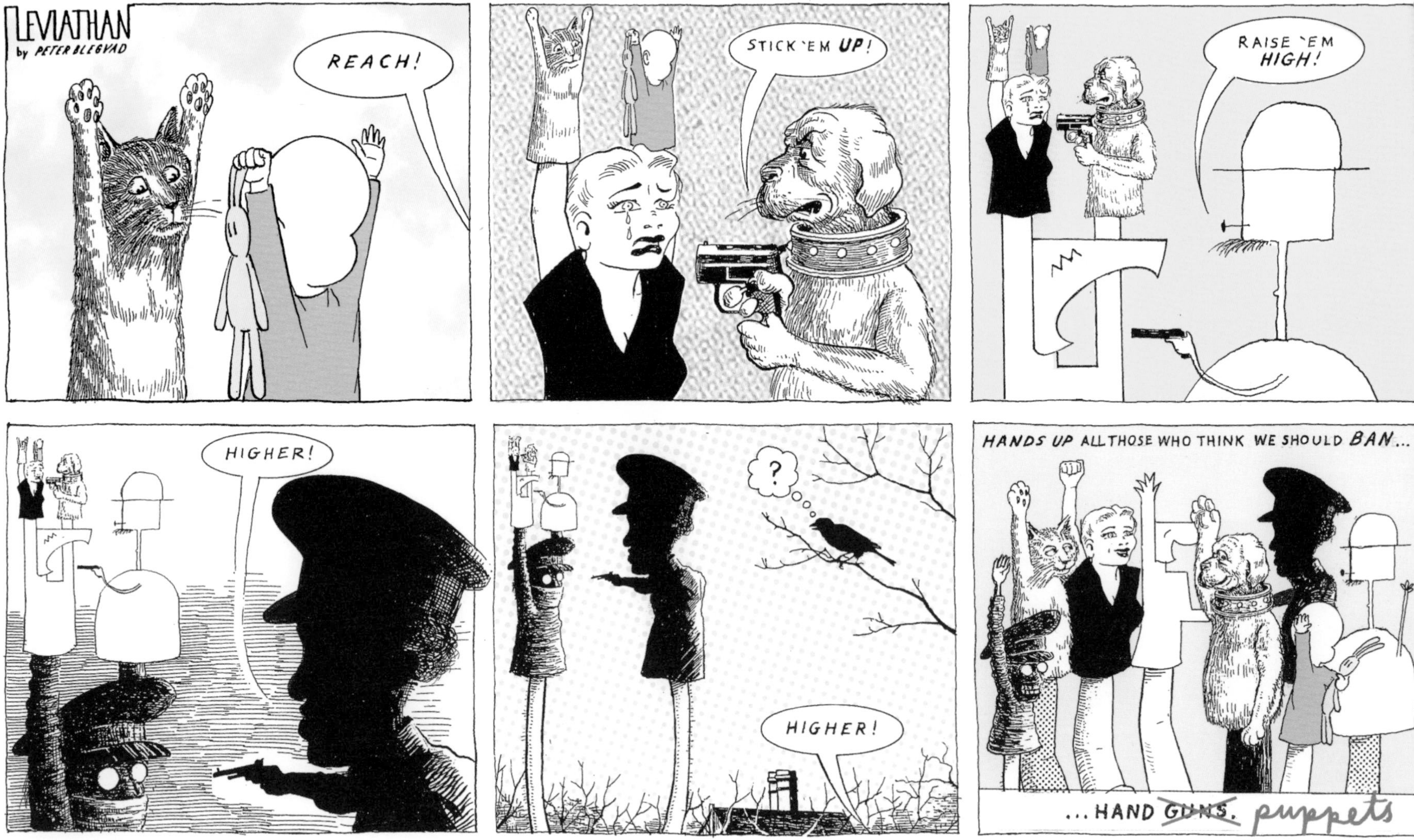
LEVIATHAN
by PETER BLEGVAD
REACH!
STICK 'EM UP!
RAISE 'EM HIGH!
HIGHER!
?
HIGHER!
HANDS UP ALL THOSE WHO THINK WE SHOULD BAN...
...HAND GUNS. puppets

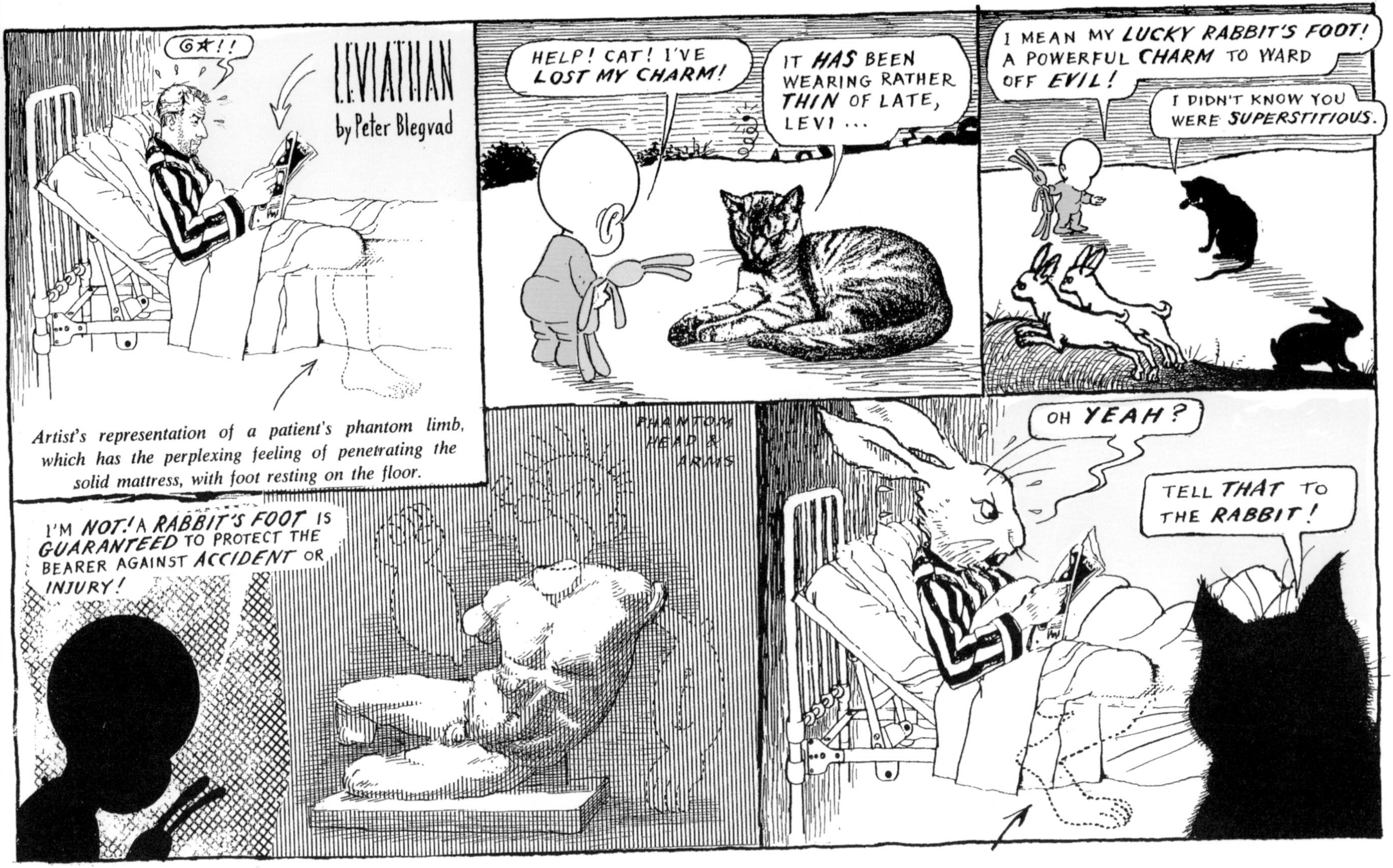

LEVIATHAN
by Peter Blegvad
G☆!!
Artist's representation of a patient's phantom limb, which has the perplexing feeling of penetrating the solid mattress, with foot resting on the floor.
HELP! CAT! I'VE LOST MY CHARM!
IT HAS BEEN WEARING RATHER THIN OF LATE, LEVI ...
I MEAN MY LUCKY RABBIT'S FOOT! A POWERFUL CHARM TO WARD OFF EVIL!
I DIDN'T KNOW YOU WERE SUPERSTITIOUS.
I'M NOT! A RABBIT'S FOOT IS GUARANTEED TO PROTECT THE BEARER AGAINST ACCIDENT OR INJURY!
PHANTOM HEAD & ARMS
OH YEAH?
TELL THAT TO THE RABBIT!

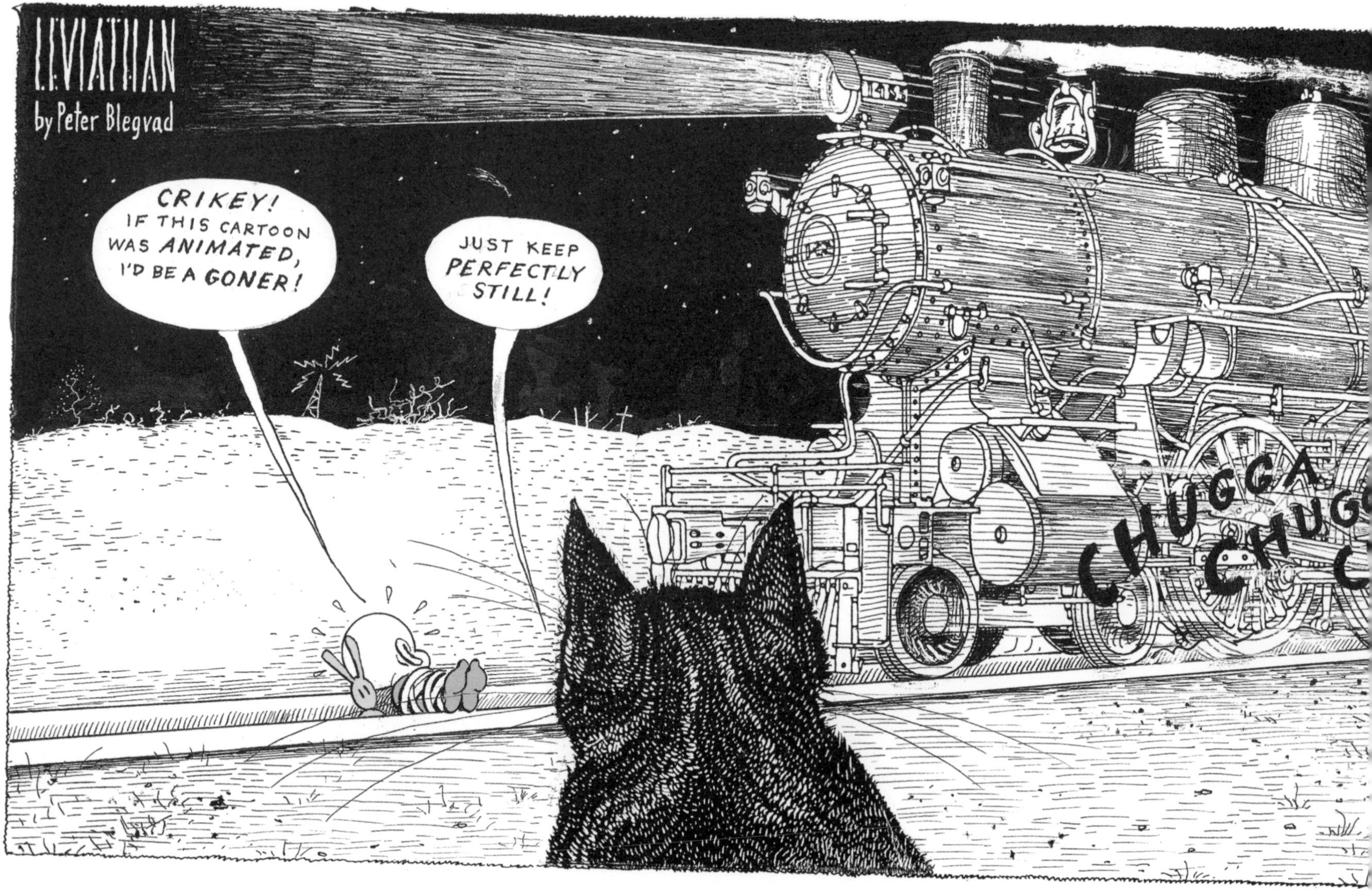
LEVIATHAN
by Peter Blegvad
CRIKEY! IF THIS CARTOON WAS ANIMATED, I'D BE A GONER!
JUST KEEP PERFECTLY STILL!
CHUGGA CHUG

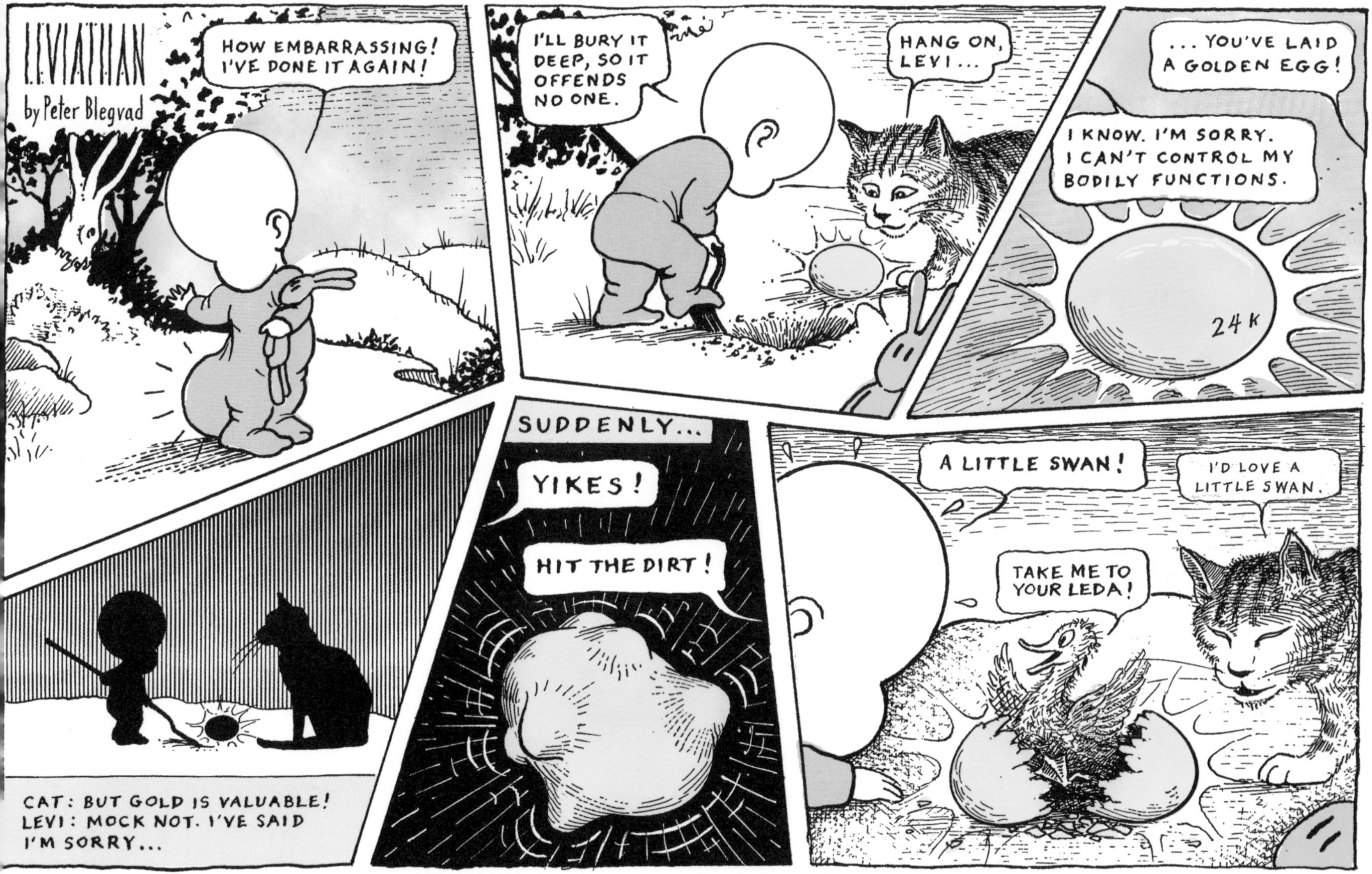
LEVIATHAN
by Peter Blegvad
HOW EMBARRASSING! I'VE DONE IT AGAIN!
I'LL BURY IT DEEP, SO IT OFFENDS NO ONE.
HANG ON, LEVI...
... YOU'VE LAID A GOLDEN EGG!
I KNOW. I'M SORRY. I CAN'T CONTROL MY BODILY FUNCTIONS.
24 K
CAT: BUT GOLD IS VALUABLE!
LEVI: MOCK NOT. I'VE SAID I'M SORRY...
SUDDENLY...
YIKES!
HIT THE DIRT!
A LITTLE SWAN!
I'D LOVE A LITTLE SWAN.
TAKE ME TO YOUR LEDA!

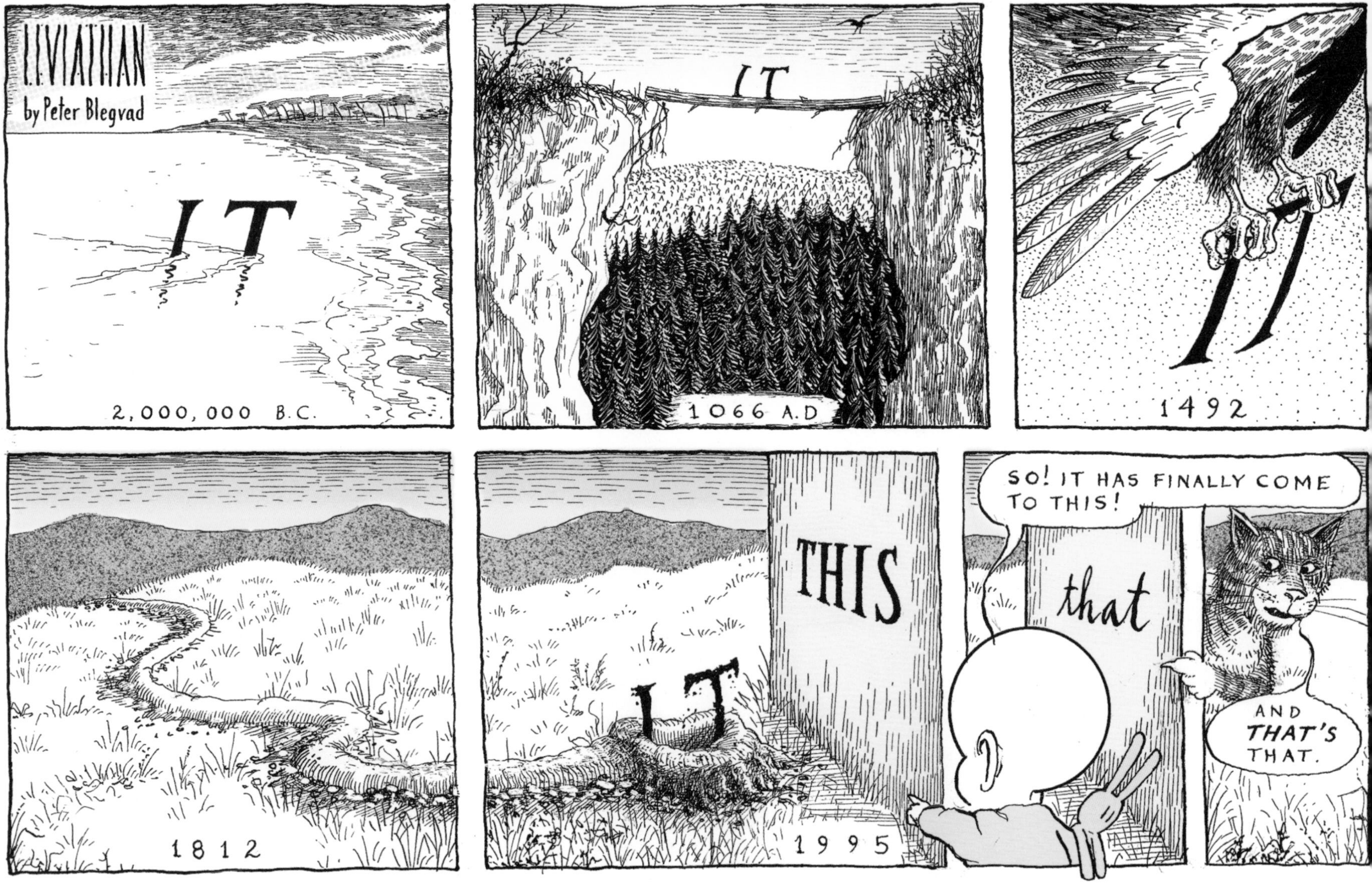
LEVIATHAN
by Peter Blegvad
IT
2,000,000 B.C.
IT
1066 A.D
1492
1812
IT
THIS
1995
SO! IT HAS FINALLY COME TO THIS!
that
AND *THAT'S* THAT.

# XI. HELL

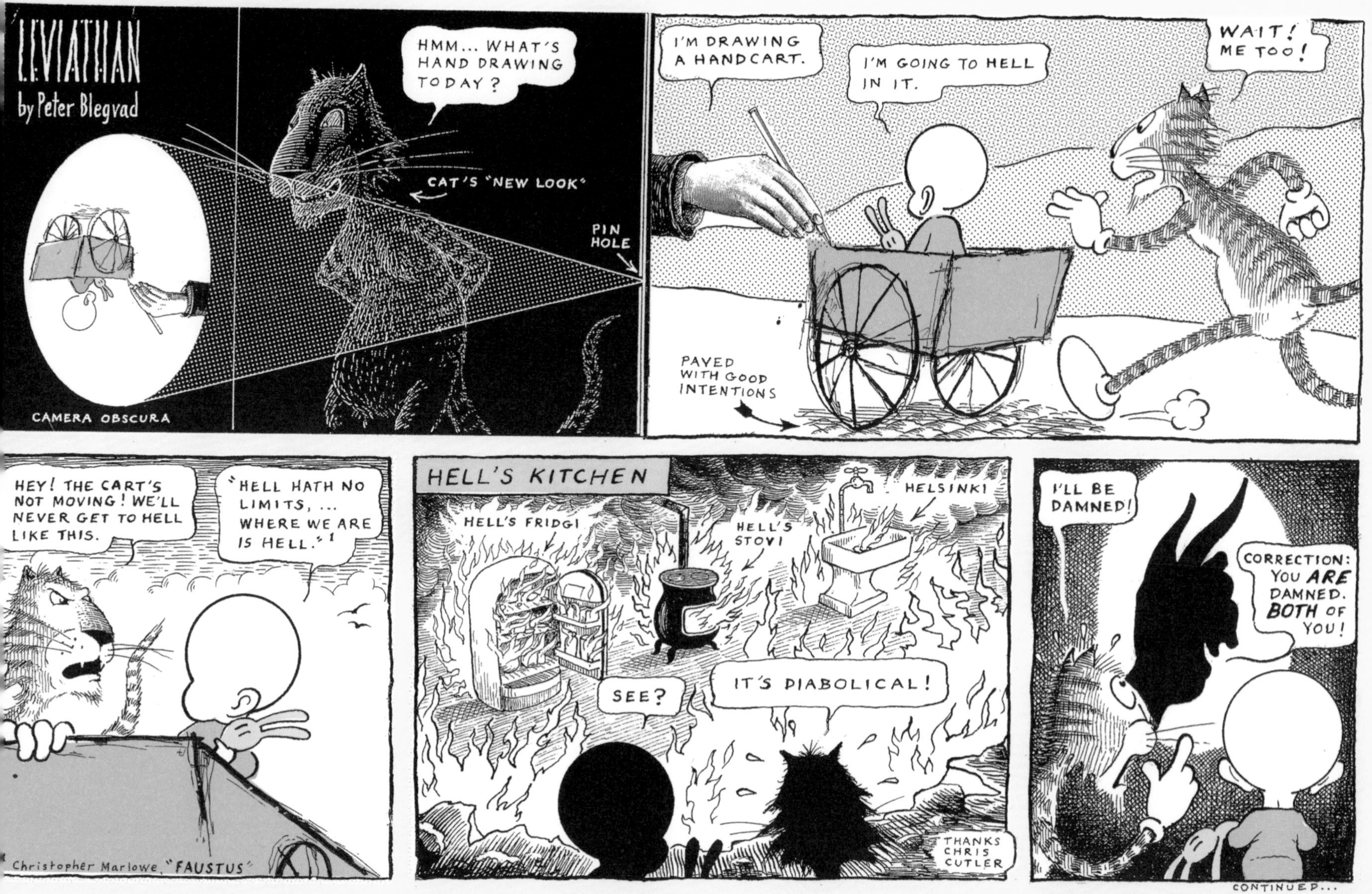
LEVIATHAN
by Peter Blegvad
HMM... WHAT'S HAND DRAWING TODAY?
CAT'S "NEW LOOK"
PIN HOLE
CAMERA OBSCURA
I'M DRAWING A HANDCART.
I'M GOING TO HELL IN IT.
WAIT! ME TOO!
PAYED WITH GOOD INTENTIONS
HEY! THE CART'S NOT MOVING! WE'LL NEVER GET TO HELL LIKE THIS.
"HELL HATH NO LIMITS, ... WHERE WE ARE IS HELL." 1
1 Christopher Marlowe, "FAUSTUS"
HELL'S KITCHEN
HELL'S FRIDGI
HELL'S STOVI
HELSINKI
SEE?
IT'S DIABOLICAL!
THANKS CHRIS CUTLER
I'LL BE DAMNED!
CORRECTION: YOU ARE DAMNED. BOTH OF YOU!
CONTINUED...

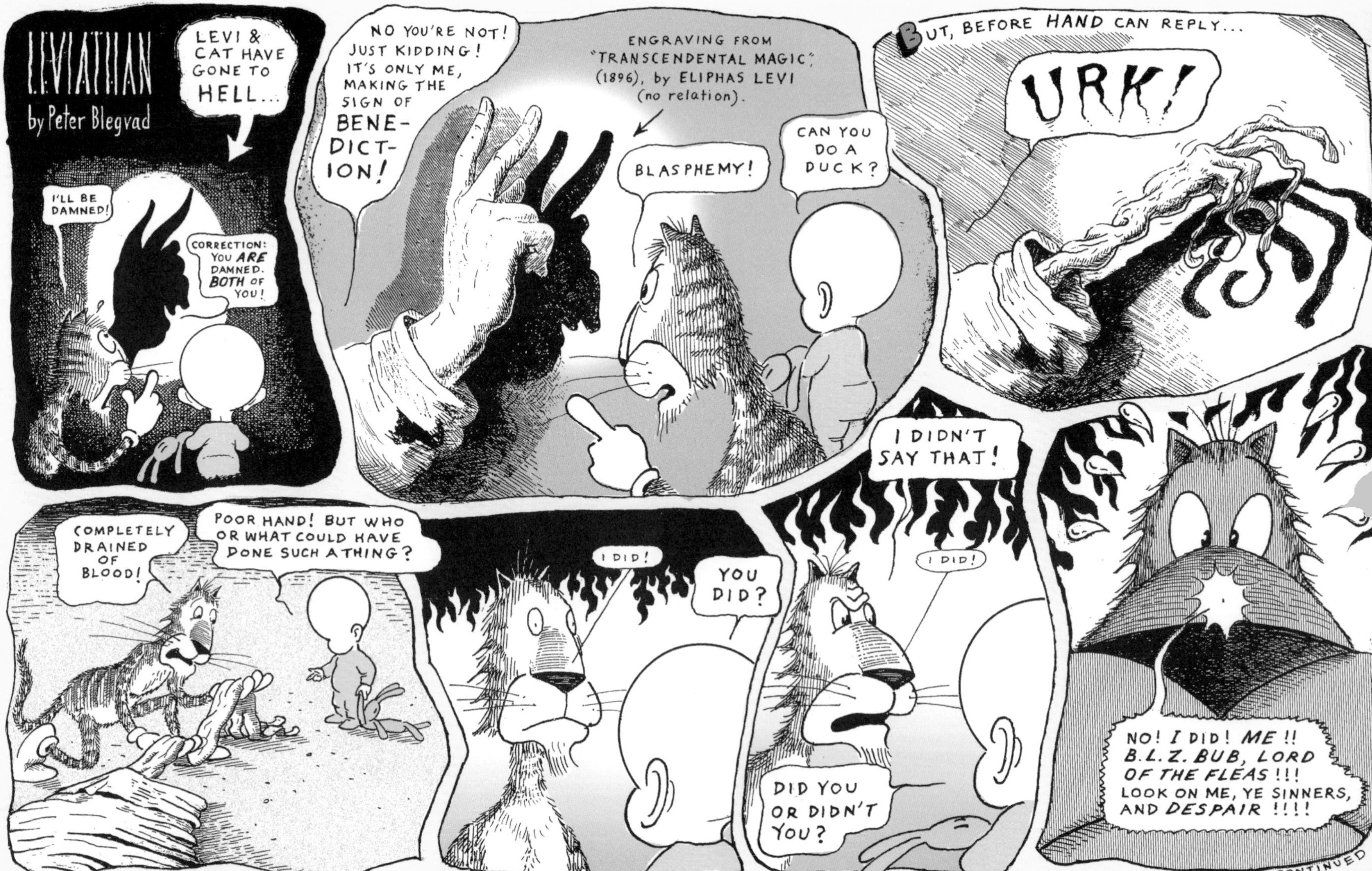
LEVIATHAN
by Peter Blegvad
LEVI & CAT HAVE GONE TO HELL...
I'LL BE DAMNED!
CORRECTION: YOU ARE DAMNED. BOTH OF YOU!
NO YOU'RE NOT! JUST KIDDING! IT'S ONLY ME, MAKING THE SIGN OF BENE-DICT-ION!
ENGRAVING FROM "TRANSCENDENTAL MAGIC", (1896), by ELIPHAS LEVI (no relation).
BLASPHEMY!
CAN YOU DO A DUCK?
BUT, BEFORE HAND CAN REPLY...
URK!
COMPLETELY DRAINED OF BLOOD!
POOR HAND! BUT WHO OR WHAT COULD HAVE DONE SUCH A THING?
I DID!
YOU DID?
I DIDN'T SAY THAT!
I DID!
DID YOU OR DIDN'T YOU?
NO! I DID! ME!! B.L.Z. BUB, LORD OF THE FLEAS!!! LOOK ON ME, YE SINNERS, AND DESPAIR!!!!
CONTINUED

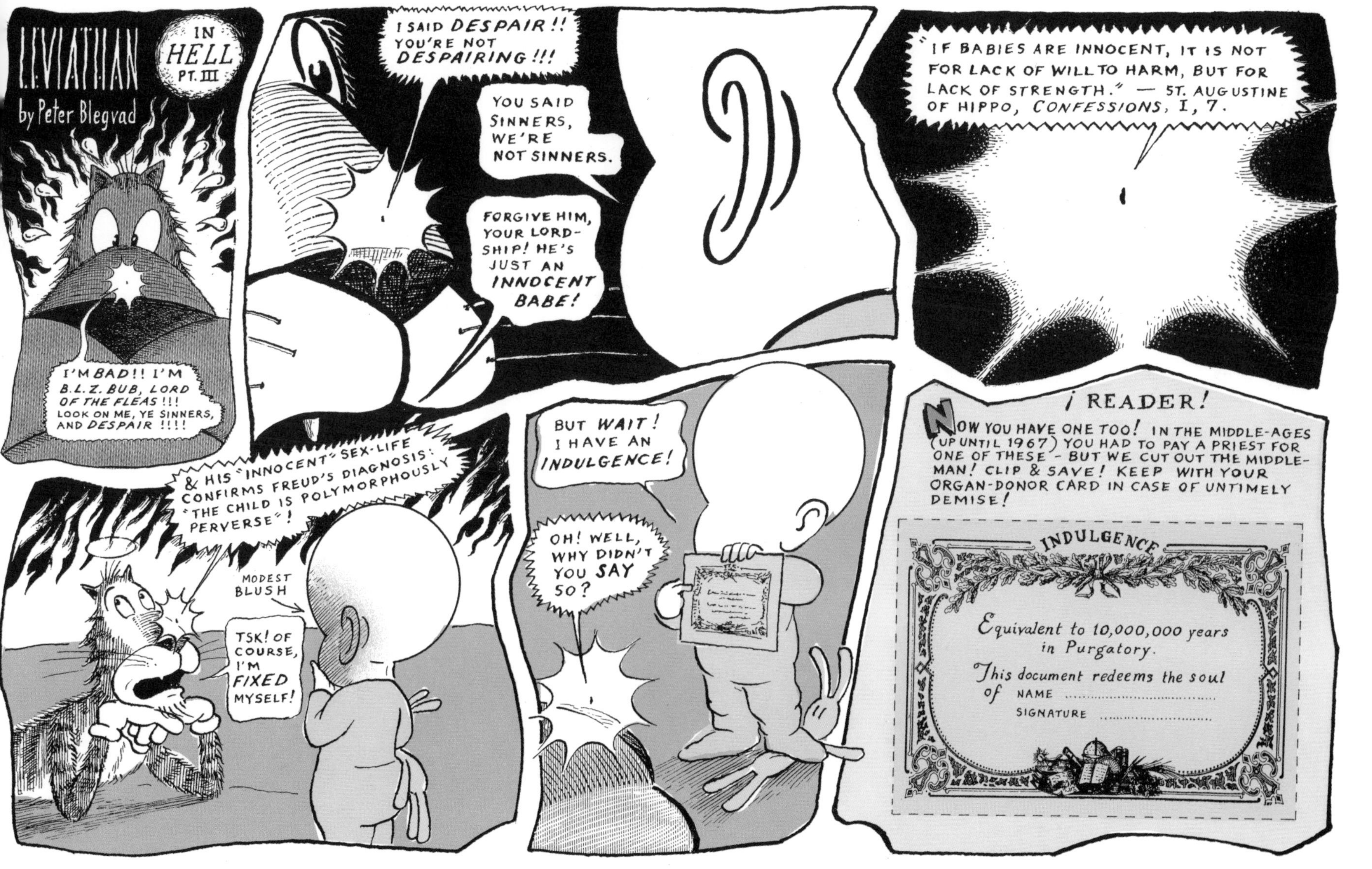

LEVIATHAN
IN HELL PT. III
by Peter Blegvad
I'M BAD!! I'M B.L.Z. BUB, LORD OF THE FLEAS!!! LOOK ON ME, YE SINNERS, AND DESPAIR!!!!
I SAID DESPAIR!! YOU'RE NOT DESPAIRING!!!
YOU SAID SINNERS, WE'RE NOT SINNERS.
FORGIVE HIM, YOUR LORDSHIP! HE'S JUST AN INNOCENT BABE!
"IF BABIES ARE INNOCENT, IT IS NOT FOR LACK OF WILL TO HARM, BUT FOR LACK OF STRENGTH." — ST. AUGUSTINE OF HIPPO, CONFESSIONS, I, 7.
& HIS "INNOCENT" SEX-LIFE CONFIRMS FREUD'S DIAGNOSIS: "THE CHILD IS POLYMORPHOUSLY PERVERSE"!
MODEST BLUSH
TSK! OF COURSE, I'M FIXED MYSELF!
BUT WAIT! I HAVE AN INDULGENCE!
OH! WELL, WHY DIDN'T YOU SAY SO?
¡READER!
NOW YOU HAVE ONE TOO! IN THE MIDDLE-AGES (UP UNTIL 1967) YOU HAD TO PAY A PRIEST FOR ONE OF THESE - BUT WE CUT OUT THE MIDDLE-MAN! CLIP & SAVE! KEEP WITH YOUR ORGAN-DONOR CARD IN CASE OF UNTIMELY DEMISE!
INDULGENCE
Equivalent to 10,000,000 years in Purgatory.
This document redeems the soul of NAME ..............
SIGNATURE ..............

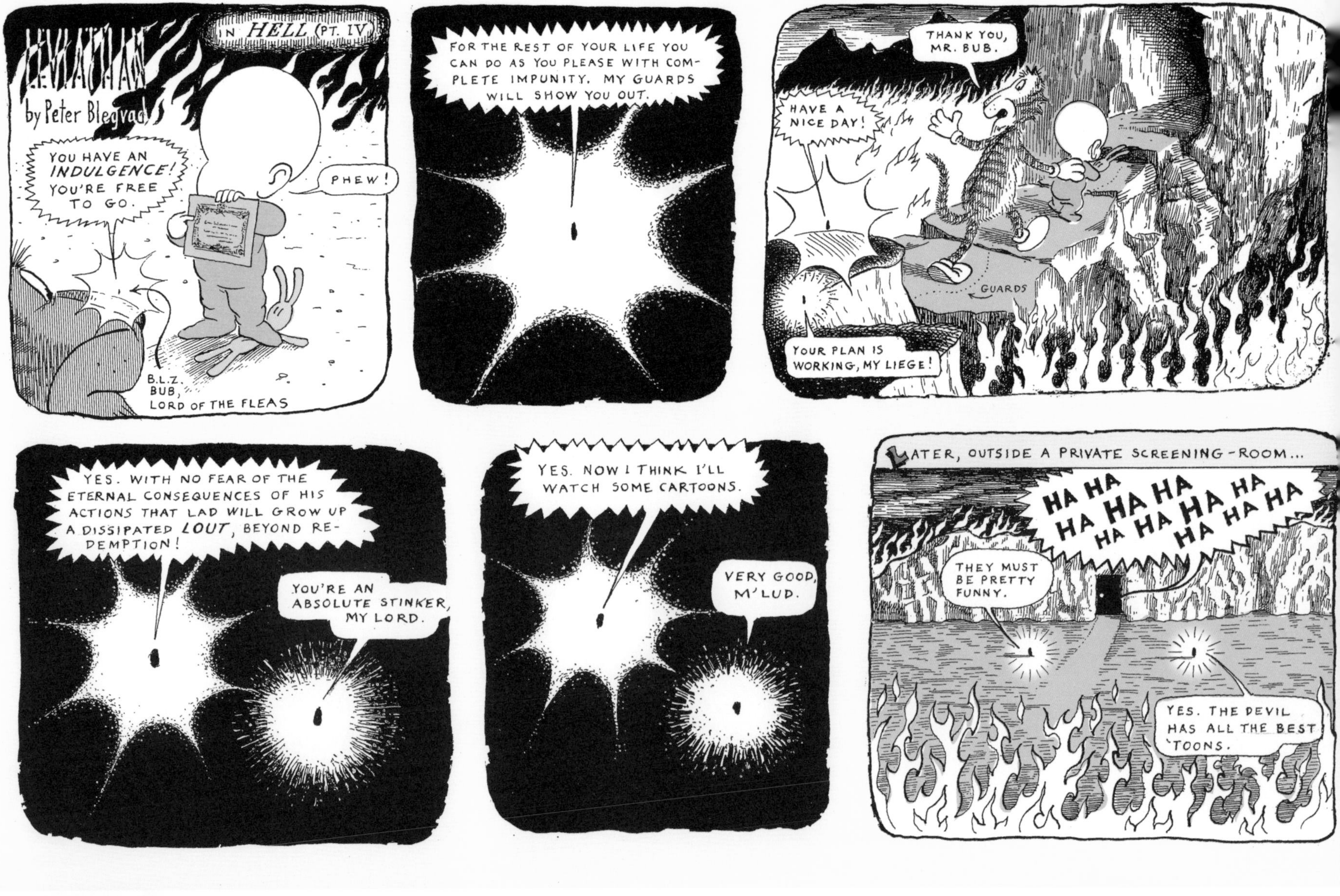
LEVIATHAN
IN HELL PT. IV
by Peter Blegvad
YOU HAVE AN INDULGENCE! YOU'RE FREE TO GO.
PHEW!
B.L.Z. BUB, LORD OF THE FLEAS
FOR THE REST OF YOUR LIFE YOU CAN DO AS YOU PLEASE WITH COMPLETE IMPUNITY. MY GUARDS WILL SHOW YOU OUT.
THANK YOU, MR. BUB.
HAVE A NICE DAY!
GUARDS
YOUR PLAN IS WORKING, MY LIEGE!
YES. WITH NO FEAR OF THE ETERNAL CONSEQUENCES OF HIS ACTIONS THAT LAD WILL GROW UP A DISSIPATED LOUT, BEYOND REDEMPTION!
YOU'RE AN ABSOLUTE STINKER, MY LORD.
YES. NOW I THINK I'LL WATCH SOME CARTOONS.
VERY GOOD, M'LUD.
LATER, OUTSIDE A PRIVATE SCREENING-ROOM...
HA HA HA HA HA HA HA HA HA HA HA HA HA HA HA HA HA HA
THEY MUST BE PRETTY FUNNY.
YES. THE DEVIL HAS ALL THE BEST 'TOONS.

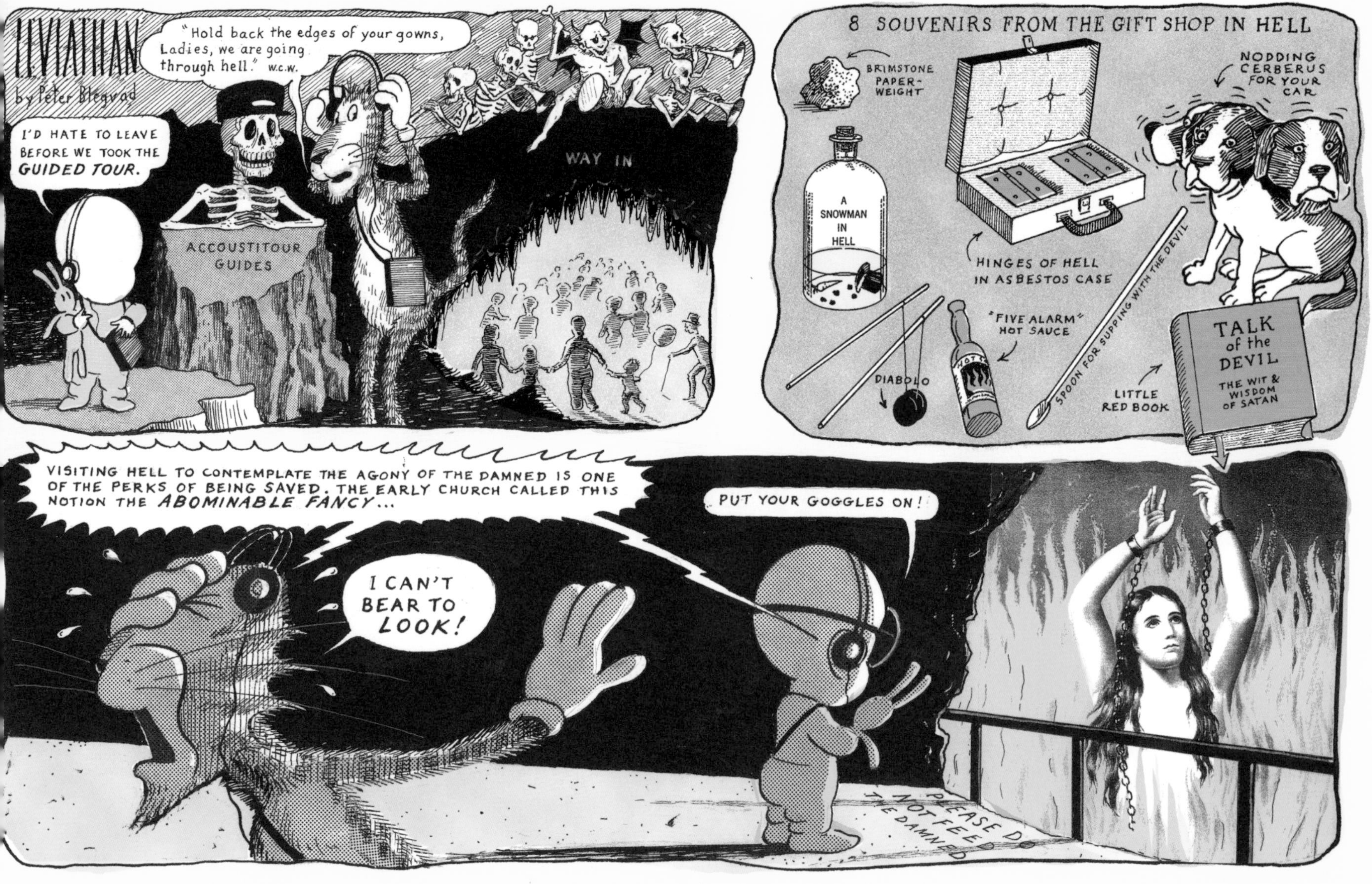
LEVIATHAN
by Peter Blegvad
"Hold back the edges of your gowns, Ladies, we are going through hell." W.C.W.
I'D HATE TO LEAVE BEFORE WE TOOK THE GUIDED TOUR.
ACCOUSTITOUR GUIDES
WAY IN
8 SOUVENIRS FROM THE GIFT SHOP IN HELL
BRIMSTONE PAPER-WEIGHT
A SNOWMAN IN HELL
HINGES OF HELL IN ASBESTOS CASE
NODDING CERBERUS FOR YOUR CAR
SPOON FOR SUPPING WITH THE DEVIL
"FIVE ALARM" HOT SAUCE
DIABOLO
LITTLE RED BOOK
TALK of the DEVIL THE WIT & WISDOM OF SATAN
VISITING HELL TO CONTEMPLATE THE AGONY OF THE DAMNED IS ONE OF THE PERKS OF BEING SAVED. THE EARLY CHURCH CALLED THIS NOTION THE ABOMINABLE FANCY...
PUT YOUR GOGGLES ON!
I CAN'T BEAR TO LOOK!
PLEASE DO NOT FEED THE DAMNED

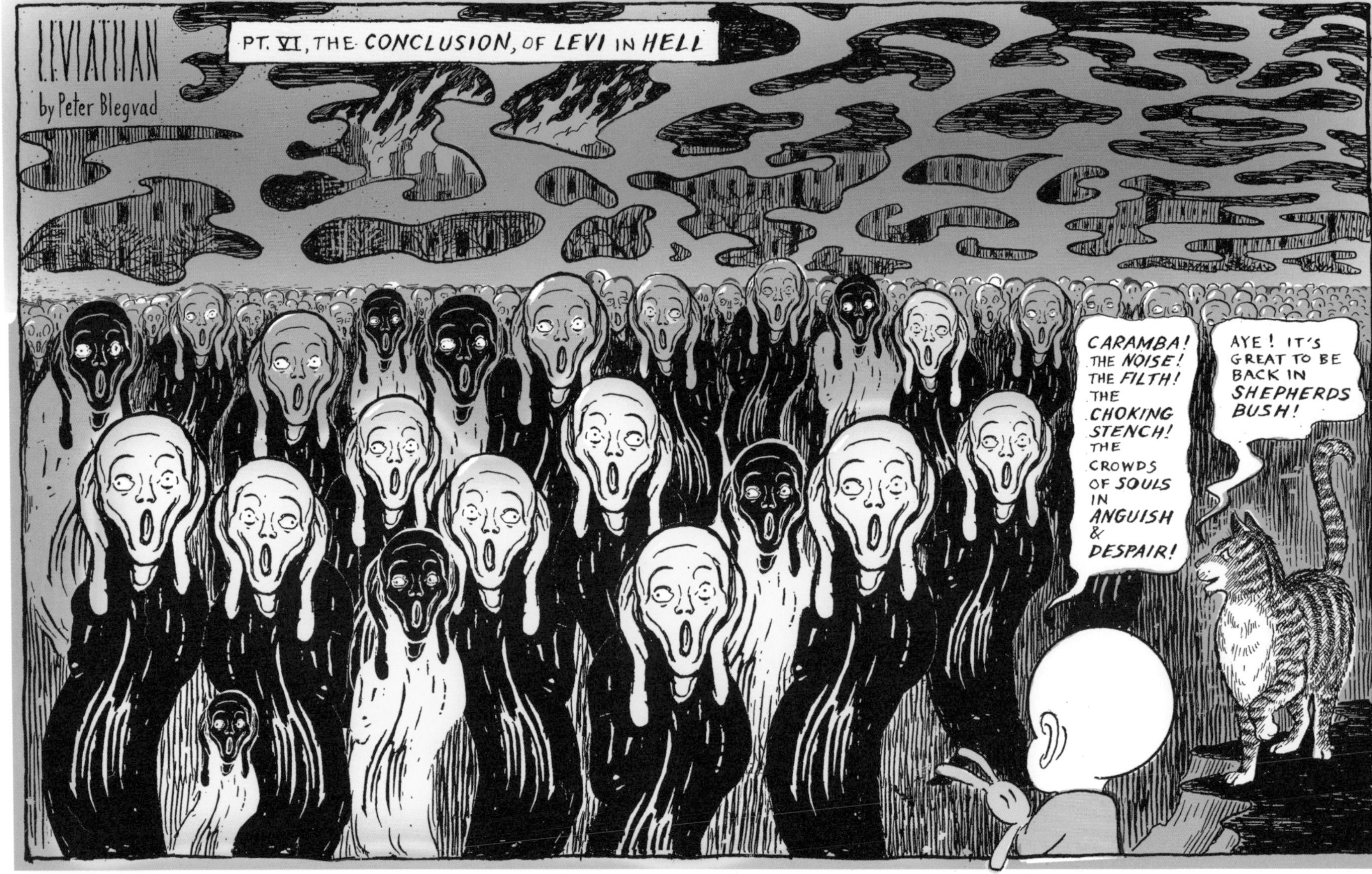
LEVIATHAN
by Peter Blegvad
PT. VI, THE CONCLUSION, OF LEVI IN HELL
CARAMBA! THE NOISE! THE FILTH! THE CHOKING STENCH! THE CROWDS OF SOULS IN ANGUISH & DESPAIR!
AYE! IT'S GREAT TO BE BACK IN SHEPHERDS BUSH!

# XII. ESCAPE

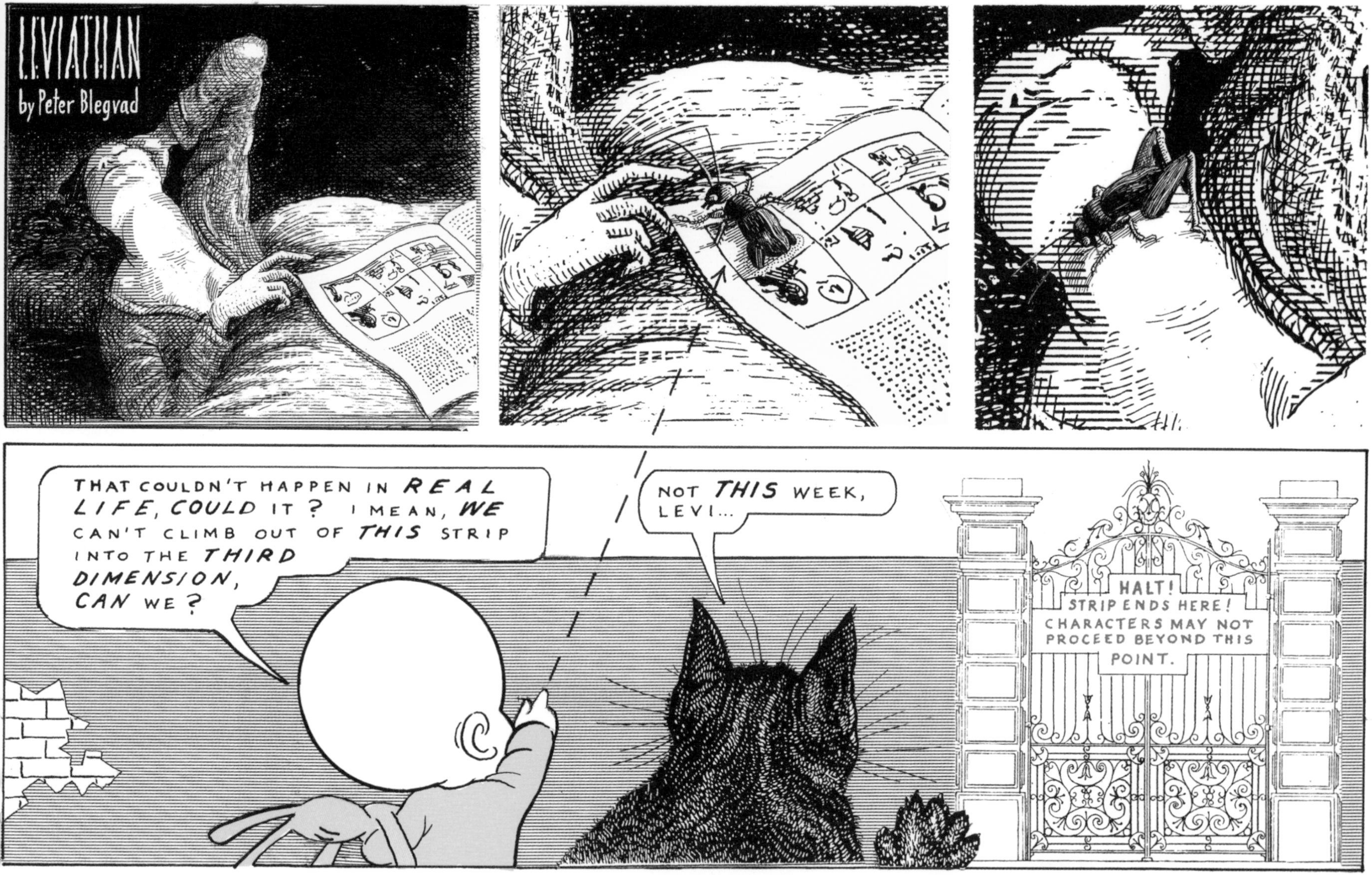
LEVIATHAN
by Peter Blegvad
THAT COULDN'T HAPPEN IN REAL LIFE, COULD IT? I MEAN, WE CAN'T CLIMB OUT OF THIS STRIP INTO THE THIRD DIMENSION, CAN WE?
NOT THIS WEEK, LEVI...
HALT! STRIP ENDS HERE! CHARACTERS MAY NOT PROCEED BEYOND THIS POINT.

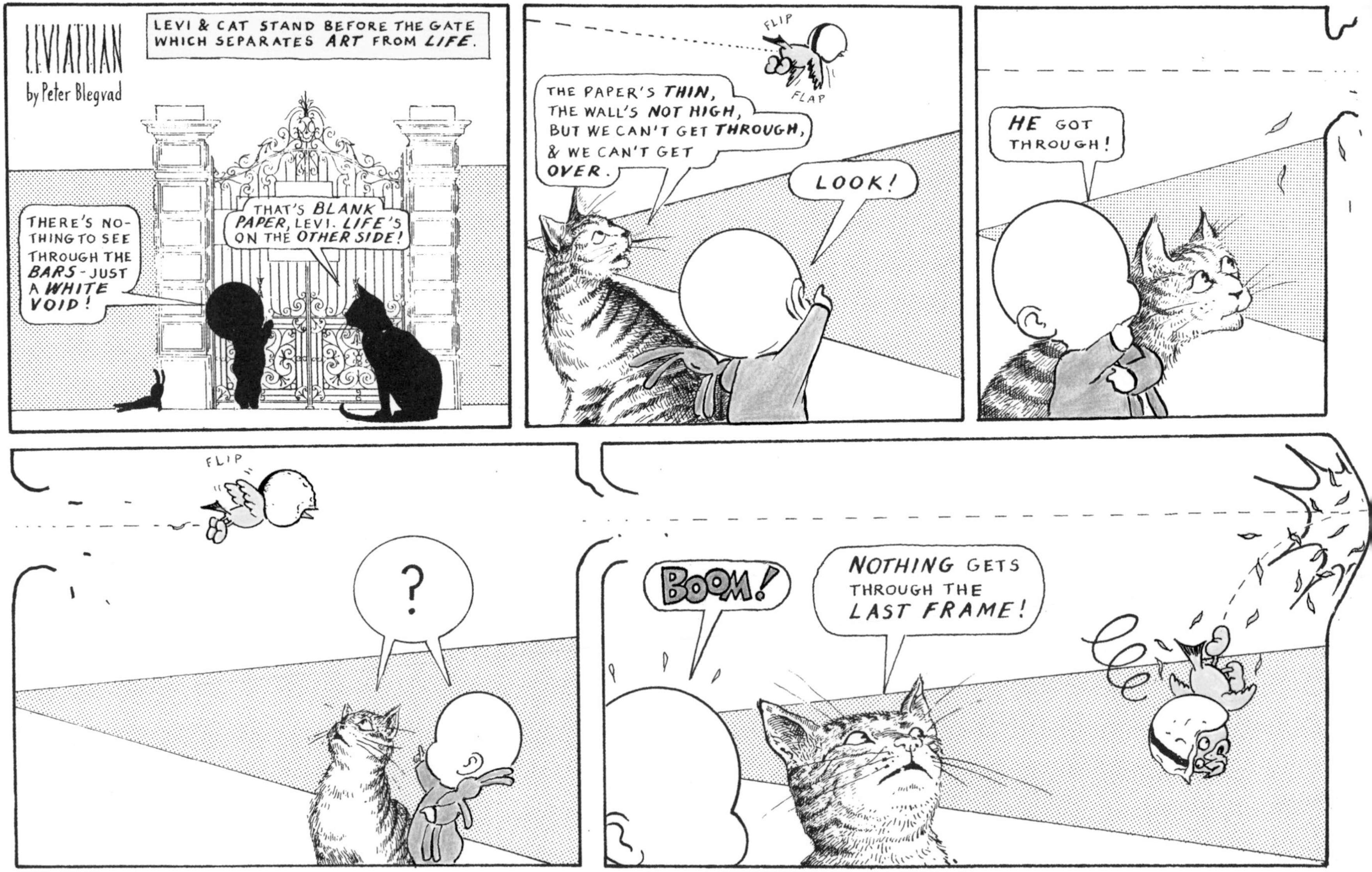
LEVIATHAN
by Peter Blegvad
LEVI & CAT STAND BEFORE THE GATE WHICH SEPARATES ART FROM LIFE.
THERE'S NOTHING TO SEE THROUGH THE BARS - JUST A WHITE VOID!
THAT'S BLANK PAPER, LEVI. LIFE'S ON THE OTHER SIDE!
FLIP
FLAP
THE PAPER'S THIN, THE WALL'S NOT HIGH, BUT WE CAN'T GET THROUGH, & WE CAN'T GET OVER.
LOOK!
HE GOT THROUGH!
FLIP
?
BOOM!
NOTHING GETS THROUGH THE LAST FRAME!

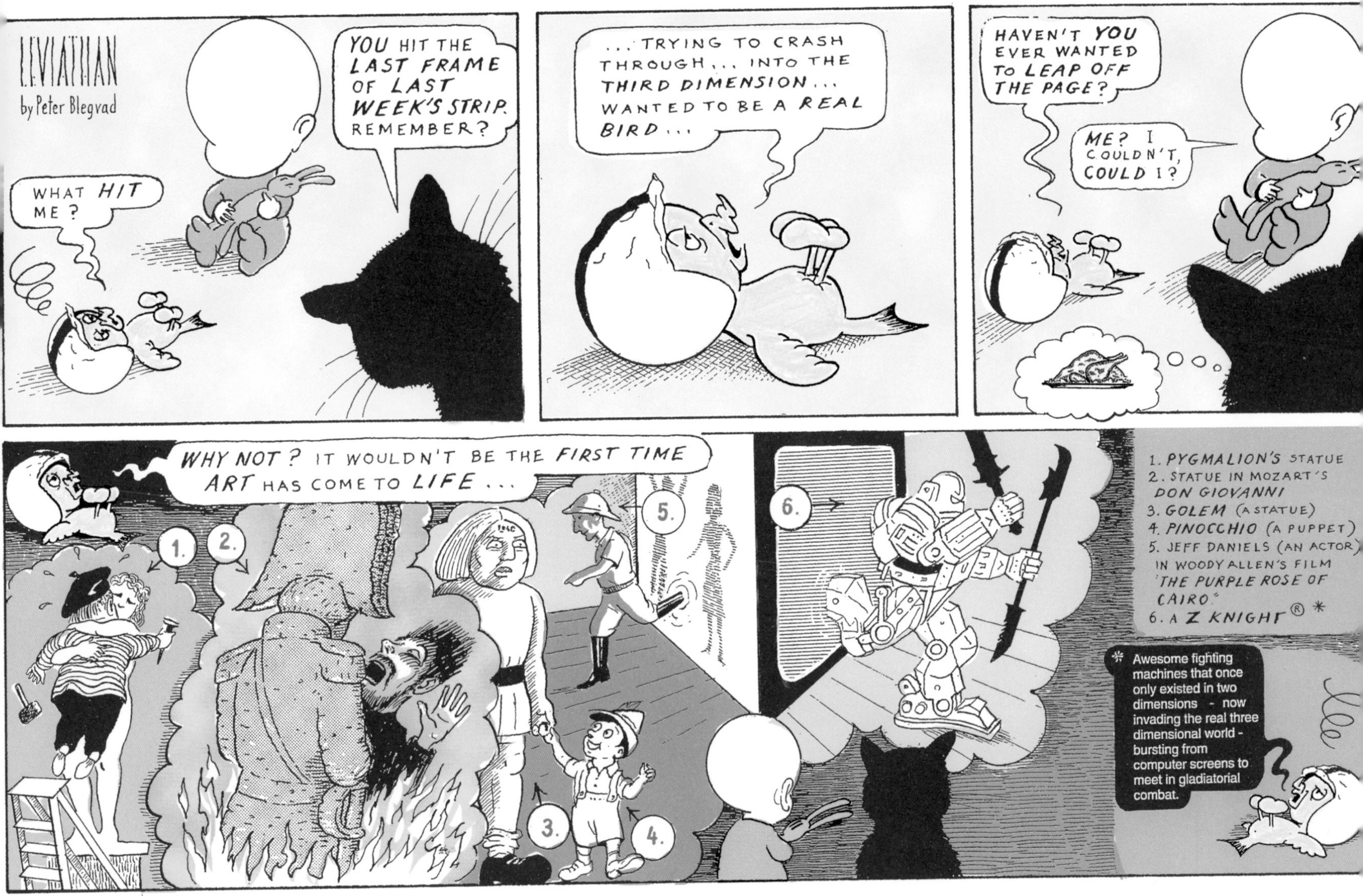
LEVIATHAN
by Peter Blegvad
WHAT HIT ME?
YOU HIT THE LAST FRAME OF LAST WEEK'S STRIP. REMEMBER?
... TRYING TO CRASH THROUGH ... INTO THE THIRD DIMENSION ... WANTED TO BE A REAL BIRD ...
HAVEN'T YOU EVER WANTED TO LEAP OFF THE PAGE?
ME? I COULDN'T, COULD I?
WHY NOT? IT WOULDN'T BE THE FIRST TIME ART HAS COME TO LIFE ...
1.
2.
3.
4.
5.
6.
1. PYGMALION'S STATUE
2. STATUE IN MOZART'S DON GIOVANNI
3. GOLEM (A STATUE)
4. PINOCCHIO (A PUPPET)
5. JEFF DANIELS (AN ACTOR) IN WOODY ALLEN'S FILM "THE PURPLE ROSE OF CAIRO."
6. A Z KNIGHT® *
* Awesome fighting machines that once only existed in two dimensions - now invading the real three dimensional world - bursting from computer screens to meet in gladiatorial combat.

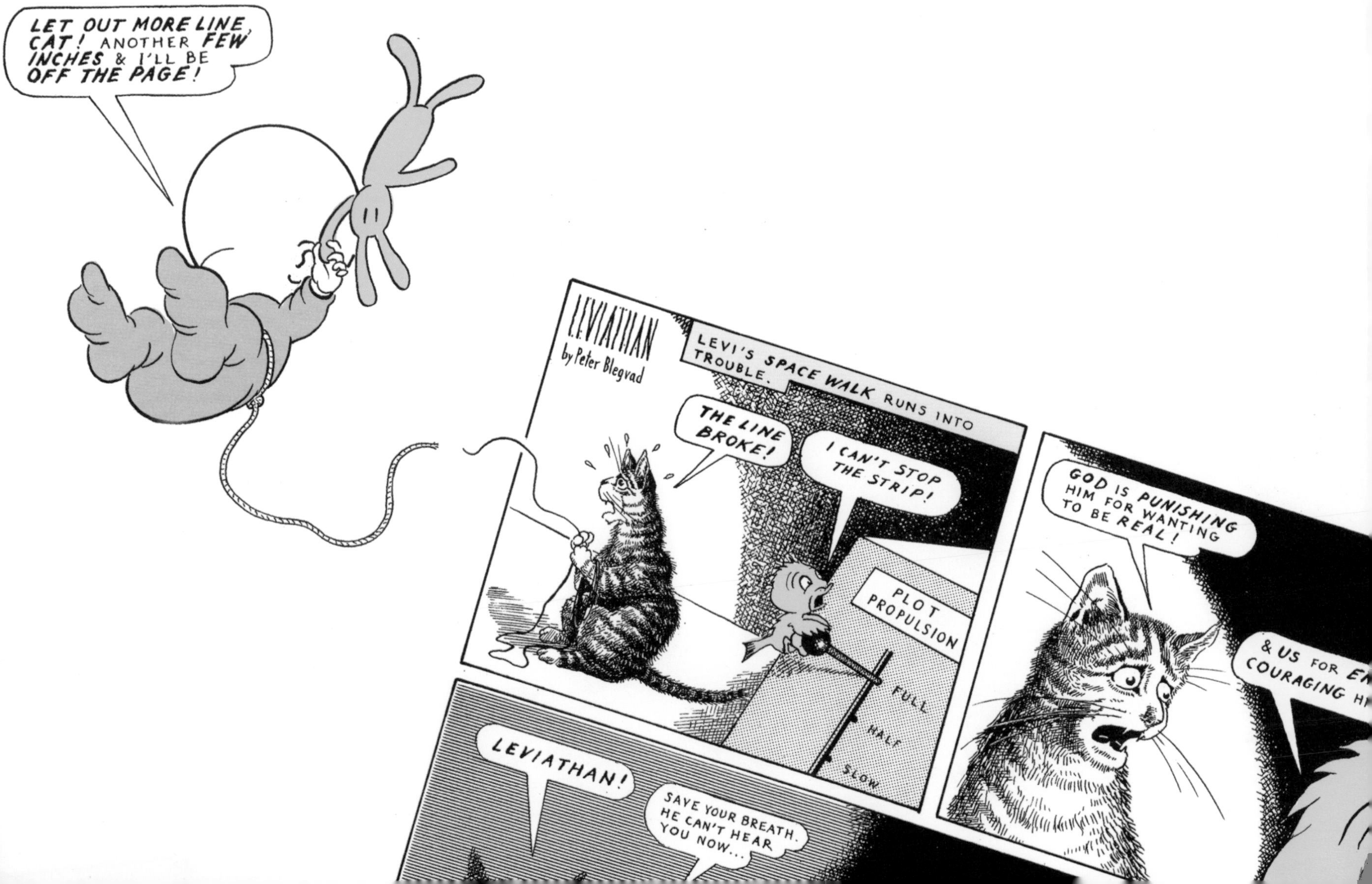
LET OUT MORE LINE, CAT! ANOTHER FEW INCHES & I'LL BE OFF THE PAGE!
LEVIATHAN
by Peter Blegvad
LEVI'S SPACE WALK RUNS INTO TROUBLE.
THE LINE BROKE!
I CAN'T STOP THE STRIP!
PLOT PROPULSION
FULL
HALF
SLOW
GOD IS PUNISHING HIM FOR WANTING TO BE REAL!
LEVIATHAN!
SAVE YOUR BREATH. HE CAN'T HEAR YOU NOW...

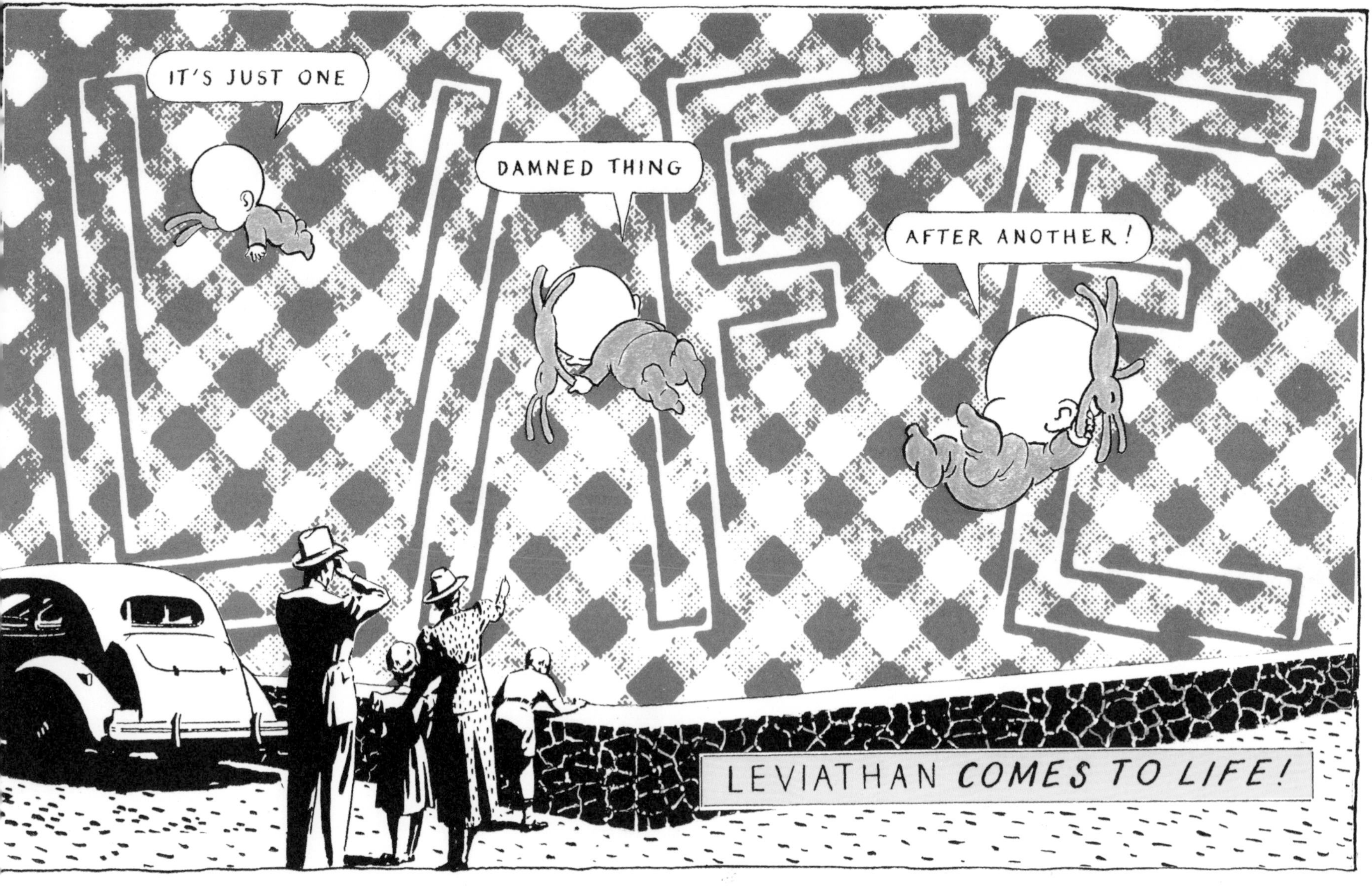
IT'S JUST ONE
DAMNED THING
AFTER ANOTHER!
LEVIATHAN COMES TO LIFE!

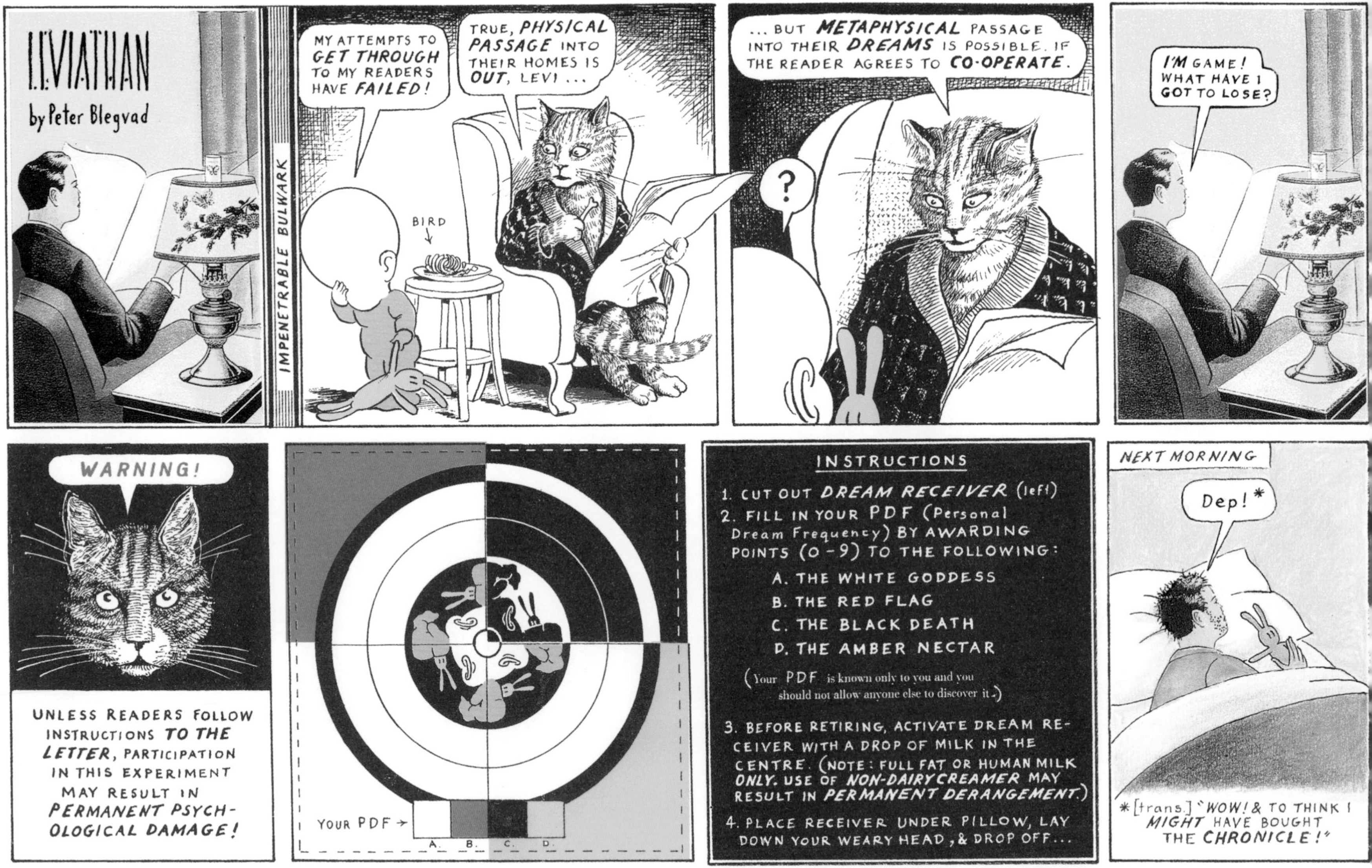
LEVIATHAN
by Peter Blegvad
IMPENETRABLE BULWARK
MY ATTEMPTS TO GET THROUGH TO MY READERS HAVE FAILED!
TRUE, PHYSICAL PASSAGE INTO THEIR HOMES IS OUT, LEVI ...
BIRD
... BUT METAPHYSICAL PASSAGE INTO THEIR DREAMS IS POSSIBLE, IF THE READER AGREES TO CO-OPERATE.
?
I'M GAME! WHAT HAVE I GOT TO LOSE?
WARNING!
UNLESS READERS FOLLOW INSTRUCTIONS TO THE LETTER, PARTICIPATION IN THIS EXPERIMENT MAY RESULT IN PERMANENT PSYCHOLOGICAL DAMAGE!
YOUR PDF →
A. B. C. D.
INSTRUCTIONS
1. CUT OUT DREAM RECEIVER (left)
2. FILL IN YOUR PDF (Personal Dream Frequency) BY AWARDING POINTS (0 - 9) TO THE FOLLOWING:
A. THE WHITE GODDESS
B. THE RED FLAG
C. THE BLACK DEATH
D. THE AMBER NECTAR
(Your PDF is known only to you and you should not allow anyone else to discover it.)
3. BEFORE RETIRING, ACTIVATE DREAM RECEIVER WITH A DROP OF MILK IN THE CENTRE. (NOTE: FULL FAT OR HUMAN MILK ONLY. USE OF NON-DAIRY CREAMER MAY RESULT IN PERMANENT DERANGEMENT.)
4. PLACE RECEIVER UNDER PILLOW, LAY DOWN YOUR WEARY HEAD, & DROP OFF...
NEXT MORNING
Dep!*
* [trans.] "WOW! & TO THINK I MIGHT HAVE BOUGHT THE CHRONICLE!"

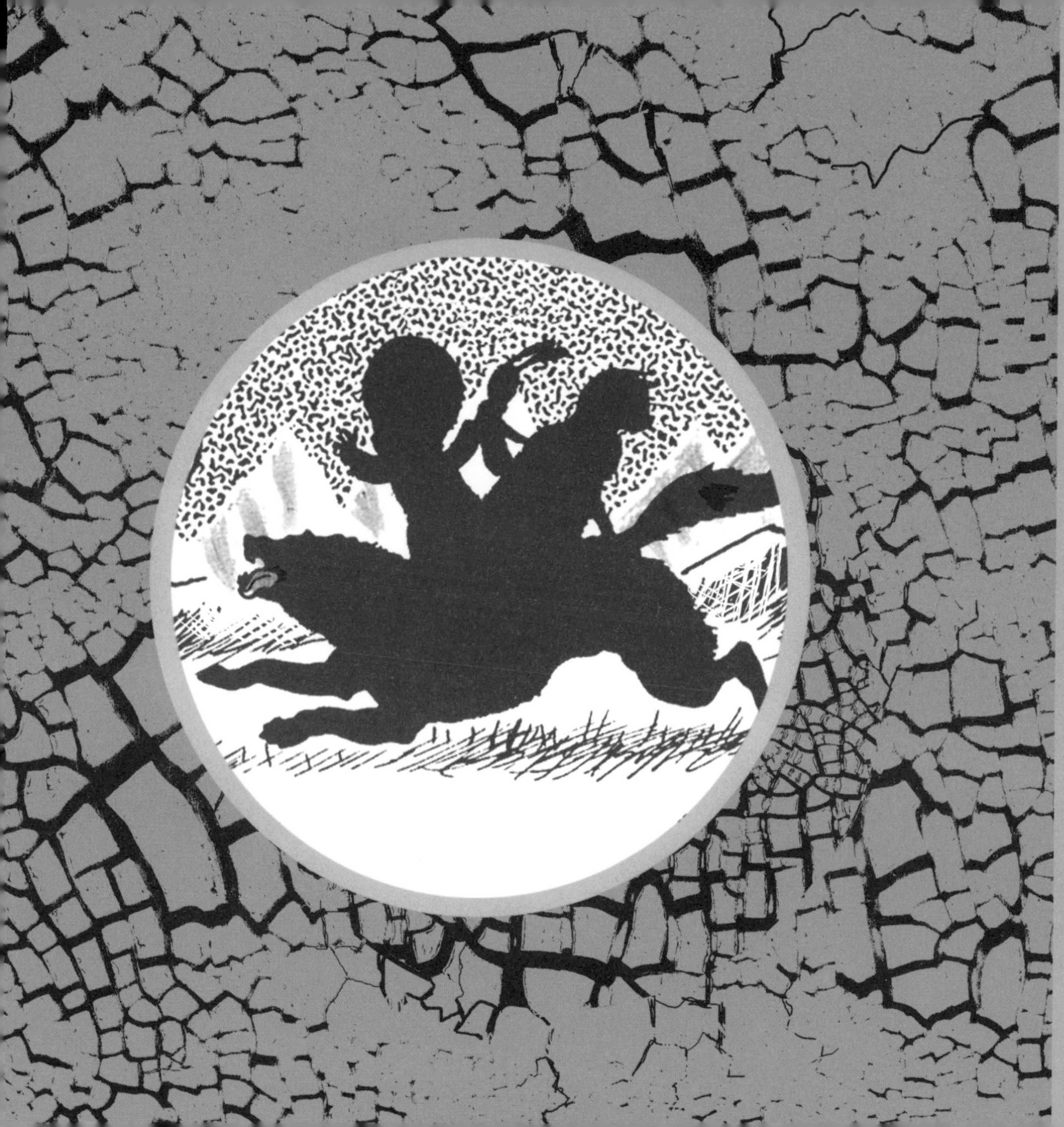

# XIII. TELL ME A STORY

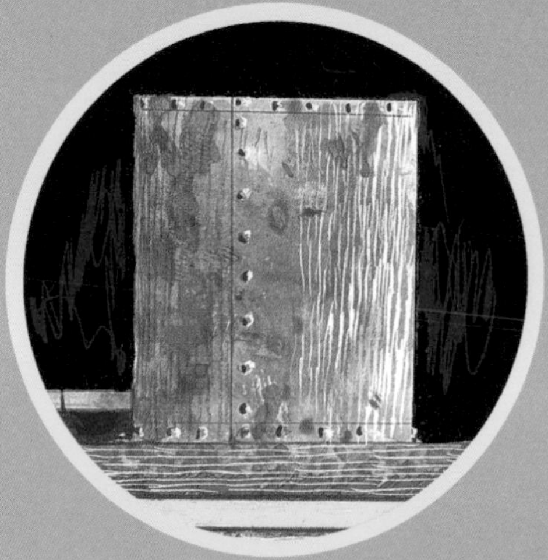

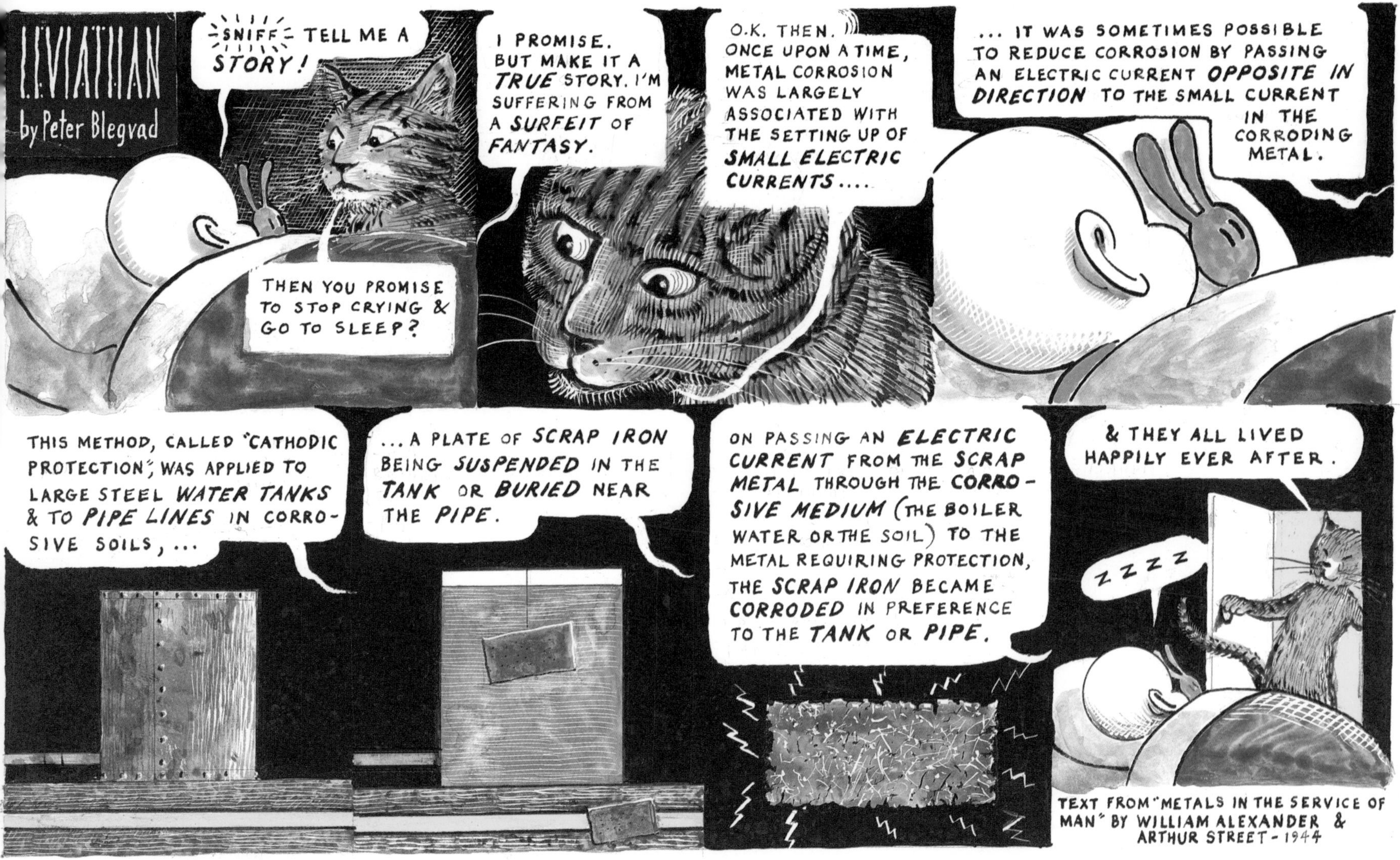
LEVIATHAN
by Peter Blegvad
SNIFF TELL ME A STORY!
THEN YOU PROMISE TO STOP CRYING & GO TO SLEEP?
I PROMISE. BUT MAKE IT A TRUE STORY. I'M SUFFERING FROM A SURFEIT OF FANTASY.
O.K. THEN. ONCE UPON A TIME, METAL CORROSION WAS LARGELY ASSOCIATED WITH THE SETTING UP OF SMALL ELECTRIC CURRENTS....
... IT WAS SOMETIMES POSSIBLE TO REDUCE CORROSION BY PASSING AN ELECTRIC CURRENT OPPOSITE IN DIRECTION TO THE SMALL CURRENT IN THE CORRODING METAL.
THIS METHOD, CALLED "CATHODIC PROTECTION", WAS APPLIED TO LARGE STEEL WATER TANKS & TO PIPE LINES IN CORROSIVE SOILS, ...
... A PLATE OF SCRAP IRON BEING SUSPENDED IN THE TANK OR BURIED NEAR THE PIPE.
ON PASSING AN ELECTRIC CURRENT FROM THE SCRAP METAL THROUGH THE CORROSIVE MEDIUM (THE BOILER WATER OR THE SOIL) TO THE METAL REQUIRING PROTECTION, THE SCRAP IRON BECAME CORRODED IN PREFERENCE TO THE TANK OR PIPE.
& THEY ALL LIVED HAPPILY EVER AFTER.
Z Z Z Z
TEXT FROM "METALS IN THE SERVICE OF MAN" BY WILLIAM ALEXANDER & ARTHUR STREET - 1944

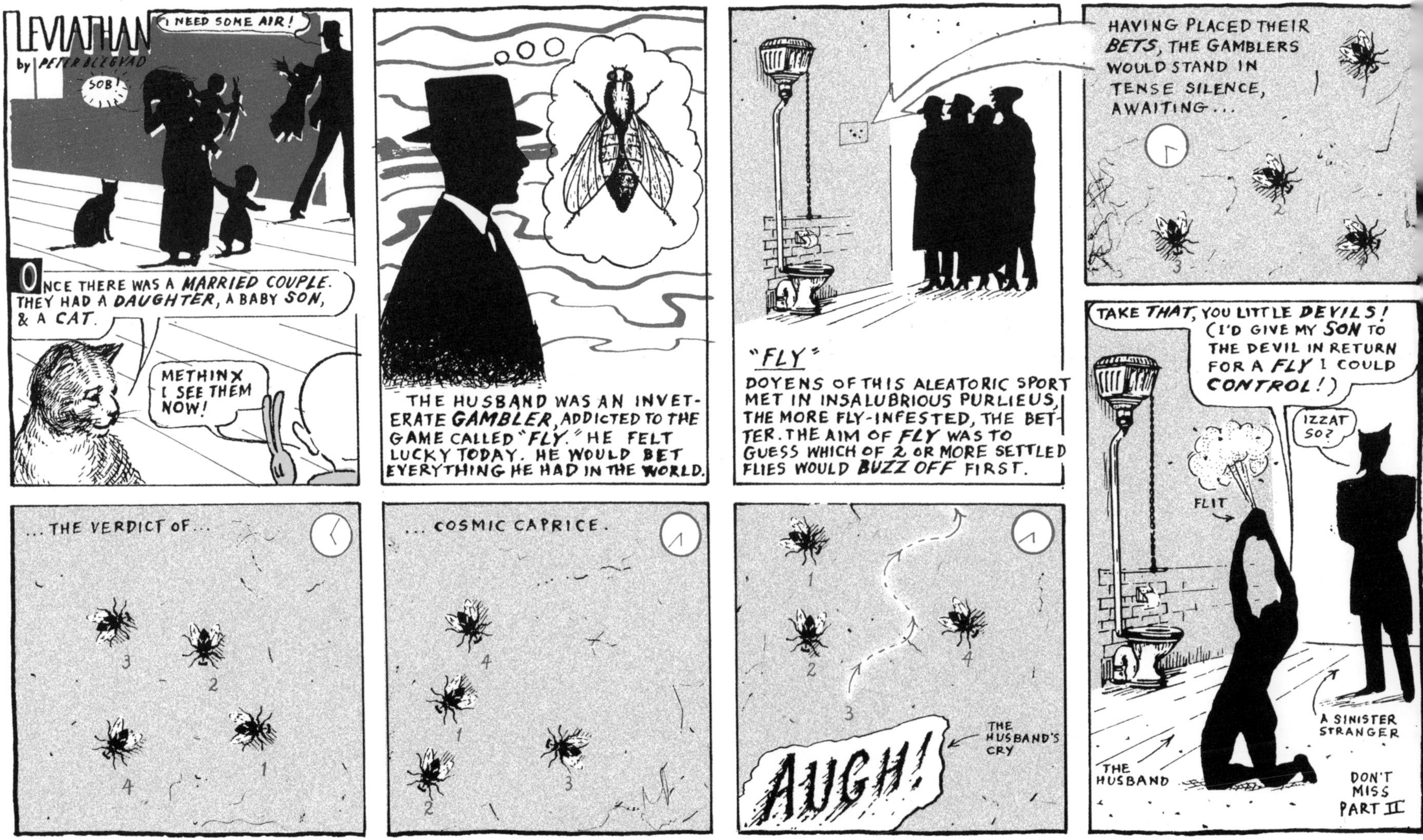

LEVIATHAN
by PETER BLEGVAD
I NEED SOME AIR!
SOB!
ONCE THERE WAS A MARRIED COUPLE. THEY HAD A DAUGHTER, A BABY SON, & A CAT.
METHINX I SEE THEM NOW!
THE HUSBAND WAS AN INVETERATE GAMBLER, ADDICTED TO THE GAME CALLED "FLY." HE FELT LUCKY TODAY. HE WOULD BET EVERYTHING HE HAD IN THE WORLD.
"FLY"
DOYENS OF THIS ALEATORIC SPORT MET IN INSALUBRIOUS PURLIEUS, THE MORE FLY-INFESTED, THE BETTER. THE AIM OF FLY WAS TO GUESS WHICH OF 2 OR MORE SETTLED FLIES WOULD BUZZ OFF FIRST.
HAVING PLACED THEIR BETS, THE GAMBLERS WOULD STAND IN TENSE SILENCE, AWAITING...
... THE VERDICT OF ...
... COSMIC CAPRICE.
AUGH!
THE HUSBAND'S CRY
TAKE THAT, YOU LITTLE DEVILS! (I'D GIVE MY SON TO THE DEVIL IN RETURN FOR A FLY I COULD CONTROL!)
IZZAT SO?
FLIT
A SINISTER STRANGER
THE HUSBAND
DON'T MISS PART II

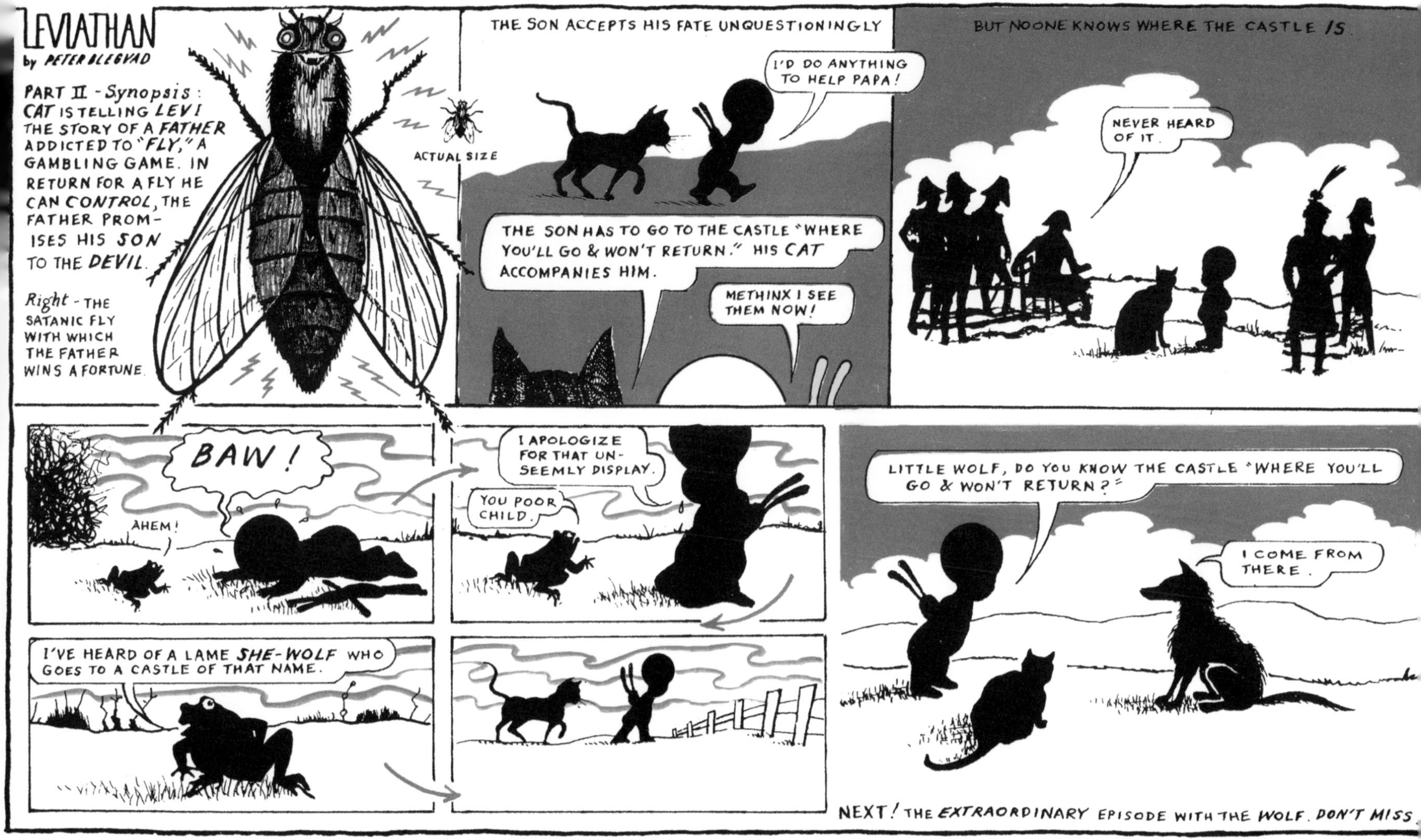
LEVIATHAN
by PETER BLEGVAD
PART II - Synopsis: CAT IS TELLING LEVI THE STORY OF A FATHER ADDICTED TO "FLY," A GAMBLING GAME. IN RETURN FOR A FLY HE CAN CONTROL, THE FATHER PROMISES HIS SON TO THE DEVIL.
Right - THE SATANIC FLY WITH WHICH THE FATHER WINS A FORTUNE.
ACTUAL SIZE
THE SON ACCEPTS HIS FATE UNQUESTIONINGLY
I'D DO ANYTHING TO HELP PAPA!
THE SON HAS TO GO TO THE CASTLE "WHERE YOU'LL GO & WON'T RETURN." HIS CAT ACCOMPANIES HIM.
METHINX I SEE THEM NOW!
BUT NOONE KNOWS WHERE THE CASTLE IS.
NEVER HEARD OF IT.
BAW!
AHEM!
I APOLOGIZE FOR THAT UNSEEMLY DISPLAY.
YOU POOR CHILD.
I'VE HEARD OF A LAME SHE-WOLF WHO GOES TO A CASTLE OF THAT NAME.
LITTLE WOLF, DO YOU KNOW THE CASTLE "WHERE YOU'LL GO & WON'T RETURN?"
I COME FROM THERE.
NEXT! THE EXTRAORDINARY EPISODE WITH THE WOLF. DON'T MISS

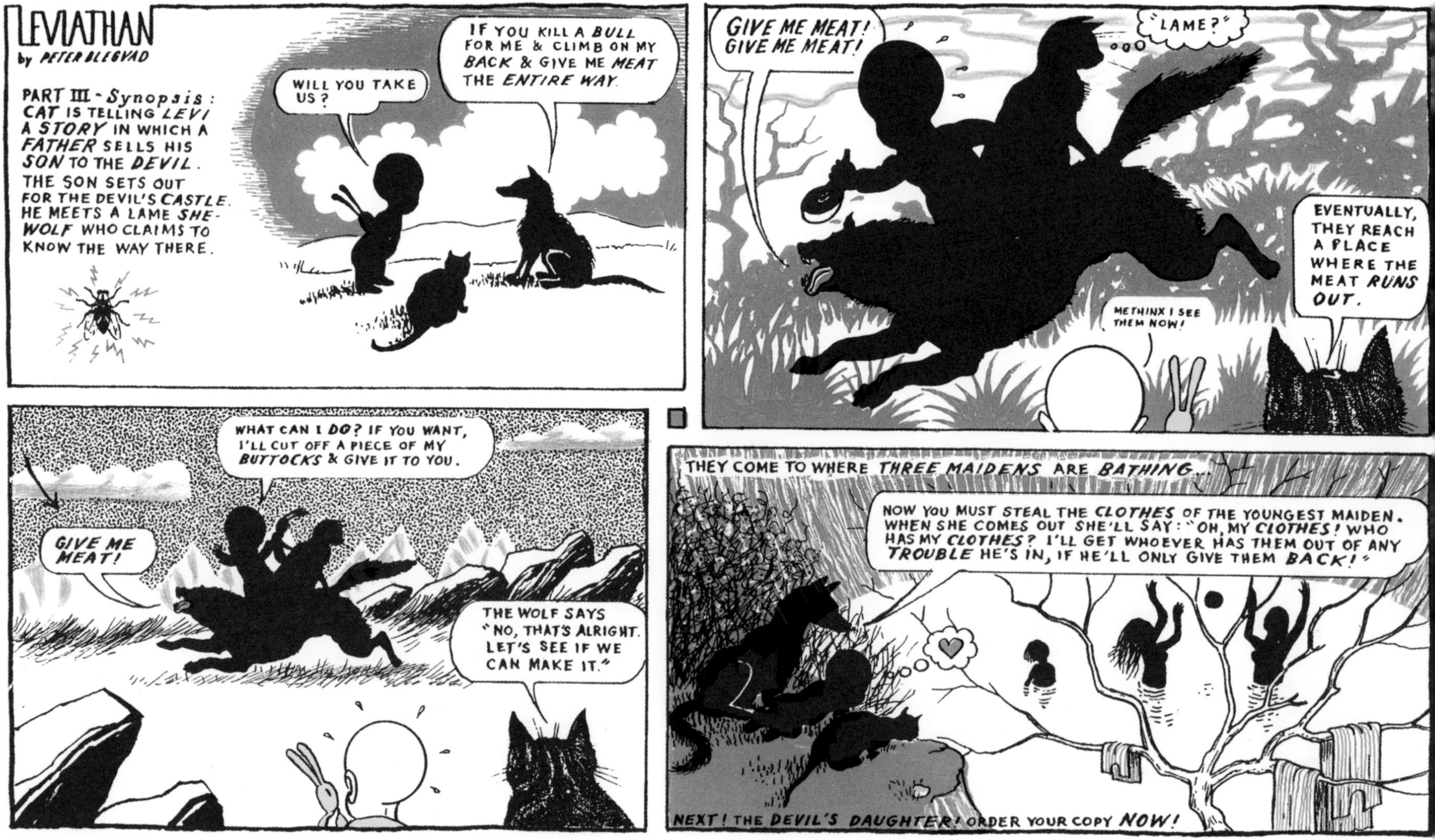

LEVIATHAN
by PETER BLEGVAD
PART III - Synopsis: CAT IS TELLING LEVI A STORY IN WHICH A FATHER SELLS HIS SON TO THE DEVIL. THE SON SETS OUT FOR THE DEVIL'S CASTLE. HE MEETS A LAME SHE-WOLF WHO CLAIMS TO KNOW THE WAY THERE.
WILL YOU TAKE US?
IF YOU KILL A BULL FOR ME & CLIMB ON MY BACK & GIVE ME MEAT THE ENTIRE WAY.
GIVE ME MEAT! GIVE ME MEAT!
"LAME?"
EVENTUALLY, THEY REACH A PLACE WHERE THE MEAT RUNS OUT.
METHINX I SEE THEM NOW!
WHAT CAN I DO? IF YOU WANT, I'LL CUT OFF A PIECE OF MY BUTTOCKS & GIVE IT TO YOU.
GIVE ME MEAT!
THE WOLF SAYS "NO, THAT'S ALRIGHT. LET'S SEE IF WE CAN MAKE IT."
THEY COME TO WHERE THREE MAIDENS ARE BATHING...
NOW YOU MUST STEAL THE CLOTHES OF THE YOUNGEST MAIDEN. WHEN SHE COMES OUT SHE'LL SAY: "OH, MY CLOTHES! WHO HAS MY CLOTHES? I'LL GET WHOEVER HAS THEM OUT OF ANY TROUBLE HE'S IN, IF HE'LL ONLY GIVE THEM BACK!"
NEXT! THE DEVIL'S DAUGHTER! ORDER YOUR COPY NOW!

# LEVIATHAN
by PETER BLEGVAD

PART IV - Synopsis: CAT IS TELLING LEVI A STORY IN WHICH A FATHER SELLS HIS SON TO THE DEVIL. A WOLF CARRIES THE SON TO WHERE THREE MAIDENS ARE BATHING.

WAIT! DON'T *TELL* ME — LET ME *GUESS*. THE *SON* STEALS THE *CLOTHES* OF THE *YOUNGEST MAIDEN* WHO TURNS OUT TO BE THE *DEVIL'S DAUGHTER*, & SHE HELPS HIM OUTWIT HER *FATHER* & THEY LIVE *HAPPILY EVER AFTER*.

THEY COME TO WHERE *THREE MAIDENS* ARE *BATHING*.

NOW YOU MUST STEAL THE *CLOTHES* OF WHEN SHE COMES OUT SHE'LL SAY: "*HAS MY CLOTHES* I'LL GET WHOEVER *TROUBLE* HE'S IN, IF HE'LL ONLY G THEM *BACK*!'

YOUNGEST MAIDEN. Y CLOTHES! WHO S THEM OUT OF ANY THEM BACK!'

YOU'VE HEARD IT *BEFORE*!

IN *SEVERAL* VARIANTS. THE *FATHERS* ALWAYS GET THE *WORST* OF IT. THE POOR *DEVIL* IS *BETRAYED* BY THE *DAUGHTER* HE LOVED & *TRUSTED*. BUT IT'S THE *HERO'S* FATHER I FEEL *SORRIEST* FOR.

BUT HE *SOLD* HIS SON TO THE *DEVIL*!

I KNOW. IN RETURN FOR A FOOLPROOF WAY TO CHEAT HIS CRONIES AT *GAMBLING* ...

RIGHT! HE WINS A *FORTUNE*! THAT'S HIS *VILLA*!

... BUT I DON'T THINK HE'S IN ANY *FRAME OF MIND* TO *ENJOY* HIS *RICHES*! THINK OF HIS *REMORSE*! IMAGINE THE *ABHORENCE* HIS *WIFE & DAUGHTER* WOULD FEEL FOR HIM! HAVING *RUINED* HIS FORMER *CRONIES*, HE'D BE LEFT *ALONE* WITH HIS HORRID *FLY* — NO DOUBT SEEKING *JUSTIFICATION* FOR HIS *SELFISHNESS* BY BLAMING HIS *OWN* FATHER'S INDIFFERENCE TO HIM, & HIS *FATHER'S FATHER'S* INDIFFERENCE, & *SO ON*, BACK TO *ADAM* — A LEGACY OF *MORAL FAILURE* WHICH ULTIMATELY *POINTS THE FINGER* AT A CALLOUS, JEALOUS, SMALL-MINDED *GOD*. THE *MORAL* OF THE TALE IS CLEAR; FROM *HENCEFORTH*, WHENEVER I HEAR THE *BUZZING* OF A *FLY*, I'LL BE *STEELED* IN MY *RESOLVE* TO *NEVER* HAVE *CHILDREN*.

The End

HELP ME! PLEEZE!

DO YOU KNOW THE ONE ABOUT THE *THREE BEARS*?

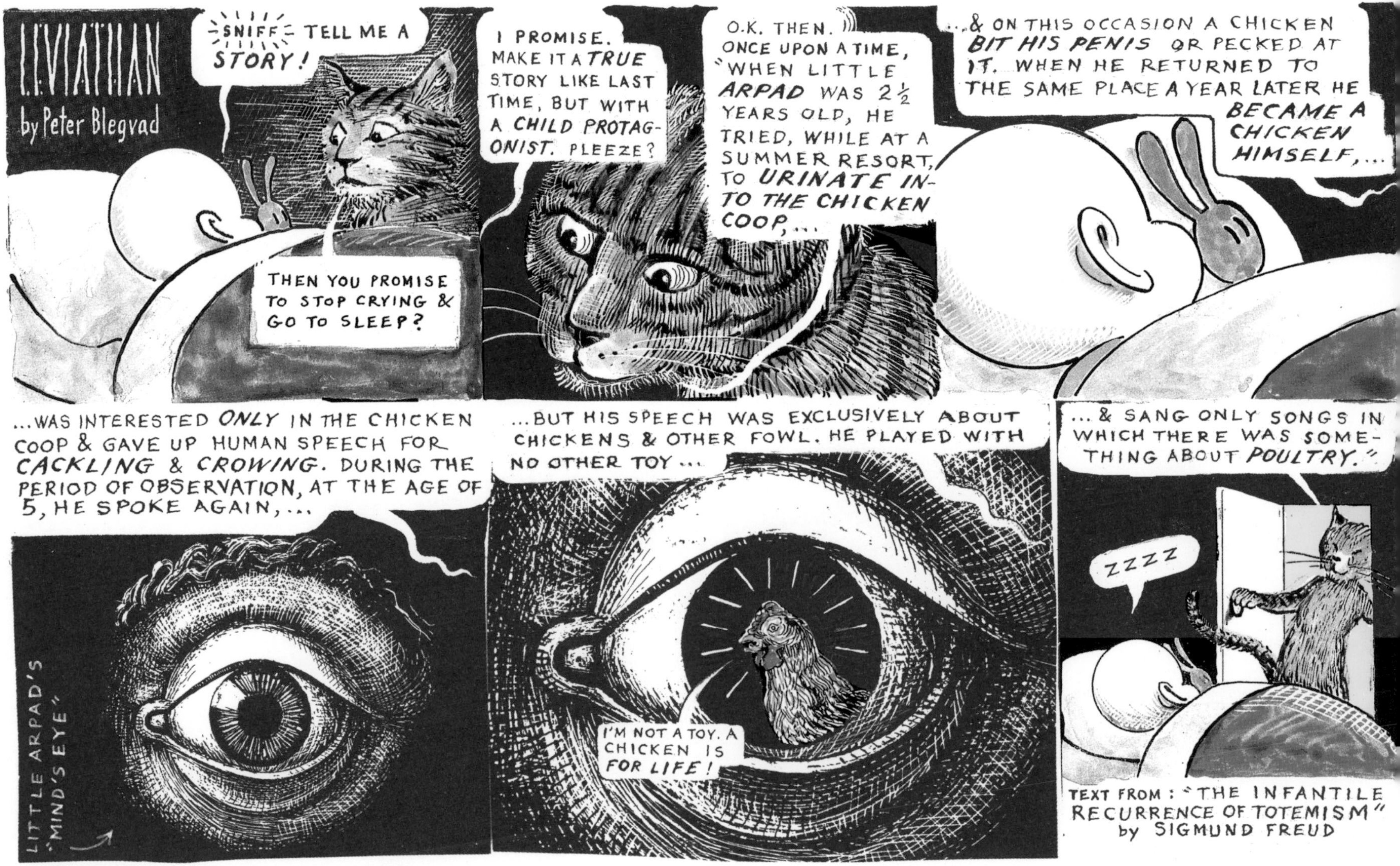

LEVIATHAN
by Peter Blegvad
SNIFF — TELL ME A STORY!
THEN YOU PROMISE TO STOP CRYING & GO TO SLEEP?
I PROMISE. MAKE IT A TRUE STORY LIKE LAST TIME, BUT WITH A CHILD PROTAGONIST. PLEEZE?
O.K. THEN. ONCE UPON A TIME, "WHEN LITTLE ARPAD WAS 2½ YEARS OLD, HE TRIED, WHILE AT A SUMMER RESORT, TO URINATE INTO THE CHICKEN COOP, ...
...& ON THIS OCCASION A CHICKEN BIT HIS PENIS OR PECKED AT IT. WHEN HE RETURNED TO THE SAME PLACE A YEAR LATER HE BECAME A CHICKEN HIMSELF, ...
...WAS INTERESTED ONLY IN THE CHICKEN COOP & GAVE UP HUMAN SPEECH FOR CACKLING & CROWING. DURING THE PERIOD OF OBSERVATION, AT THE AGE OF 5, HE SPOKE AGAIN, ...
LITTLE ARPAD'S "MIND'S EYE"
...BUT HIS SPEECH WAS EXCLUSIVELY ABOUT CHICKENS & OTHER FOWL. HE PLAYED WITH NO OTHER TOY ...
I'M NOT A TOY. A CHICKEN IS FOR LIFE!
...& SANG ONLY SONGS IN WHICH THERE WAS SOMETHING ABOUT POULTRY."
ZZZZ
TEXT FROM: "THE INFANTILE RECURRENCE OF TOTEMISM" by SIGMUND FREUD

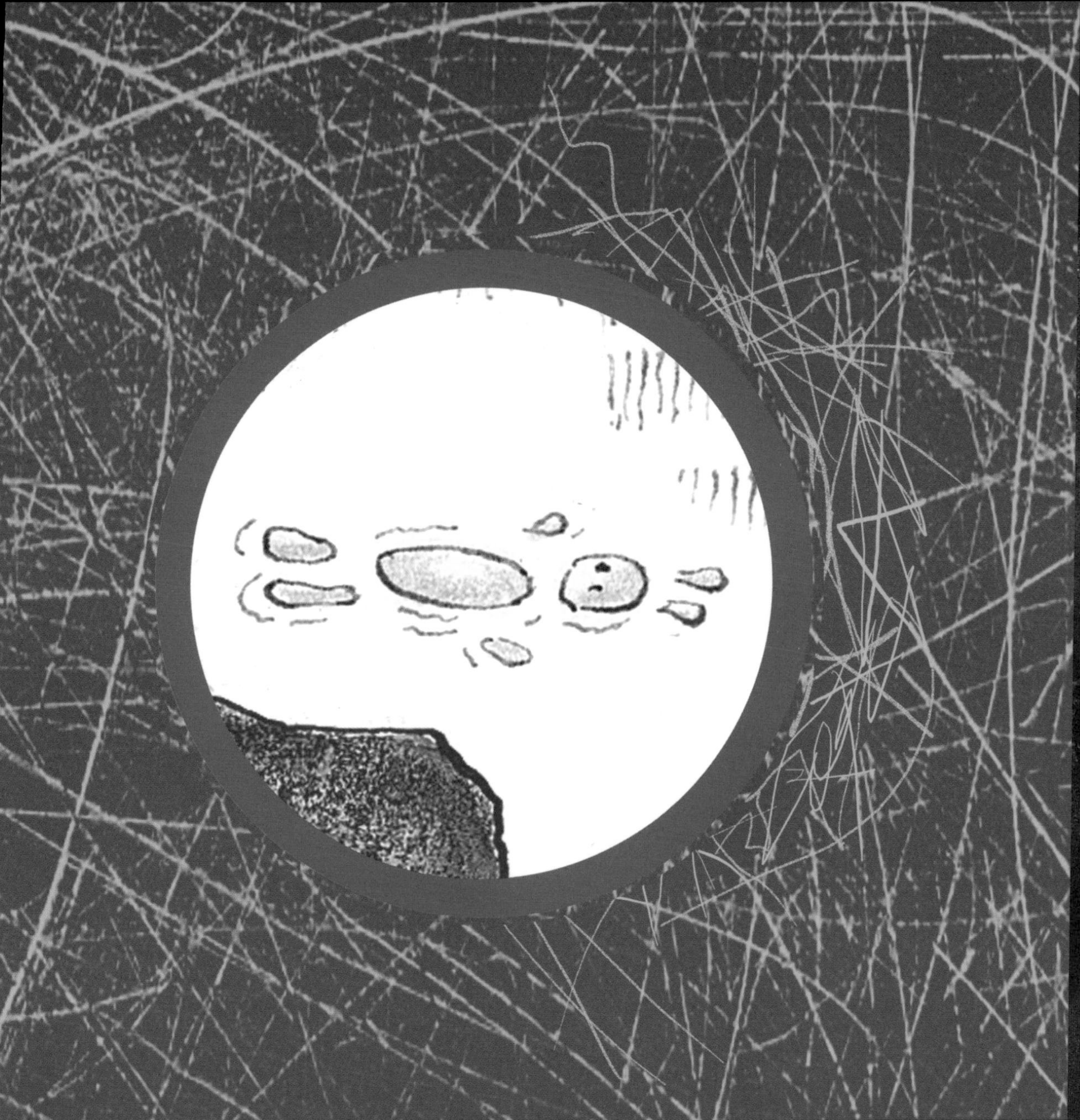

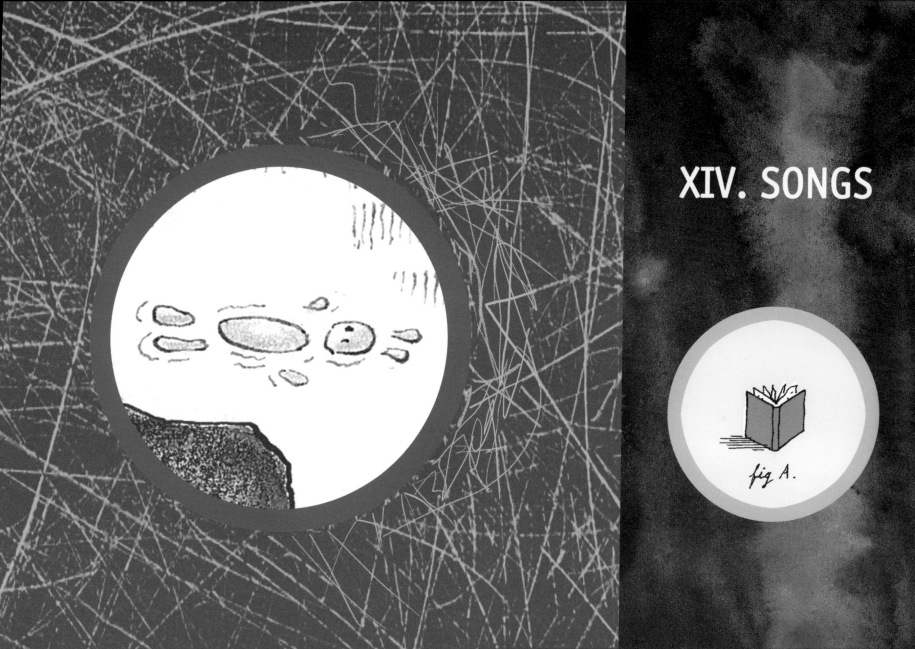

# XIV. SONGS

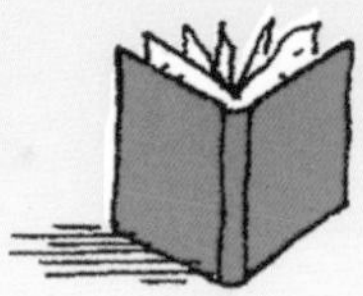

fig A.

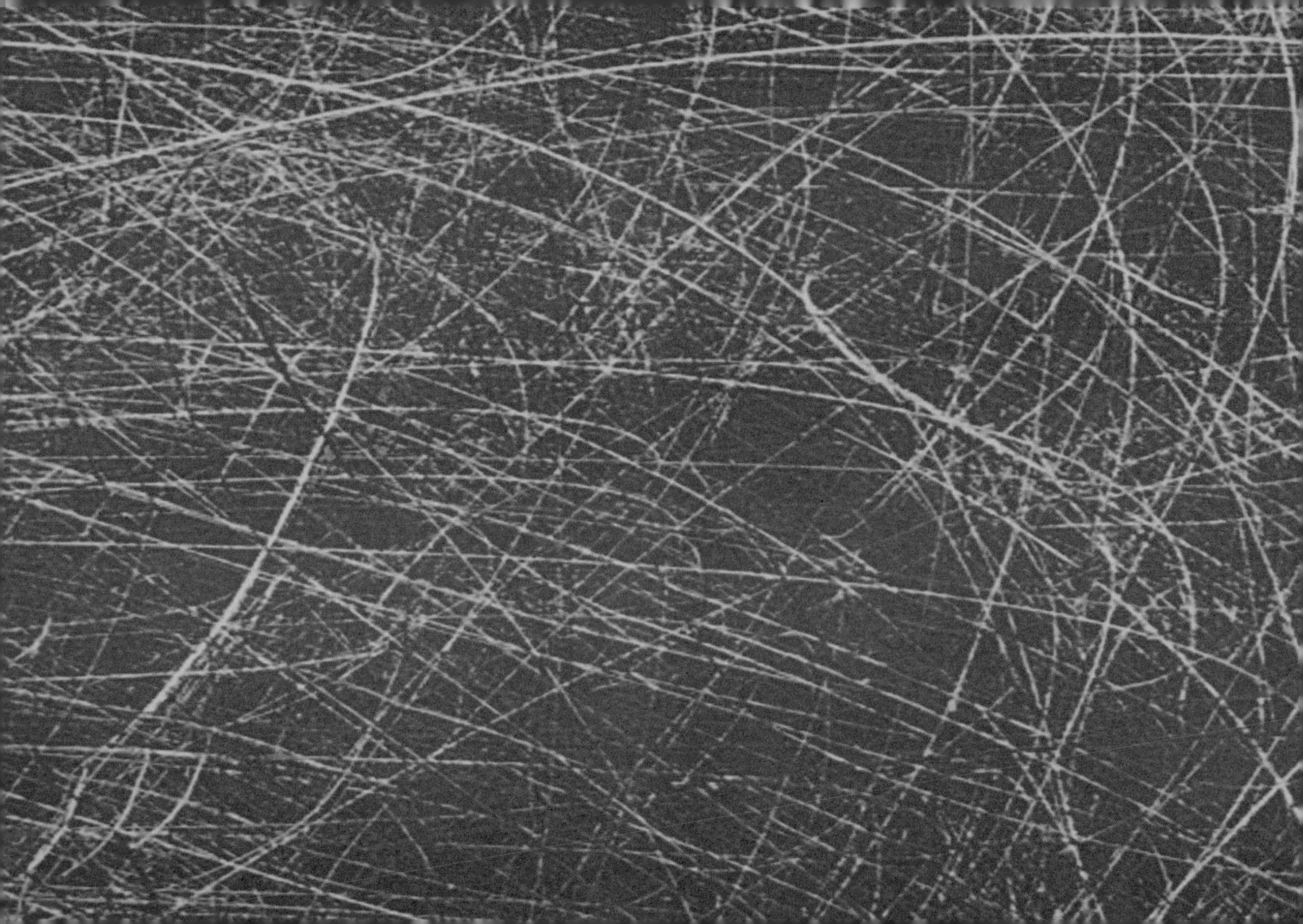

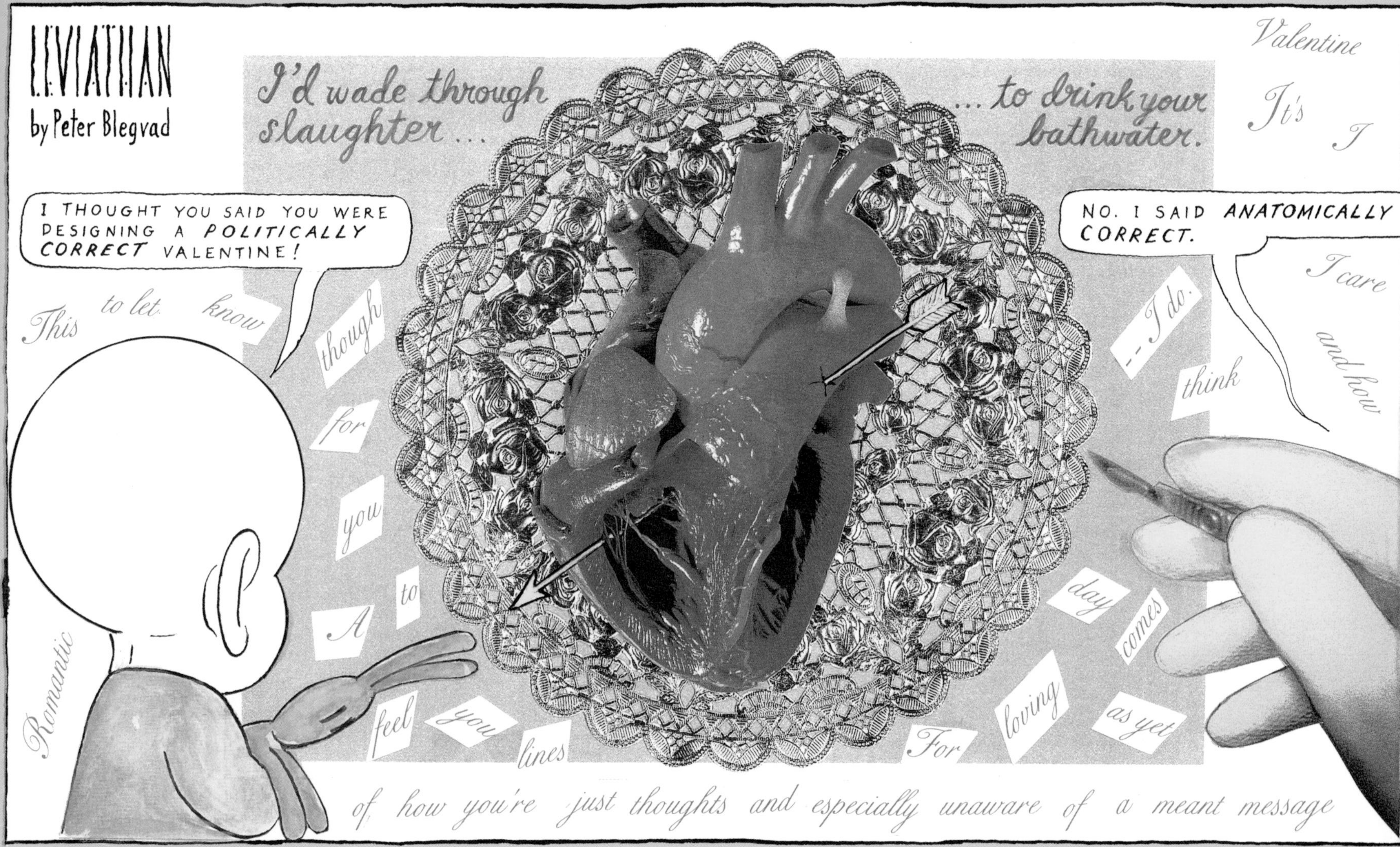
LEVIATHAN
by Peter Blegvad
I'd wade through slaughter...
...to drink your bathwater.
I THOUGHT YOU SAID YOU WERE DESIGNING A POLITICALLY CORRECT VALENTINE!
NO. I SAID ANATOMICALLY CORRECT.
Valentine
It's
I
This
to let
know
though
for
you
A
to
feel
you
lines
--I do.
think
I care
and how
day
comes
loving
as yet
For
Romantic
of how you're just thoughts and especially unaware of a meant message

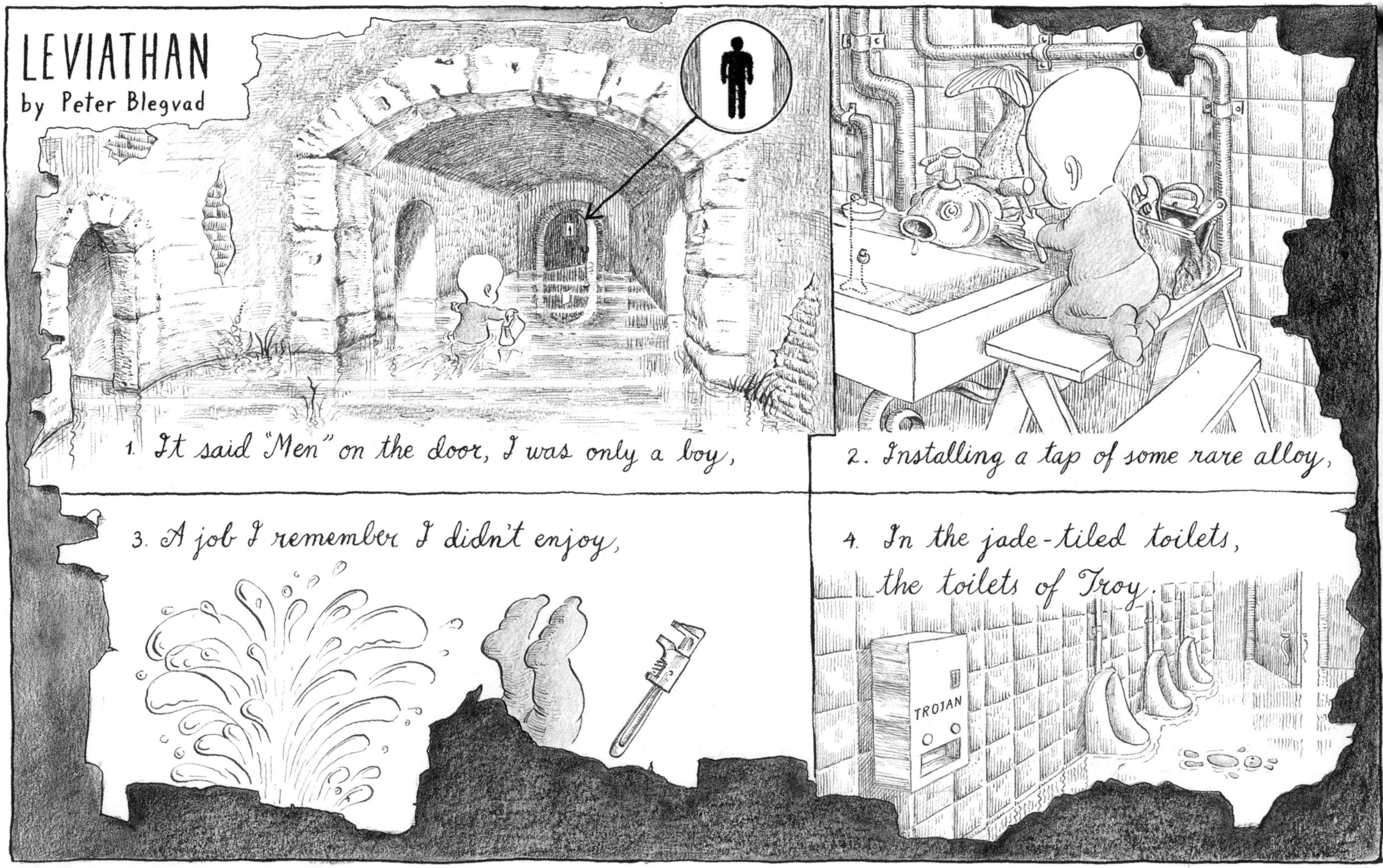
LEVIATHAN
by Peter Blegvad
1. It said "Men" on the door, I was only a boy,
2. Installing a tap of some rare alloy,
3. A job I remember I didn't enjoy,
4. In the jade-tiled toilets,
the toilets of Troy.
TROJAN

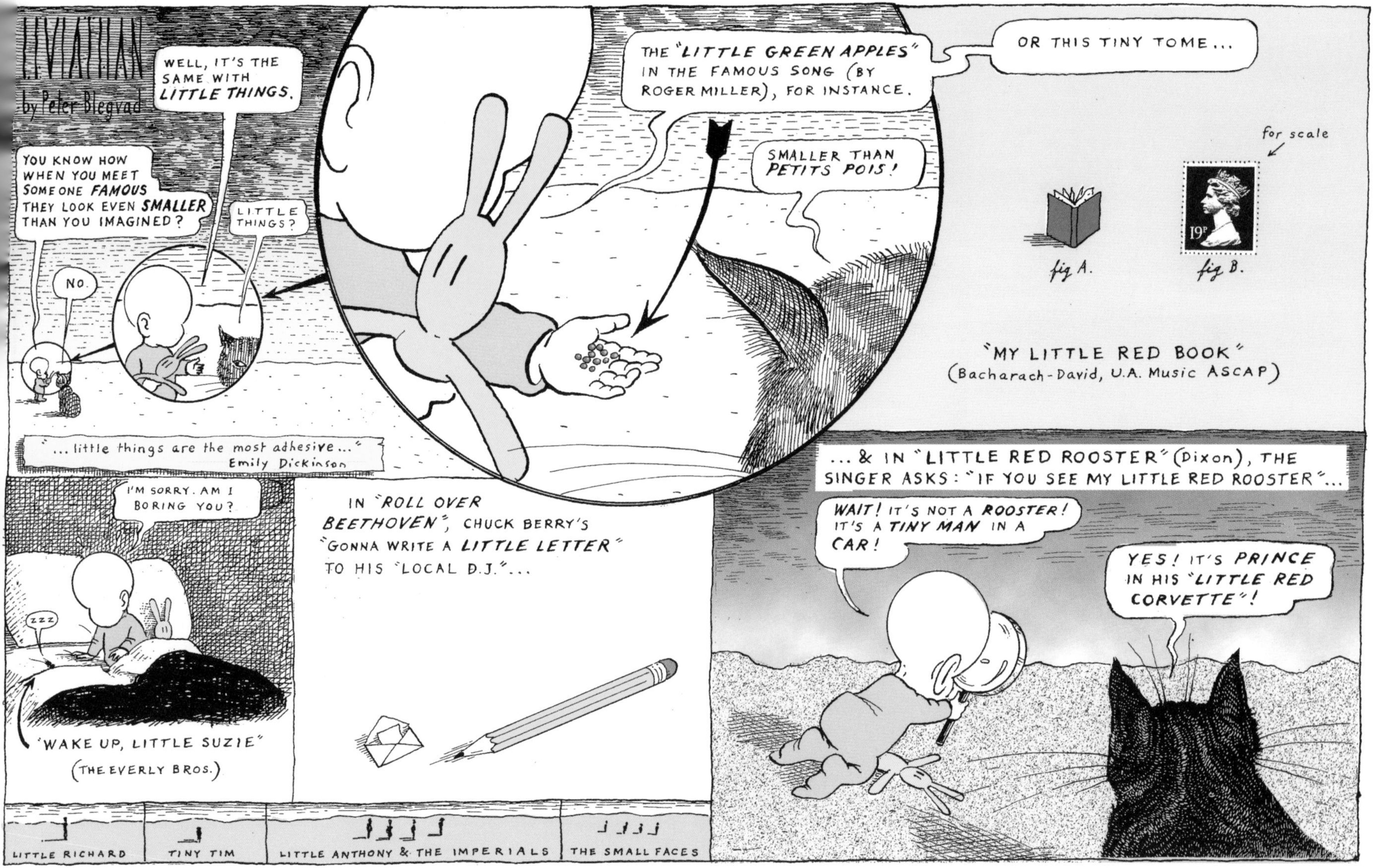

LEVIATHAN
by Peter Blegvad
WELL, IT'S THE SAME WITH LITTLE THINGS.
YOU KNOW HOW WHEN YOU MEET SOME ONE FAMOUS THEY LOOK EVEN SMALLER THAN YOU IMAGINED?
LITTLE THINGS?
NO.
THE "LITTLE GREEN APPLES" IN THE FAMOUS SONG (BY ROGER MILLER), FOR INSTANCE.
SMALLER THAN PETITS POIS!
OR THIS TINY TOME...
for scale
19p
fig A.
fig B.
"MY LITTLE RED BOOK"
(Bacharach-David, U.A. Music ASCAP)
"... little things are the most adhesive..."
Emily Dickinson
I'M SORRY. AM I BORING YOU?
ZZZ
"WAKE UP, LITTLE SUZIE"
(THE EVERLY BROS.)
IN "ROLL OVER BEETHOVEN", CHUCK BERRY'S "GONNA WRITE A LITTLE LETTER" TO HIS "LOCAL D.J."...
... & IN "LITTLE RED ROOSTER" (Dixon), THE SINGER ASKS: "IF YOU SEE MY LITTLE RED ROOSTER"...
WAIT! IT'S NOT A ROOSTER! IT'S A TINY MAN IN A CAR!
YES! IT'S PRINCE IN HIS "LITTLE RED CORVETTE"!
LITTLE RICHARD
TINY TIM
LITTLE ANTHONY & THE IMPERIALS
THE SMALL FACES

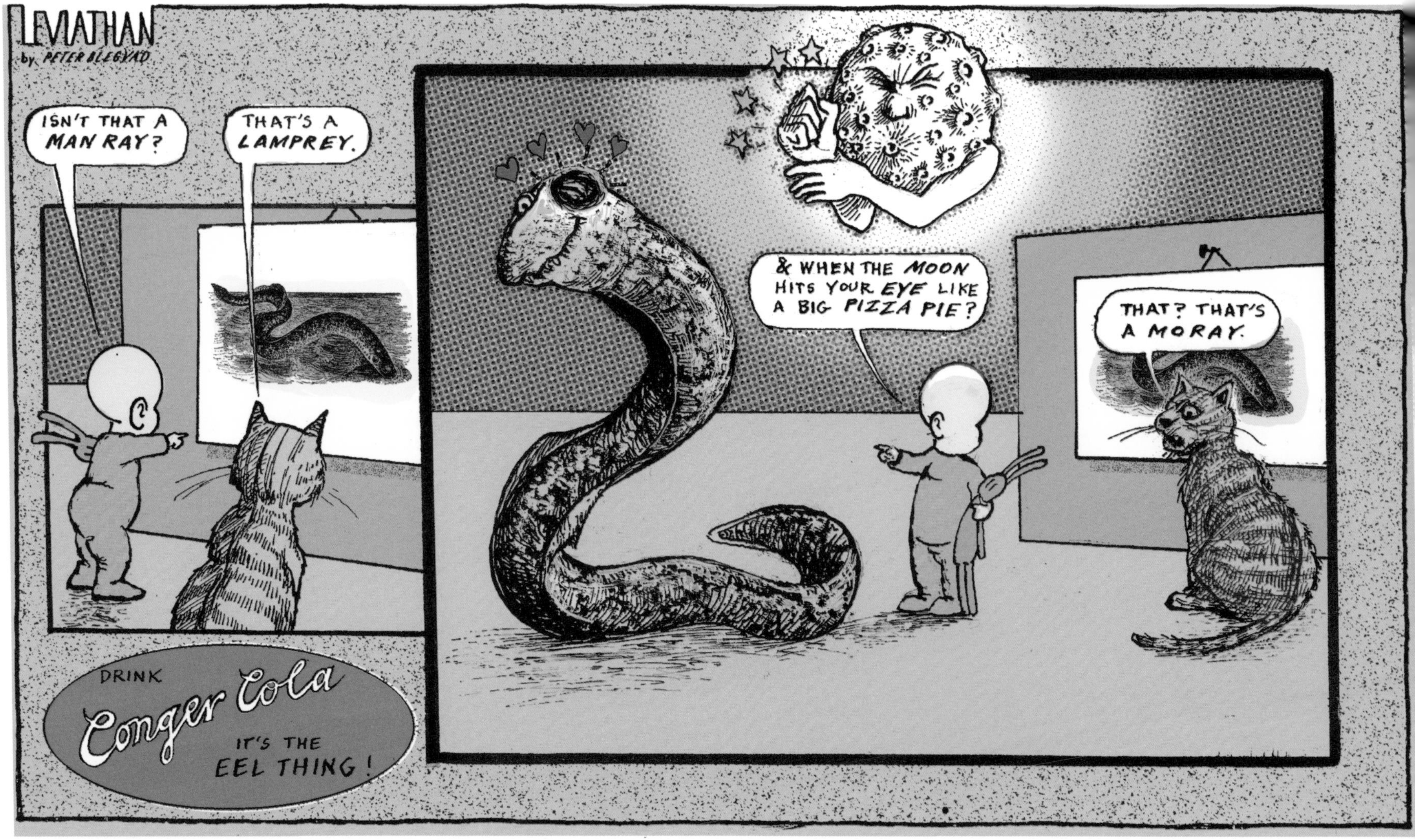
LEVIATHAN
by PETER BLEGVAD
ISN'T THAT A MAN RAY?
THAT'S A LAMPREY.
& WHEN THE MOON HITS YOUR EYE LIKE A BIG PIZZA PIE?
THAT? THAT'S A MORAY.
DRINK Conger Cola IT'S THE EEL THING!

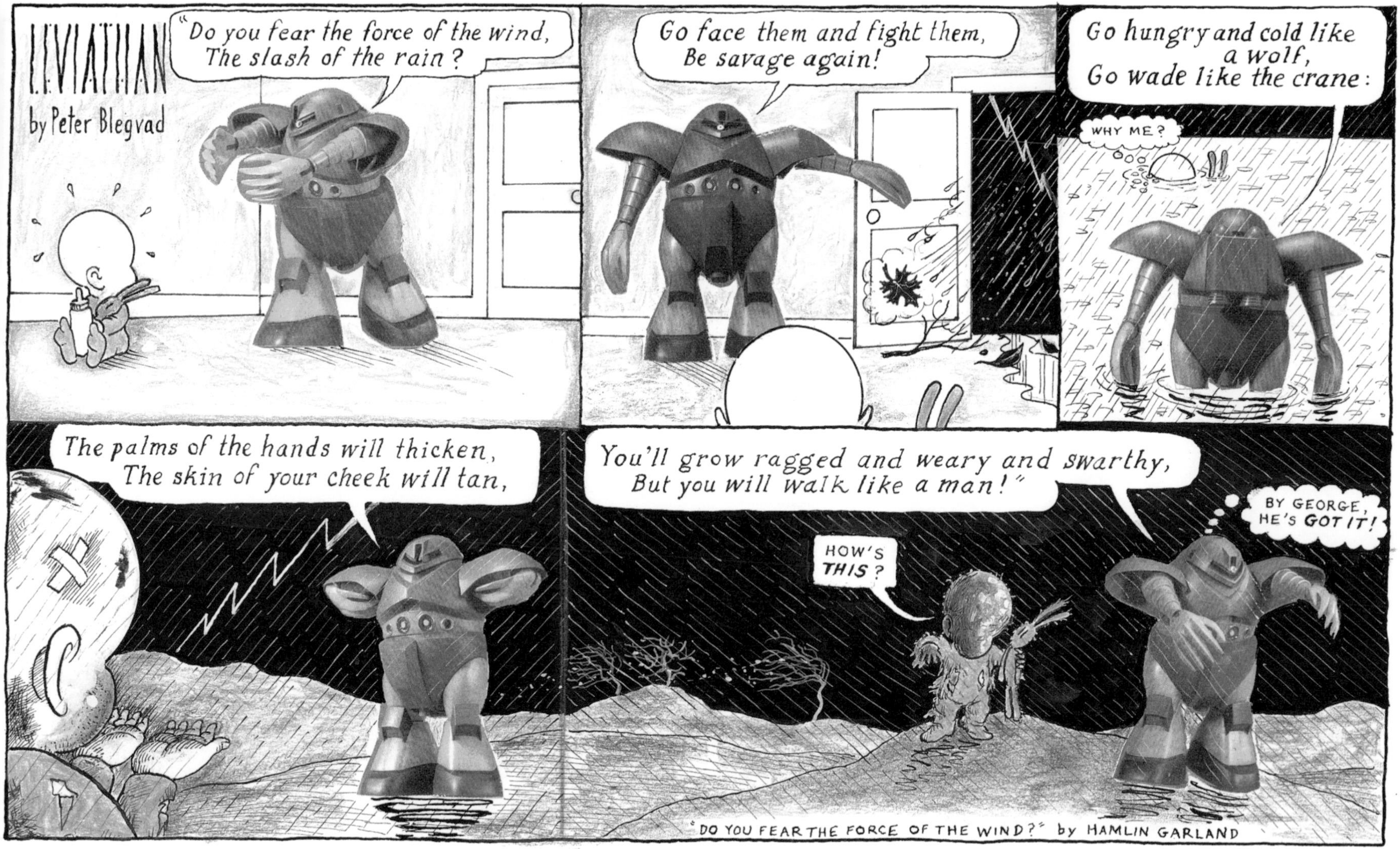
LEVIATHAN
by Peter Blegvad
"Do you fear the force of the wind, The slash of the rain?
Go face them and fight them, Be savage again!
Go hungry and cold like a wolf, Go wade like the crane:
WHY ME?
The palms of the hands will thicken, The skin of your cheek will tan,
You'll grow ragged and weary and swarthy, But you will walk like a man!"
HOW'S THIS?
BY GEORGE, HE'S GOT IT!
"DO YOU FEAR THE FORCE OF THE WIND?" by HAMLIN GARLAND

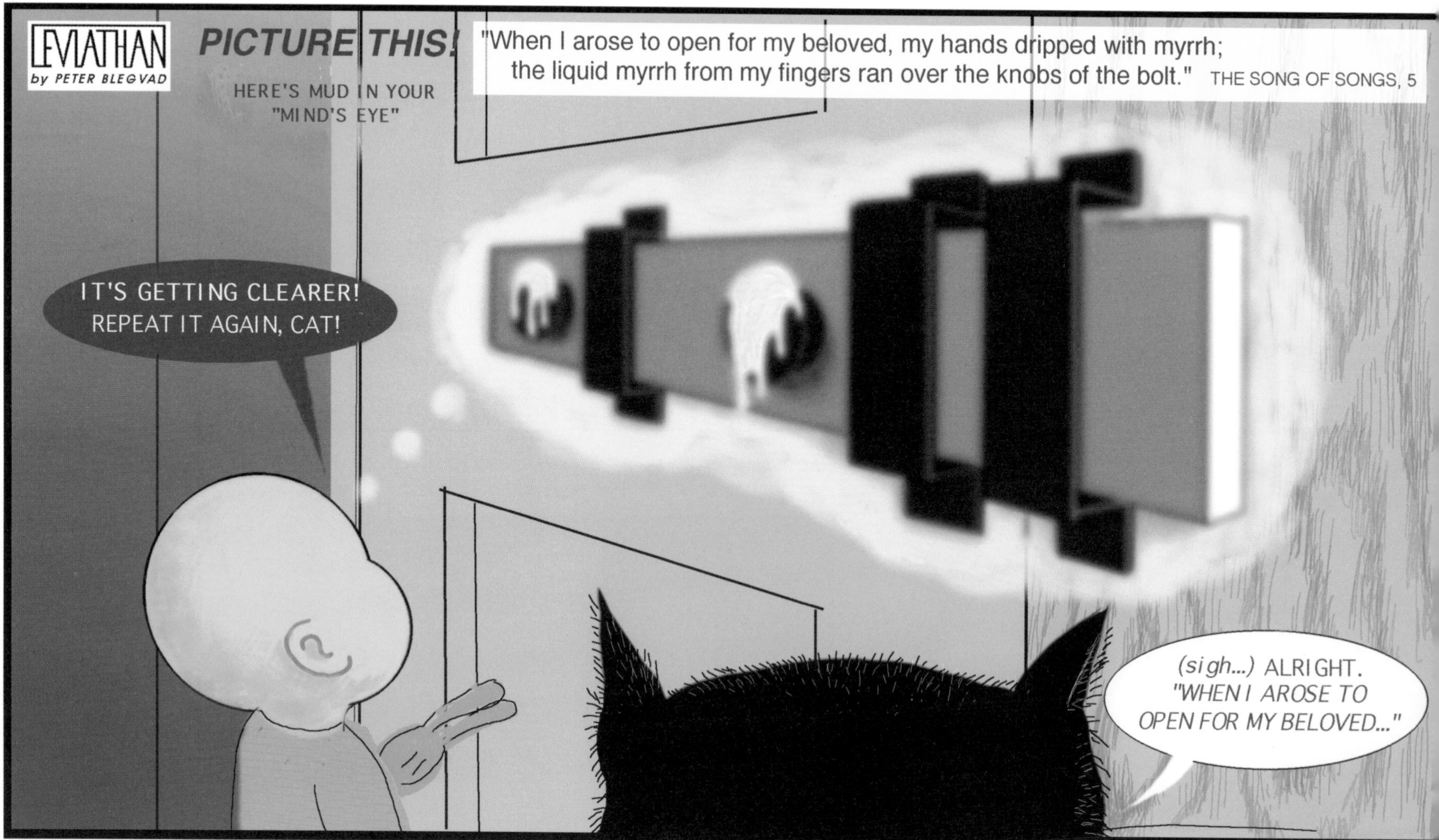
LEVIATHAN
by PETER BLEGVAD
PICTURE THIS!
HERE'S MUD IN YOUR "MIND'S EYE"
"When I arose to open for my beloved, my hands dripped with myrrh; the liquid myrrh from my fingers ran over the knobs of the bolt." THE SONG OF SONGS, 5
IT'S GETTING CLEARER! REPEAT IT AGAIN, CAT!
(sigh...) ALRIGHT. "WHEN I AROSE TO OPEN FOR MY BELOVED..."

# XV. THIS WAY UP

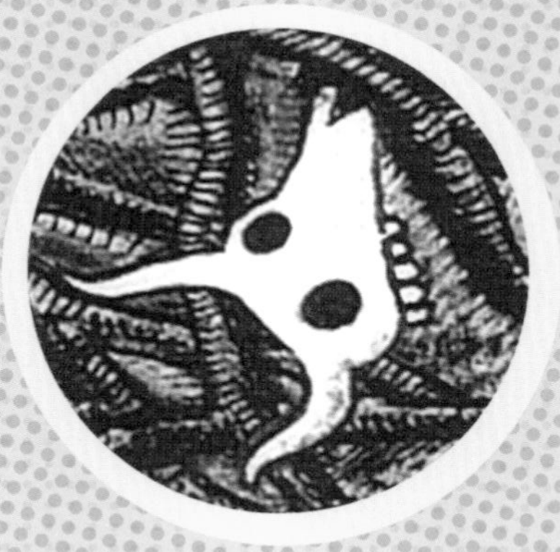

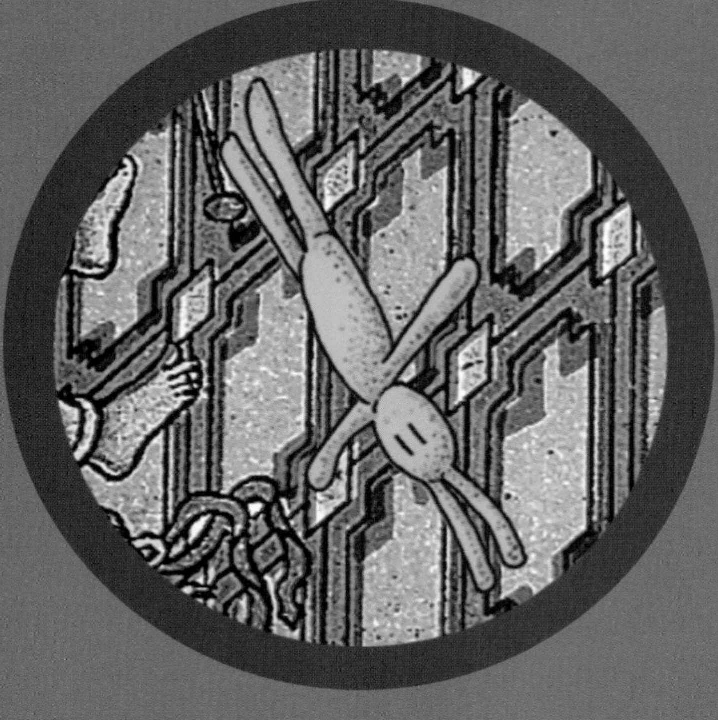

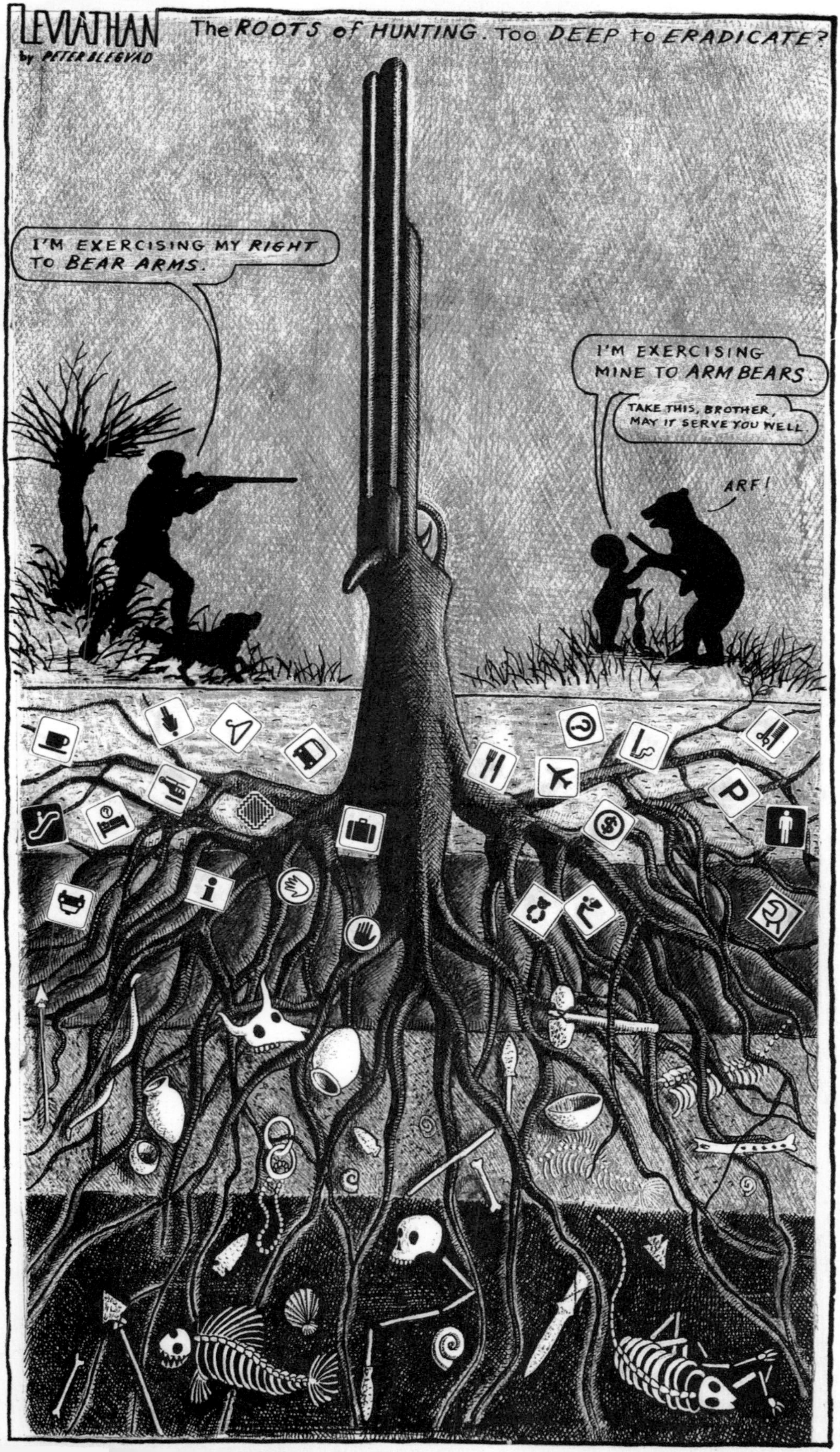
LEVIATHAN
by PETER BLEGVAD
The ROOTS of HUNTING. Too DEEP to ERADICATE?
I'M EXERCISING MY RIGHT TO BEAR ARMS.
I'M EXERCISING MINE TO ARM BEARS.
TAKE THIS, BROTHER, MAY IT SERVE YOU WELL.
ARF!

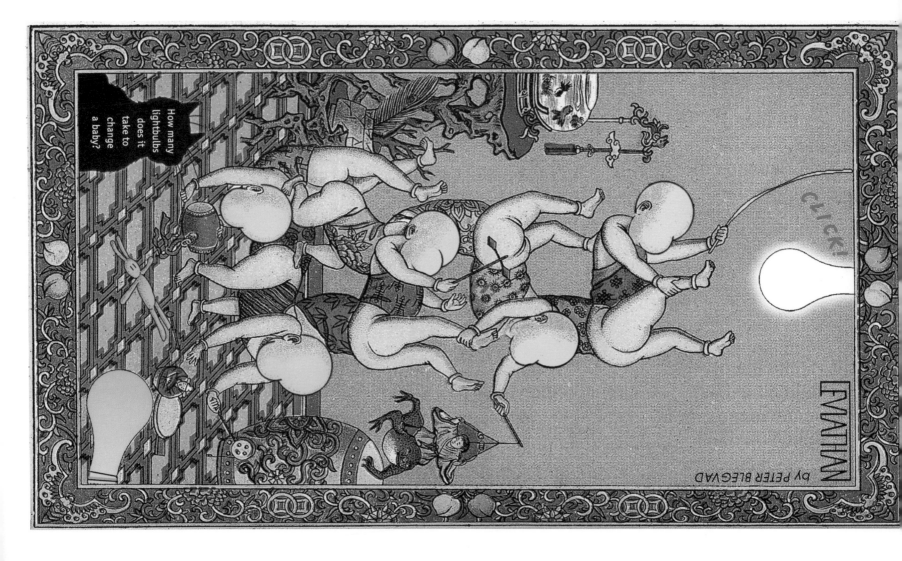

How many lightbulbs does it take to change a baby?

LEVIATHAN

by PETER BLEGVAD

CLICK!

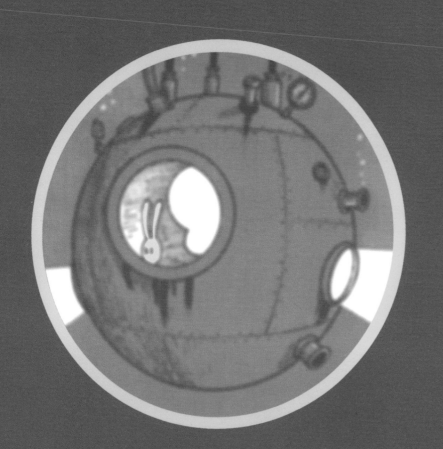

# XVI. A PROBLEM AIRED

LEVIATHAN
BY PETER BLEGVAD
TUNNEL OR MINE?
BOTH.
FROM THIS TUNNEL-MINE ...
... MAN HACKS THE MINERAL HE MAKES...
...BLINKERS OF.
WOW! WITH THESE ON MY TUNNEL-VISION IS 20/20!
A REAL LOOKER (& A SEER)
SO MUCH FOR MAN. & WOMAN?
SHE TENDS TO TAKE THE BROAD VIEW.

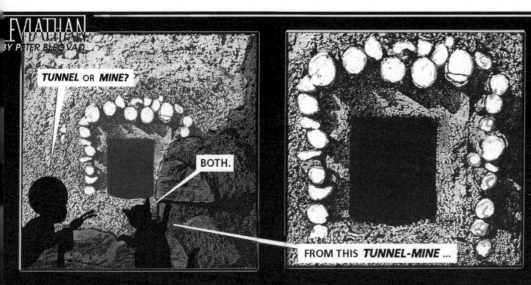

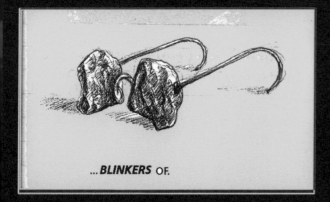

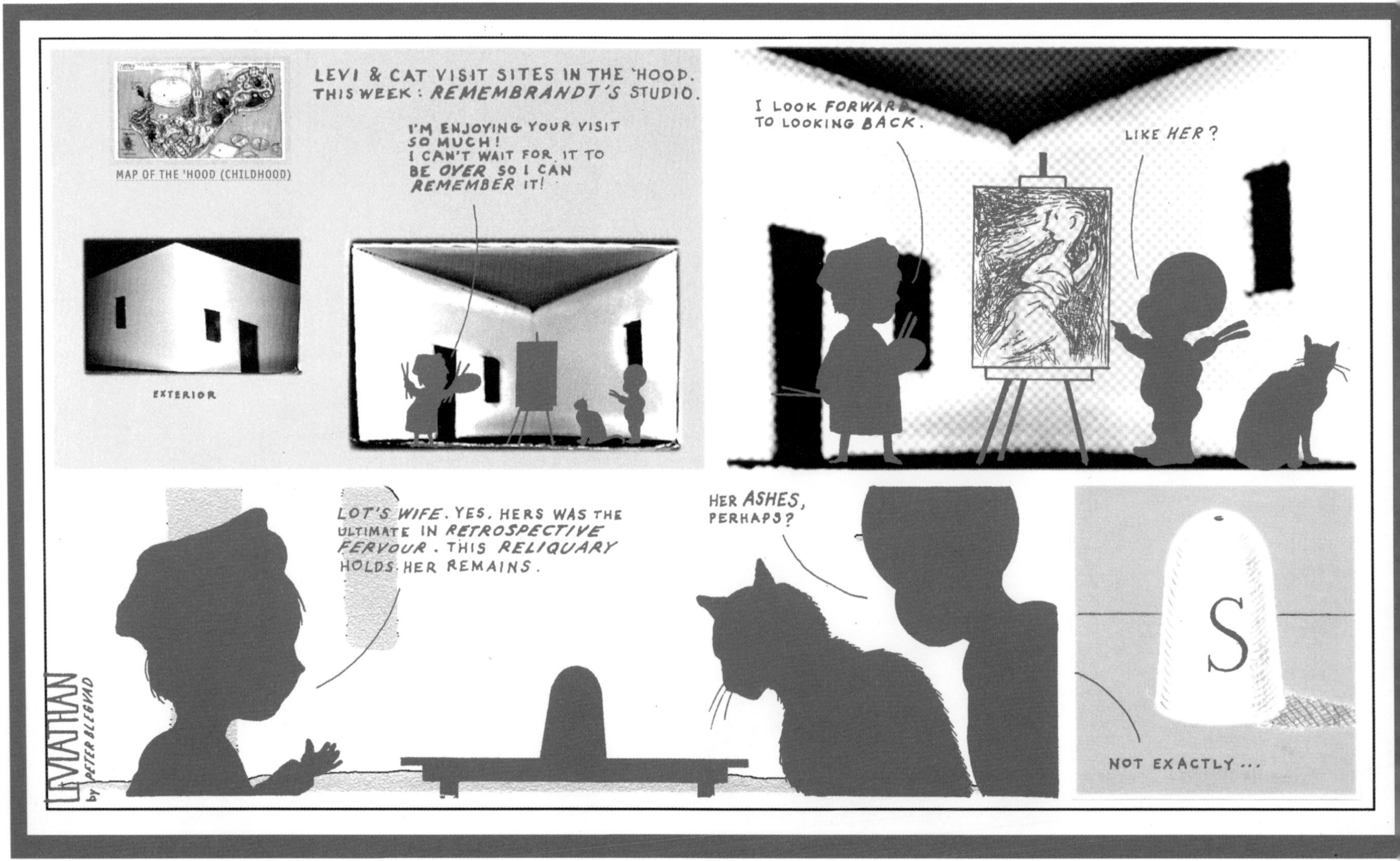

MAP OF THE 'HOOD (CHILDHOOD)
LEVI & CAT VISIT SITES IN THE 'HOOD. THIS WEEK: REMEMBRANDT'S STUDIO.
EXTERIOR
I'M ENJOYING YOUR VISIT SO MUCH! I CAN'T WAIT FOR IT TO BE OVER SO I CAN REMEMBER IT!
I LOOK FORWARD TO LOOKING BACK.
LIKE HER?
LOT'S WIFE. YES. HERS WAS THE ULTIMATE IN RETROSPECTIVE FERVOUR. THIS RELIQUARY HOLDS HER REMAINS.
HER ASHES, PERHAPS?
S
NOT EXACTLY...
LEVIATHAN by PETER BLEGVAD

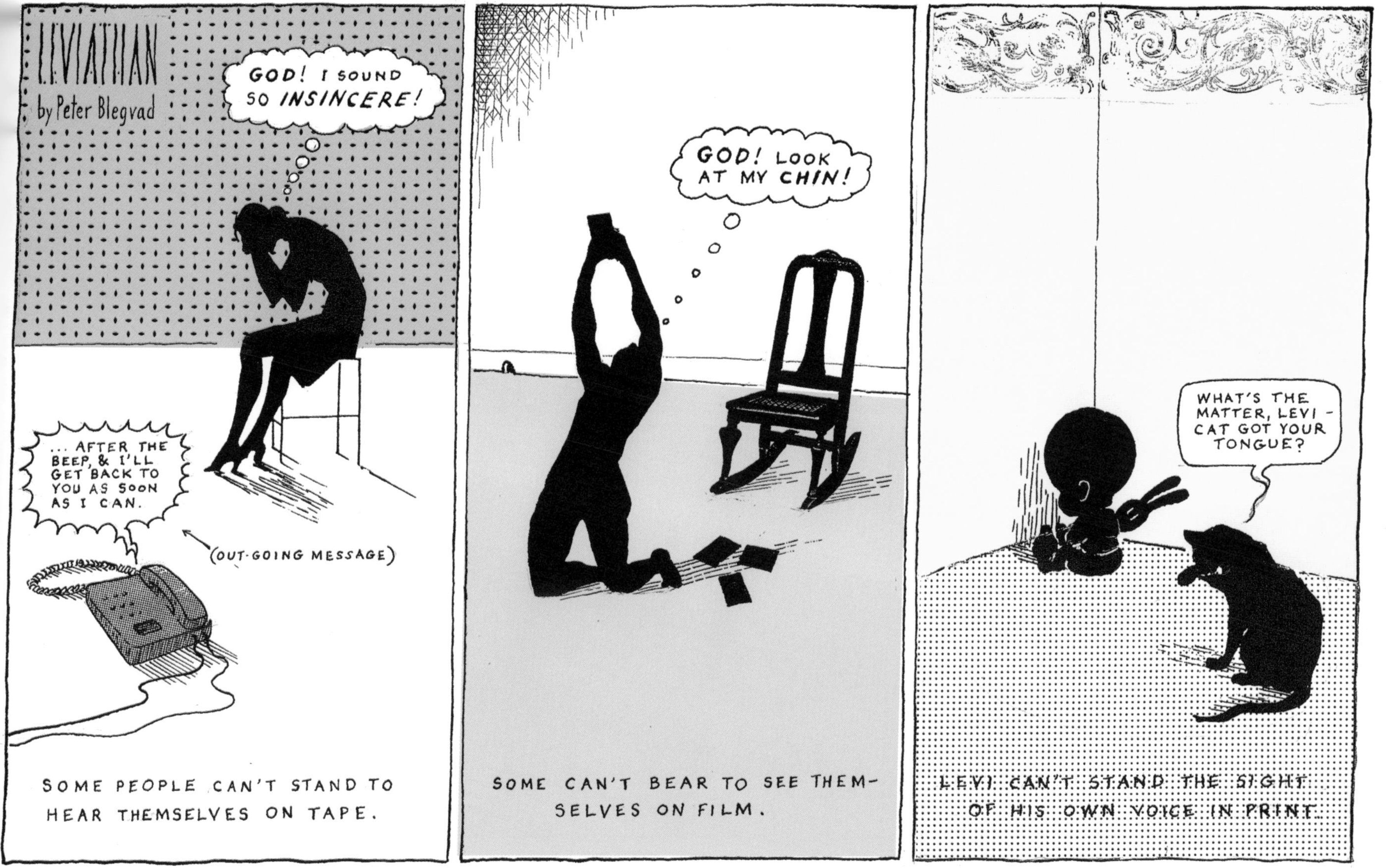
LEVIATHAN
by Peter Blegvad
GOD! I SOUND SO INSINCERE!
... AFTER THE BEEP, & I'LL GET BACK TO YOU AS SOON AS I CAN.
(OUT-GOING MESSAGE)
SOME PEOPLE CAN'T STAND TO HEAR THEMSELVES ON TAPE.
GOD! LOOK AT MY CHIN!
SOME CAN'T BEAR TO SEE THEM-SELVES ON FILM.
WHAT'S THE MATTER, LEVI - CAT GOT YOUR TONGUE?
LEVI CAN'T STAND THE SIGHT OF HIS OWN VOICE IN PRINT.

# LEVIATHAN

## by Peter Blegvad

Q: WHAT DEFINES "CHARACTER"?

A: THE CHOICES A PERSON MAKES UNDER PRESSURE.

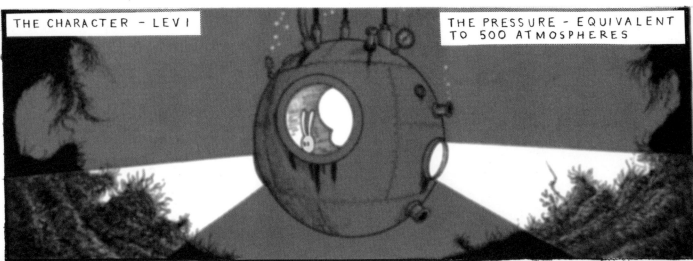

THE CHARACTER – LEVI

THE PRESSURE – EQUIVALENT TO 500 ATMOSPHERES

## THE CHOICES

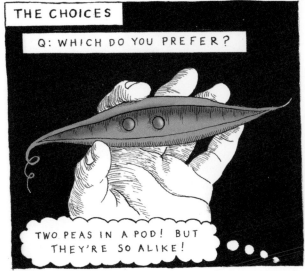

Q: WHICH DO YOU PREFER?

TWO PEAS IN A POD! BUT THEY'RE SO ALIKE!

Q: WHICH WOULD YOU SAVE FROM A BURNING BUILDING?

*a.*

*b.*

CHALK & CHEESE! BUT THEY'RE SO DIFFERENT!

WITH HIS OXYGEN RUNNING OUT, KNOWING HIS DECISIONS, ONCE MADE, WILL BE IRREVOCABLE, LEVI INVOKES A HIGHER POWER TO ENLIGHTEN HIS JUDGEMENT.

EENIE MEENIE MINIE MO...

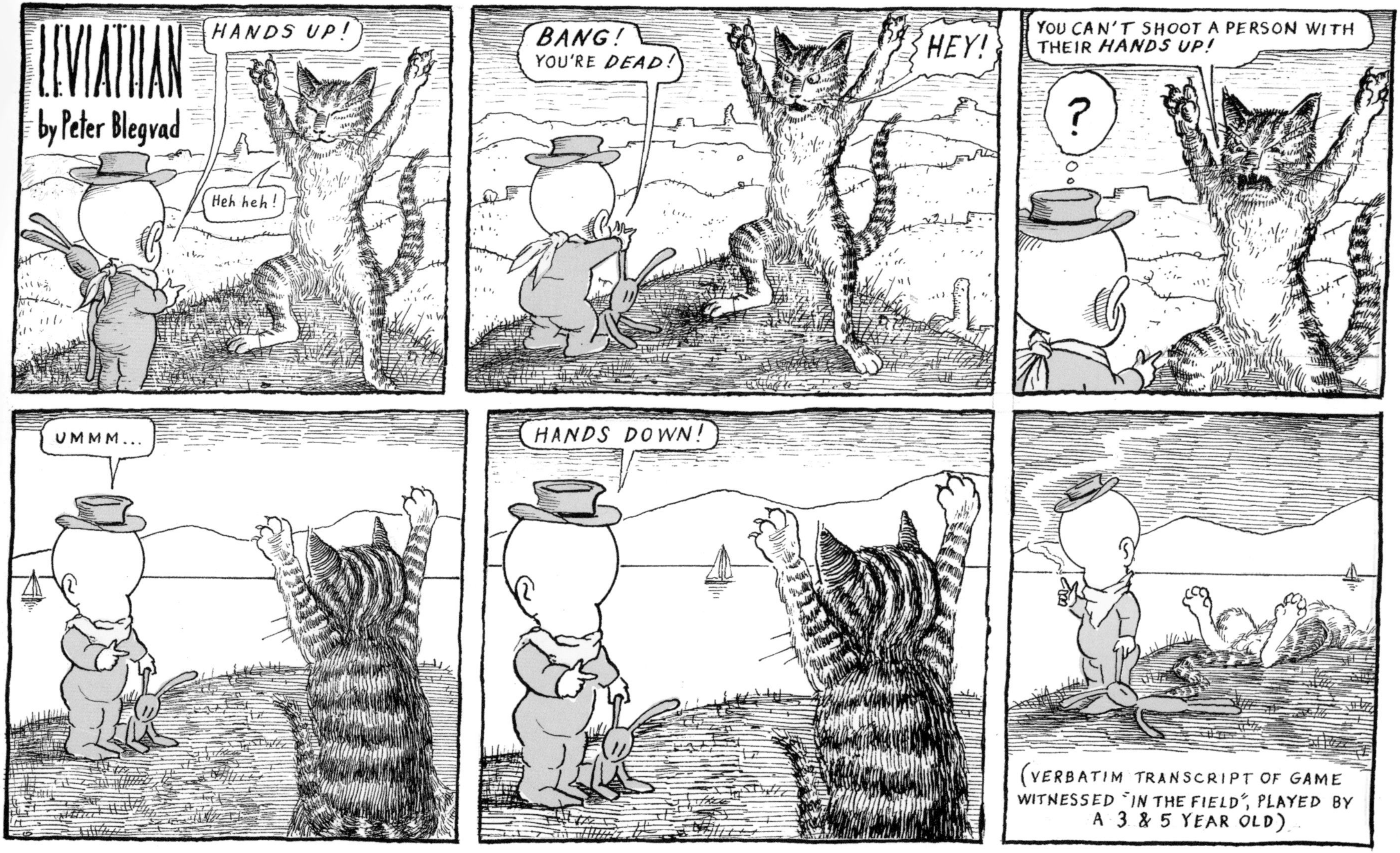
LEVIATHAN
by Peter Blegvad
HANDS UP!
Heh heh!
BANG! YOU'RE DEAD!
HEY!
YOU CAN'T SHOOT A PERSON WITH THEIR HANDS UP!
?
UMMM...
HANDS DOWN!
(VERBATIM TRANSCRIPT OF GAME WITNESSED "IN THE FIELD", PLAYED BY A 3 & 5 YEAR OLD)

# LEVIATHAN
## by PETER BLEGVAD

ERWIN SCHRÖDINGER, NOBEL-PRIZEWINNING PHYCISIST, PROPOSES AN *EXPERIMENT* TO ILLUSTRATE THE *PECULIAR* THEORY THAT AN *ATOM* CAN OCCUPY *2 STATES* AT THE *SAME TIME!* (ALTHOUGH ANY ATTEMPT TO *OBSERVE* IT WILL FORCE THE ATOM TO ADOPT *ONE* STATE OR THE *OTHER!*)

(AHEM!) *LADIES & GENTLEMEN!* I PROPOSE THAT WE SHUT AN *IMAGINARY CAT* IN A BOX WITH A *CANNISTER* OF *CYANIDE* TRIGGERED TO *OPEN* BY THE *DECAY* OF A *RADIOACTIVE ATOM.*

HE'S BEHIND THIS STONE.

!

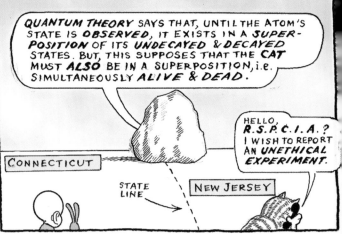

*QUANTUM THEORY* SAYS THAT, UNTIL THE ATOM'S STATE IS *OBSERVED*, IT EXISTS IN A *SUPERPOSITION* OF ITS *UNDECAYED & DECAYED* STATES. BUT, THIS SUPPOSES THAT THE *CAT* MUST *ALSO* BE IN A *SUPERPOSITION*, i.e. SIMULTANEOUSLY *ALIVE & DEAD.*

CONNECTICUT

STATE LINE

NEW JERSEY

HELLO, *R.S.P.C.I.A.?* I WISH TO REPORT AN *UNETHICAL EXPERIMENT.*

I USE THIS *PARADOX* TO ILLUSTRATE THE *DIFFICULTY* OF CONNECTING *QUANTUM MECHANICS...*

AHH, *GOOD!* I *THOUGHT* SO, BUT I WANTED TO BE *SURE.* THANK YOU! GOOD BYE.

...WITH THE LAWS OF *CLASSICAL PHYS...* * HEY! GET *BACK! NO! NICE* KITTY... *HELP! AUGGGHHH!!!*

SHOULDN'T WE LEND A *HAND?*

THE *R.S.P.C.I.A.* ASSURED ME THERE'S NO NEED...

* TEXT ADAPTED FROM MARK WARD'S ARTICLE IN *NEW SCIENTIST*, JUNE 1, 1996

I PUT THE *BOFFIN* IN HIS *COFFIN!*

THE CAT IN THE HAT

THE *REAL* IS NO MATCH FOR THE *IMAGINARY.*

ReSPeCt Imaginary Animals!

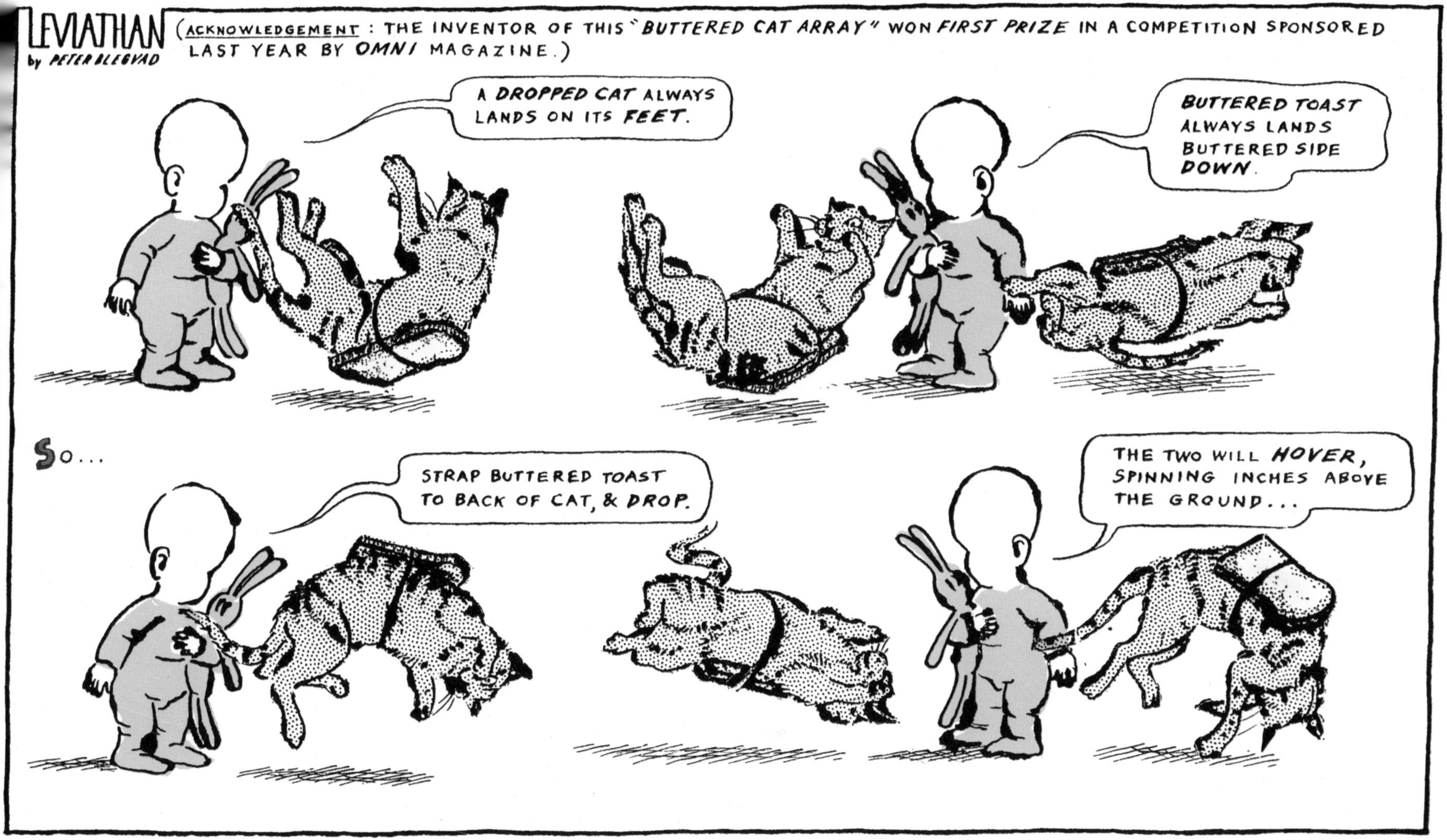
LEVIATHAN
by PETER BLEGVAD
(ACKNOWLEDGEMENT : THE INVENTOR OF THIS "BUTTERED CAT ARRAY" WON FIRST PRIZE IN A COMPETITION SPONSORED LAST YEAR BY OMNI MAGAZINE.)
A DROPPED CAT ALWAYS LANDS ON ITS FEET.
BUTTERED TOAST ALWAYS LANDS BUTTERED SIDE DOWN.
SO...
STRAP BUTTERED TOAST TO BACK OF CAT, & DROP.
THE TWO WILL HOVER, SPINNING INCHES ABOVE THE GROUND...

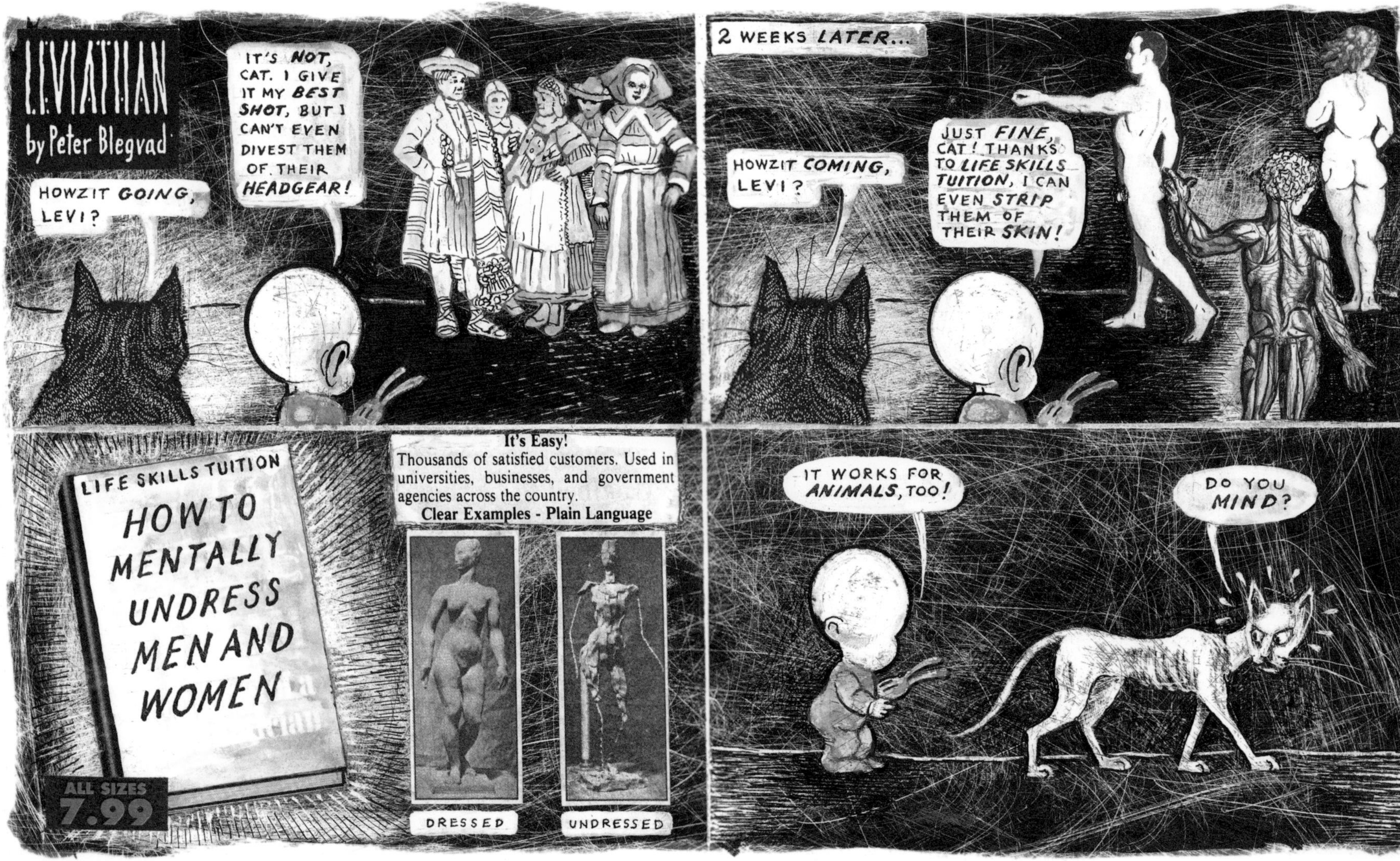
LEVIATHAN
by Peter Blegvad
HOWZIT GOING, LEVI?
IT'S NOT, CAT. I GIVE IT MY BEST SHOT, BUT I CAN'T EVEN DIVEST THEM OF THEIR HEADGEAR!
2 WEEKS LATER...
HOWZIT COMING, LEVI?
JUST FINE, CAT! THANKS TO LIFE SKILLS TUITION, I CAN EVEN STRIP THEM OF THEIR SKIN!
LIFE SKILLS TUITION
HOW TO MENTALLY UNDRESS MEN AND WOMEN
ALL SIZES 7.99
It's Easy!
Thousands of satisfied customers. Used in universities, businesses, and government agencies across the country.
Clear Examples - Plain Language
DRESSED
UNDRESSED
IT WORKS FOR ANIMALS, TOO!
DO YOU MIND?

# XVII. THE TRUCK IS STUCK

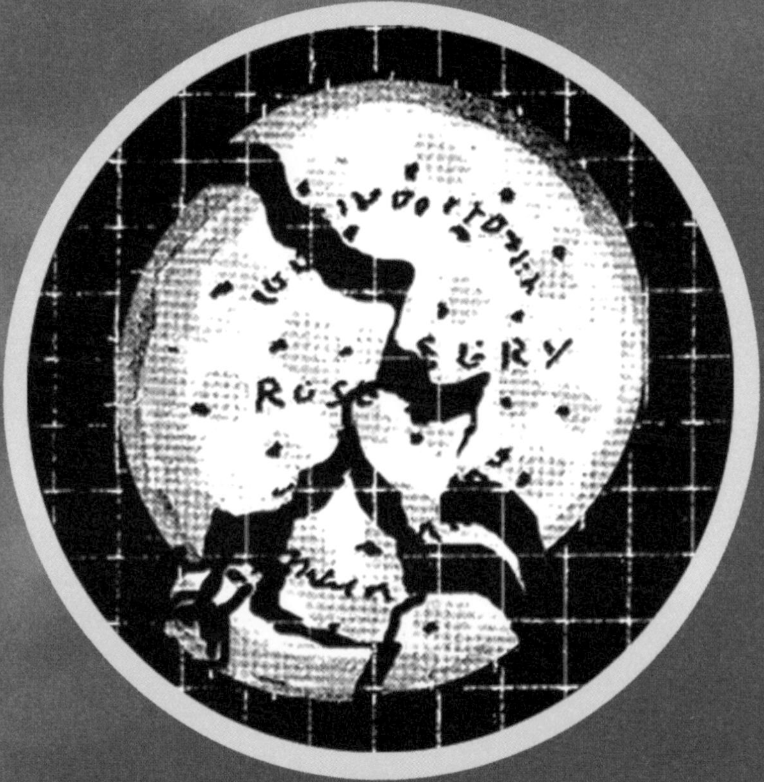

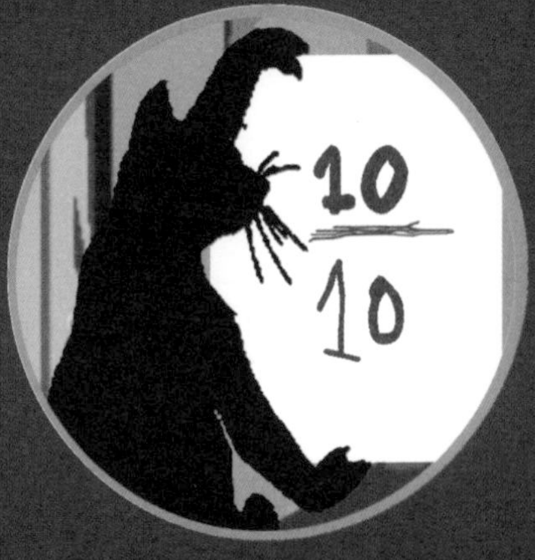
10
10

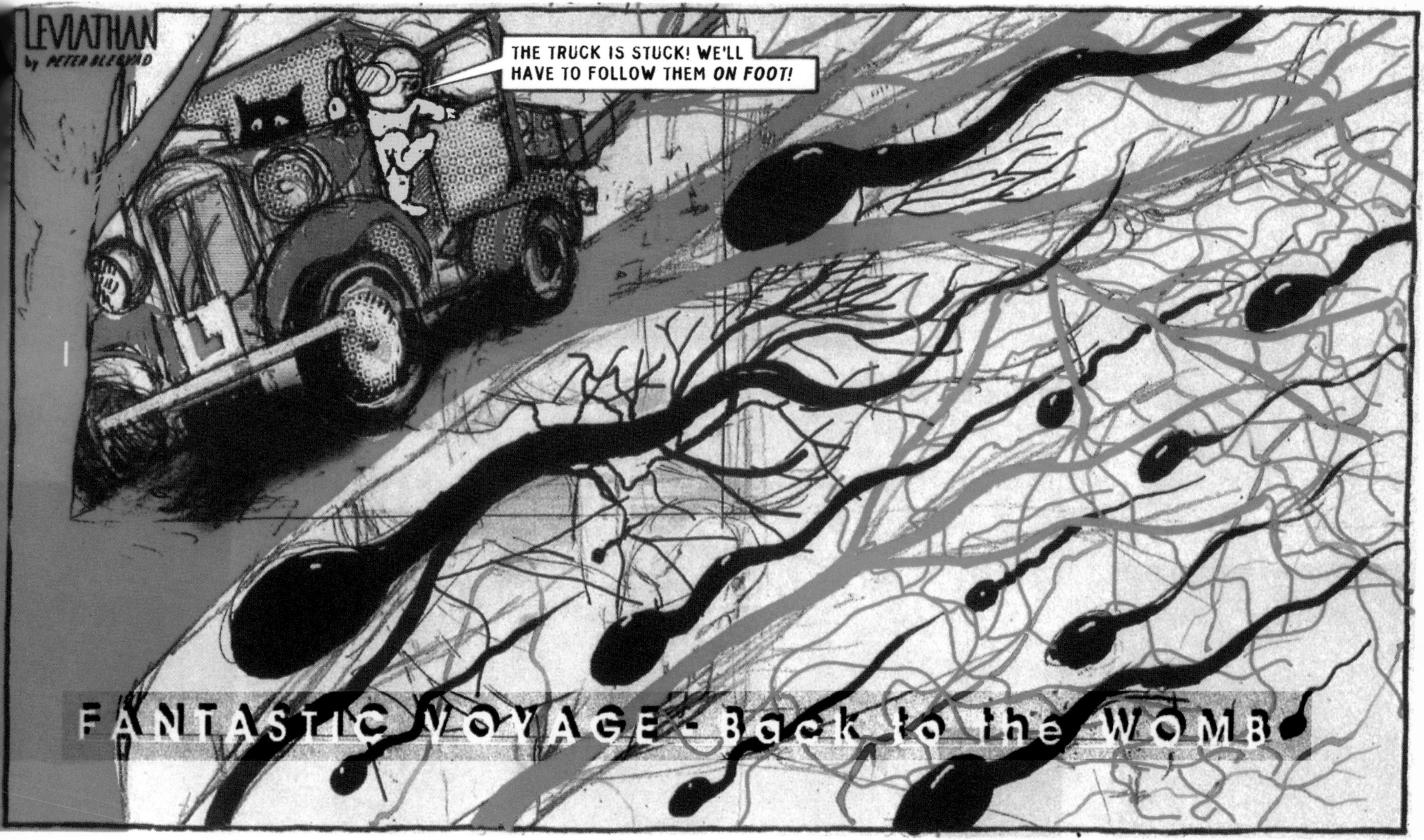
LEVIATHAN
by PETER BLEGVAD
THE TRUCK IS STUCK! WE'LL HAVE TO FOLLOW THEM ON FOOT!
FANTASTIC VOYAGE - Back to the WOMB

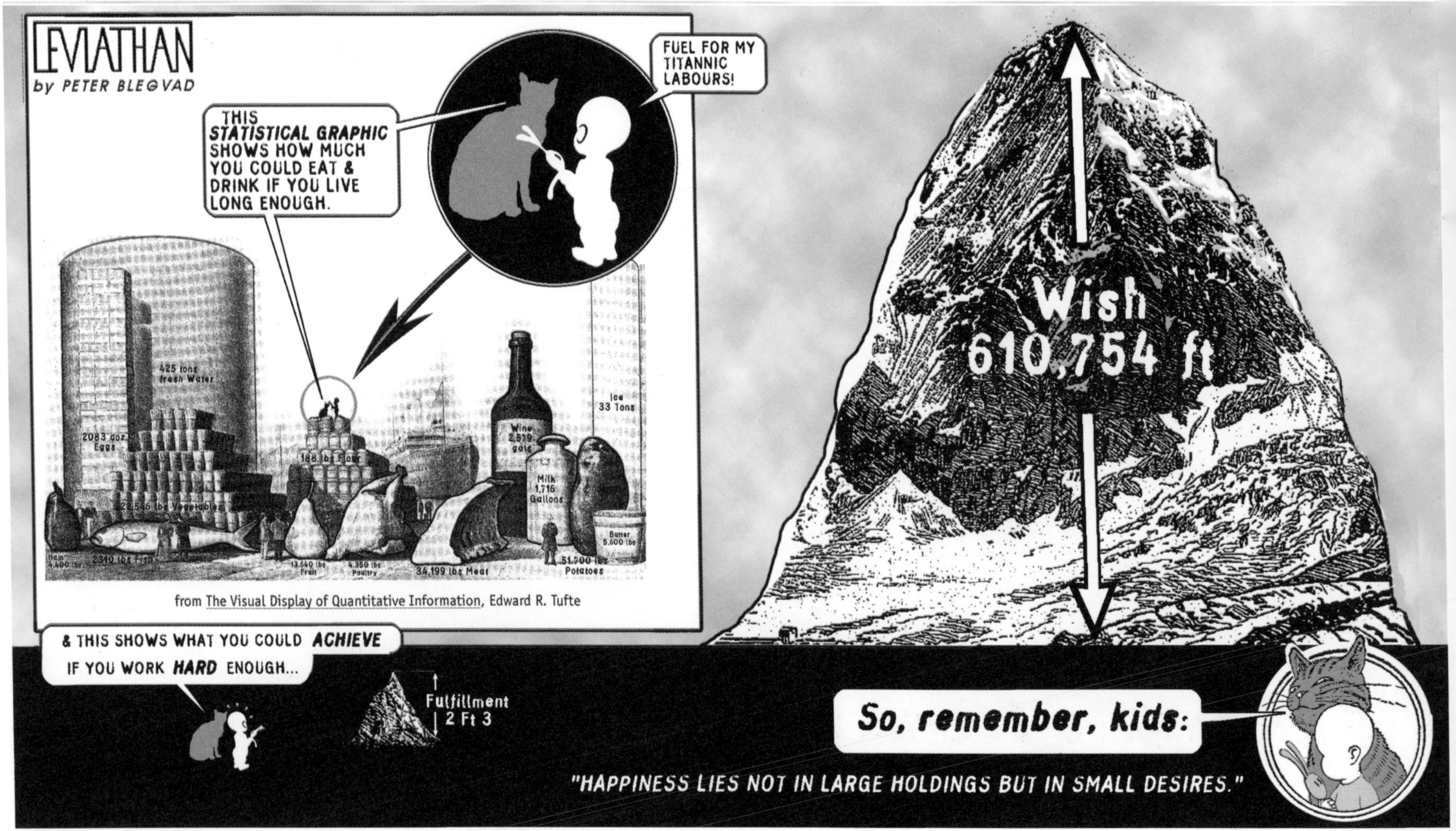
LEVIATHAN
by PETER BLEGVAD
THIS STATISTICAL GRAPHIC SHOWS HOW MUCH YOU COULD EAT & DRINK IF YOU LIVE LONG ENOUGH.
FUEL FOR MY TITANNIC LABOURS!
425 tons fresh Water
2083 doz. Eggs
188 lbs Flour
22,546 lbs Vegetables
Ham 4,400 lbs.
2310 lbs Fish
13,640 lbs Fruit
4,350 lbs Poultry
34,199 lbs Meat
Wine 2,579 gals
Milk 1,716 Gallons
Ice 33 Tons
Butter 5,600 lbs
51,700 lbs Potatoes
from The Visual Display of Quantitative Information, Edward R. Tufte
& THIS SHOWS WHAT YOU COULD ACHIEVE IF YOU WORK HARD ENOUGH...
Wish 610,754 ft
Fulfillment 2 Ft 3
So, remember, kids:
"HAPPINESS LIES NOT IN LARGE HOLDINGS BUT IN SMALL DESIRES."

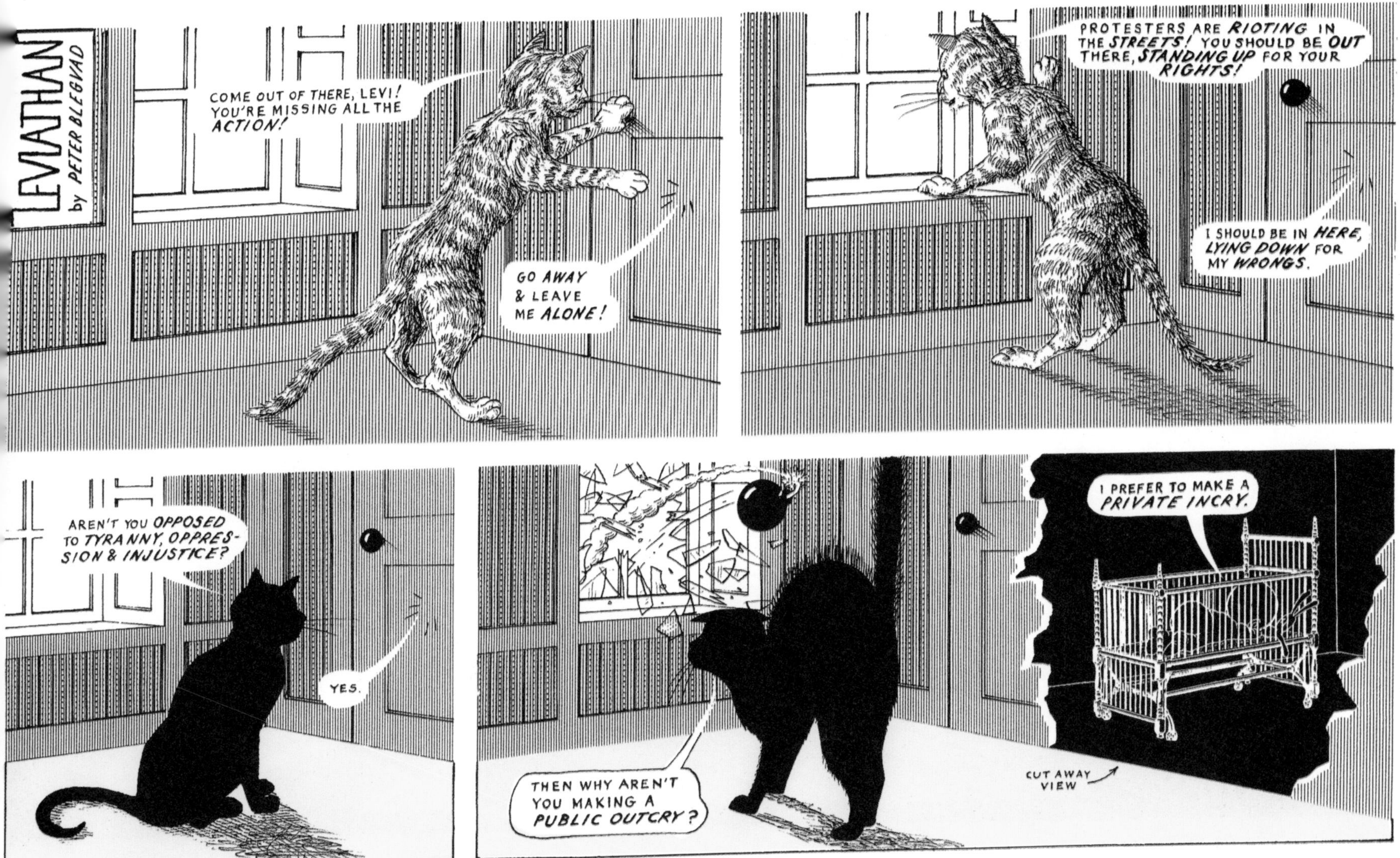
LEVIATHAN
by PETER BLEGVAD
COME OUT OF THERE, LEVI! YOU'RE MISSING ALL THE ACTION!
GO AWAY & LEAVE ME ALONE!
PROTESTERS ARE RIOTING IN THE STREETS! YOU SHOULD BE OUT THERE, STANDING UP FOR YOUR RIGHTS!
I SHOULD BE IN HERE, LYING DOWN FOR MY WRONGS.
AREN'T YOU OPPOSED TO TYRANNY, OPPRES-SION & INJUSTICE?
YES.
THEN WHY AREN'T YOU MAKING A PUBLIC OUTCRY?
I PREFER TO MAKE A PRIVATE INCRY.
CUT AWAY VIEW

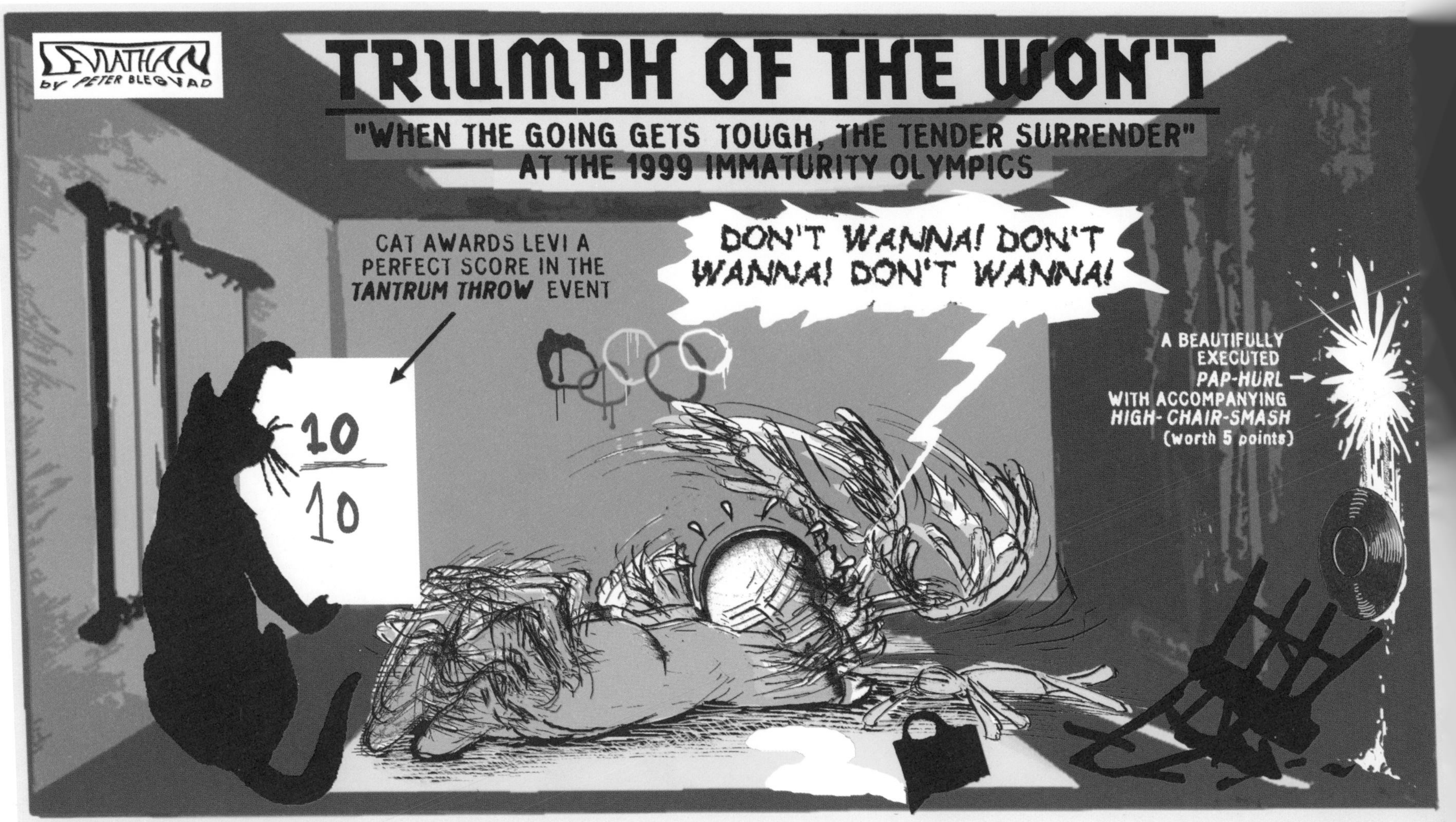
LEVIATHAN
by PETER BLEGVAD
TRIUMPH OF THE WON'T
"WHEN THE GOING GETS TOUGH, THE TENDER SURRENDER"
AT THE 1999 IMMATURITY OLYMPICS
CAT AWARDS LEVI A PERFECT SCORE IN THE TANTRUM THROW EVENT
DON'T WANNA! DON'T WANNA! DON'T WANNA!
10/10
A BEAUTIFULLY EXECUTED PAP-HURL WITH ACCOMPANYING HIGH-CHAIR-SMASH (worth 5 points)

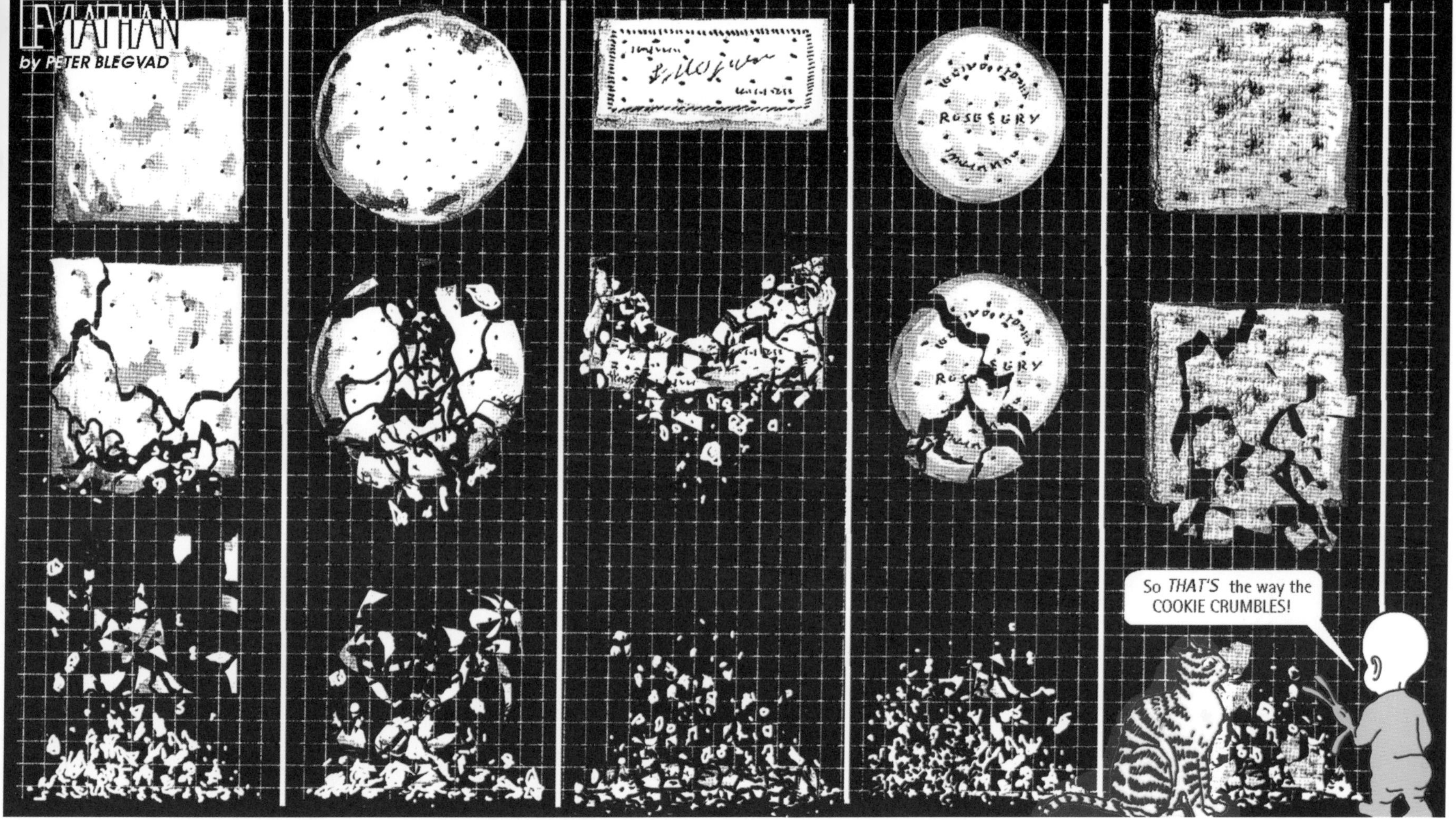
LEVIATHAN
by PETER BLEGVAD
So THAT'S the way the COOKIE CRUMBLES!

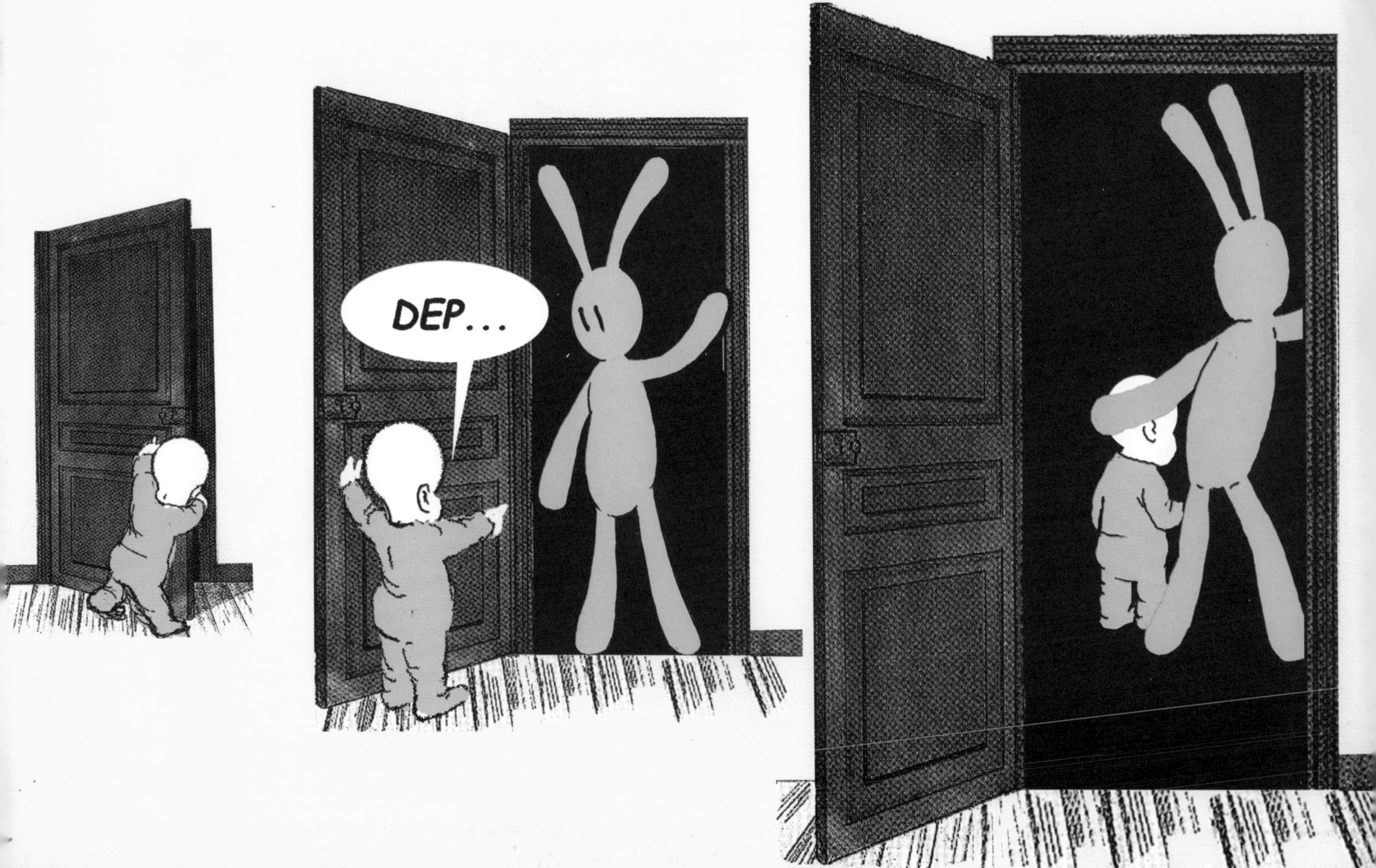
DEP...